A Fractured Relationship

Faith and the Crisis of Culture

Thomas J. Norris

VERITAS

First published 2007 by
Veritas Publications
7/8 Lower Abbey Street, Dublin 1, Ireland
Email publications@veritas.ie

Website www.veritas.ie

10 9 8 7 6 5 4 3 2 1

SS 9334

ISBN 978 185390 964 1

Scripture Quotations from the *New Revised Standard Version Bible* © 1993 and 1998 by the
Division of Christian Education of the United Council of the Churches of Christ in the
United States of America.

Designed and typeset by Paula Ryan
Printed in the Republic of Ireland by Betaprint, Dublin

*Veritas books are printed on paper made from the wood pulp of managed forests. For every tree
felled, at least one tree is planted, thereby renewing natural resources.*

Contents

To the president, priests and students of
St Kieran's College Seminary, Kilkenny,
1975–1984.

Abbreviations

Communio	International Catholic Review, Washington, D.C., 1974.
DS	H. Denzinger & Schönmetzer, Enchiridion. Symbolorum, Definitionum et Declarationum in rebus fidei et morum, Freiburg 1965.
ITQ	Irish Theological Quarterly, Maynooth, 1906; 1951 new series.
PG	J.P. Migne, Patrologia Graeca, Paris, 1857–1866: 161 volumes.
PL	J.P. Migne, Patrologia Latina, Paris, 1844–1864: 217 volumes.
SC	Sources chrétiennes, edited by H. de Lubac and Jean Danielou, Paris.

Introduction

Talking about God is Dangerous

> ... faith disturbs us and continually upsets the too beautiful balance of our mental conceptions and our social structures. Bursting into a world that perpetually tends to close in upon itself, God brings it the possibility of a harmony that is certainly superior but is to be attained only at the cost of a series of cleavages and struggles coextensive with time itself. 'I came not to bring peace, but a sword.'[1]

One of those heroic converts to Christian faith during the later Soviet era in Russia was a certain Tatjana Goritschewa. A lecturer in electronics at the University of Leningrad, as the city was then named, Tatiana wrote up the story of her exceptional discovery and conversion, in particular, how she abandoned the Marxism-Leninism of her youth and education upon the discovery of the existence of God and his self-revelation in Jesus the Christ and his Church. Costing her not less than the loss of her university career and then internment in a work camp in Kazakhstan before deportation to the outside because of the threat posed by her powerful witness of faith and love, Tatiana's ardent hope gave her a zest for living. Her life, in fact, radiated the new life received in Baptism, sealed in Confirmation and nourished by the divine Eucharist. Movingly, she describes in her autobiography the essential practical difference made by the arrival of faith in the Christ who had given himself up for her. 'My aim was to be cleverer, more capable, stronger than the others. But no one had told me that the supreme thing in life is not to overtake and to get the better of others, but to love.'[2]

Tatiana's experience, typical of others such as her great co-national and contemporary, Alexander Solzhenitsyn,[3] points towards the experience of another convert who lived in the Roman Empire – Augustine of Hippo. In particular, Tatiana's discovery that faith is both radically practical and frequently counter-cultural was an insight that had engaged the learned and passionate North-African all his life long. In fact, it inspired one of his greatest books in reflection on the meaning of the history of humankind, *The City of God*. There, Augustine proposes the view that the core struggle of humankind is the struggle to love, or rather, to welcome the God who *is* love even if that 'costs nothing less than everything' (T.S. Eliot). Augustine perceives in biblical history and in world history the struggle between two kinds of love. There is the love for God which goes as far as despising oneself, and there is the love for self which goes as far as despising God. St Augustine was particularly aware, however, that the movement of conversion from love of self to the love of God and of the neighbour is a struggle, a struggle in fact that cannot be won without the energy of grace as the free gift of God, changing the heart of stone into a heart of flesh!

Different Worlds

The religious, historical and social contexts represented by the Russian woman and the North African bishop could not be more different. While Augustine lived in a world where the existence of God was taken for granted, Tatiana lived in an Empire that was the first in history to teach and to inculcate atheism, even *antitheism*. The nineteenth century had seen a series of thinkers who systematically denied the existence of the Absolute! In the next century, the Soviet Empire translated this antitheism into all its programmes. That Empire collapsed in 1989, as gently as its beginning had been violent. However, the cruelty of its persecutions, the vista of its Gulags and the systematic violation of elementary human rights on a vast scale did not impact Western Europe. They did not gain the attention of those living beyond the wall in the West. The popular imagination did not dwell much on the horrors of the communist Gulags, nor upon the genocides of Mao Tse Tung nor the national genocide perpetrated by Pol Pot in Cambodia only two decades ago. Solzhenitsyn's voice remained isolated, even after deportation to the West in 1970, becoming a cry in the wilderness of his beloved Russia. Why did this happen?

The answer is not easy. Perhaps the collective horror and shame over hatred on such a vast scale dictated silence. It becomes even more difficult when one reflects on the further fact of the Second Vatican Council. The Council was surely the single most significant spiritual event of the twentieth century. The wall of communism fell twenty years after the Council, revealing a vacuum in society and in souls. Was this not providence providing the room for a new entry of the Gospel, an invitation to evangelise? Not only, but the Council wanted 'to endow Christianity once more with the power to shape history ... Now, following the Council, it was supposed to become evident that the faith of Christians embraces all of life, that it stands in the midst of history and in time and has relevance beyond the realm of subjective notions'.[4] With the collapse of state-sponsored atheism, it was the hope of many that a new opportunity for the Gospel and the Church had arrived. The demise of communism seemed to open the door to the programme the Council had elaborated only two decades previously.

Shaping History: The Gospel or Marx?

The Council had indeed engendered a great religious ferment. It had raised expectations among many that the prayer of 'good Pope John XXIII' for a new Pentecost in the Church would be answered. The Council, in fact, gave voice to a renewed vision of the Good News of Jesus Christ. Its sixteen texts present a 'competitive Christianity'. more rooted in divine revelation, more thoughtful in its self-understanding, and, above all, more vigorous and open in its manifold relations to other Christians, the great religions and to the men and women of goodwill. It very definitely wanted to overcome the 'ghettoisation' of the Church brought on by the pressures and struggles of the Counter-Reformation, as well as by the aftermath of the Enlightenment and the French Revolution. The Second Vatican Council wanted a Church more plain-spoken, a Church of disciples who would be open to 'the joys and the hopes, the sorrows and the struggles'[5] of all humankind.

With such fermentation in progress, many read the texts of the Council as centrally preoccupied with the search for a new relationship to the world. They took the *Pastoral Constitution on the Church in the Modern World* as the overture to the conciliar symphony, and since that text addresses in a particular way the modern world and the Church's mission *to* and *in* that world, dialogue became the catchword. Things distinctively Catholic and Christian, which thinkers such as Romano Guardini and scripture scholars such as Heinrich Schlier had been highlighting, were now sidelined, not because they were false, but because they were inappropriate in the new religious climate. The core of the Gospel lay, not in its revelation of the humble merciful love of the triune God for sinful suffering humankind, but in the capacity to alter the structures of society that kept peoples in the humiliation of a crushing poverty. The *Sermon on the Mount* became the touchstone for a revolt against the existing cultural and social order.

In the student revolts of 1968, and still more spectacularly in the phenomenon of Liberation Theology in South America, the ideal way to make Christianity socially triumphant seemed to present itself. Marx could work with the Gospel to shape the world for the better! Christ has the message and Marx has the method! Marx could do this in spite of the fact that his thought had inspired those political structures that had systematically attacked the very idea of God and the reality of the Church from Peking to Berlin. The truth that Marx had appropriated in his thought the categories of the Old Testament, all of them except the God of Israel,[6] did not seem to present a problem! The theology of the Council had the power to assimilate and to 'baptise' even Marxism.

However, economics and politics, and not the Cross and the love exhibited thereon, are the instruments of Marxism. It took time, in fact, to perceive that the agents of salvation in Marxism as employed in Liberation Theology were not *always* those of Jesus Christ. Jesus set out to *change hearts and minds* before everything else. Having challenged this overdependence, the Church approved an authentic liberation theology. It is only Christ who can usher in the Kingdom of God: the Way of the Lamb in fact is a straight and narrow way between two titanisms, that of a social programme hijacking the Gospel of love exclusively for its own use, and that of a clerical theocracy attempting to control the whole of reality according to its plans. The way of the Gospel moves to the beat of another kind: it moves, in fact, in rhythm with the heartbeat of the God-Man who brought another kind of culture into history, the culture of mutual love and of self-gift even unto death (Mk 10:45; Jn 13:34; 15:12). His Gospel may be the long way around, but it is the short way home! 'The time has come, the Kingdom of God is at hand. Repent and believe in the Gospel!' (Mk 1:15)

Re-finding the First Freshness

I have been using the great short word, 'love'. Friends tell me that the great words of the faith, even the greatest of all, love (1Cor 13:13), are so frequently used, and abused, that they fail to speak! They slip, slide and decay into imprecision. They generally let down what was intended by the writer. That's why we will always need new language, or at least renewed discourse. Otherwise what is most sublime will pass by undetected, and the stunningly beautiful go unrecognised. It was of this that Emmanuel Levinas, Jew and philosopher, was thinking when he wrote of the 'other' and concern for the other in these striking terms, 'Ethics is the recognition of 'saintliness'. Plants, animals, all living things hang onto their lives. For each one, it's a struggle for survival. And then comes the human, with the possible advent of an ontological absurdity: concern for others is greater than concern for oneself. This is what I call 'saintliness'. Our humanity consists in being able to recognise the priority of the other'.[7] The highest goal has to consist in recognising this other and in then loving the other – with deeds!

The genius of a philosopher such as Levinas lies in the ability to awaken us to the riches of familiar words, to the wonder of the other person, and to the even greater wonder of the event of living out 'concern for the other' by means of the concrete deed. Now this is most helpful in realising what is great in life, and, *a fortiori*, in Christianity, where, as the Council stressed, *the* Other 'out of the abundance of his love speaks to us as friends (see Ex 33:11; Jn 15:14-15) and lives among us (see Bar 3:38), so that he may invite and take us into fellowship with himself'.[8] The central message of Christianity, then, consists in the fact that the God of Jesus Christ recognised our humanity to the point of emptying himself in order to take on this very humanity and the human condition even to death, yes, death on the cross (Phil 2:6-8). The truth of every other person is to be read from the fact that each is the brother or sister for whom Christ died (ICor 8:11).

The glory of so great a love reflects its light over each and every person. 'O man, why do you think so little of yourself, when God shows how much he thinks of you?', is a recurring question among the Fathers of the Church. A triangle comes into view, namely, God, the other person and I. Pope Benedict puts it in these vivid terms, 'For someone who has no rapport with God, the other will never be anything more than an other'.[9] Over a millennium after the Fathers, their thinking re-echoes in Dostoievski's claim that in Christian times there was 'an idea stronger than any calamity'.[10]

'The Third Death of God'[11]

The title of a French philosopher's recent book simply shocks. How could it be that the very Europe, where the first extensive inculturation of the Gospel occurred, now wants to throw off its Christian credentials? The new constitution of the European Union does not want to mention God or Christ or the fact of the Christian roots of Europe. If Europe, so saturated historically in the Gospel and so marked in its culture by the inspiration of that same Gospel, refuses to welcome the message of Christ's death and resurrection, what will happen to it? Nor should the depth of the drama be underestimated. Addressing the Fifth Symposium of the Bishops of Europe in 1982, Pope John Paul II stressed the Christian implication of the European drama in these words, 'The crises of European man are the crises of Christian man. The crises of European culture are the crises of Christian culture ... In an even more radical sense, we can affirm that these trials, these temptations and this outcome of the European drama not only challenge Christianity and the Church as a difficulty or an external obstacle coming from the outside, they are within Christianity and the Church in a certain true sense'.[12] It is not appropriate, therefore, to read the religious and cultural landscape of contemporary Europe as if atheism and nihilism were positions that had come from outside of Christian Europe. Rather they are realities that arise from within that very religious and cultural space! We must try to understand them and address the serious questions they pose to believer and non-believer alike! This will be a primary goal of this book.

An Italian philosopher comments that 'much modern thought has become the defender of the human being against God'.[13] The plain meaning of the statement is perplexing, even dismaying. If God is love in himself (IJn 4:8; 16), how could he be a threat to Man? It is obvious from the event of the eternal Trinity that the Divine Persons *are* their very relationships of love, of infinite self-giving: each divine Person is a nothingness of love for the Other Persons. Why would we need to be defended against such a God? How could this state of affairs have emerged? Or perhaps we have to ask with Bruno Forte if 'the God of Christians is Christian. It is no exaggeration to claim that we are confronted by an exile of the Trinity from both the theory and the practice of Christians'.[14] And as Karl Barth saw, many decades ago, it is only the Trinity that makes God beautiful and so attractive!

If the central mystery of the Christian faith has fallen out of view, if what is revealed by God and worked out over the early Councils of the Church no longer enjoys presence and vigour in the minds and the lives of many believers, namely, that the one God is a communion of infinite Persons, then the core of faith has slipped out of sight like a sun setting without notice in a good month of June. As the spiritual heirs of Israel the first Christians announced the one true God, but they did so in a remarkable fashion. They proclaimed this God as a One who is Three. He was both infinite unity *and* infinite communion. He was neither unity without plurality, nor plurality without unity. And not only: One of the Three had become man, bringing the culture of mutual self-giving from heaven to earth. As the only Son 'turned towards the bosom of the Father' (Jn 1:18), the Son brought with him a total newness in the reality of mutual love among believers. 'I give you a new commandment, love one another as I have loved you' (Jn 13:34). The One opened out to humankind in a trinity of infinite Persons as the Event of Love where humankind was invited to enter. 'Father, I want those you have given me to be where I am, so that they may see the glory you have given me, because you loved me before the creation of the world' (Jn 17:24). Now if this newness has evaporated, then we have to fall back upon *our own ideas* of God and of accessing him! We will have to lose what is revealed. Voltaire's comment will be fulfilled to the letter, 'God made man in his image and likeness, and man has paid him back'.[15]

The Outline of the Book in your Hands

Part I: *Thinking and Reasoning Today*

The book has two sections which are interdependent. The first section is an encounter with contemporary culture, in particular with the phenomenon of the loss of faith. Here we describe the religious crises of Christians in the Western world. We consider the alienation of recent centuries that has now produced the phenomenon of modernity and post-modernity. The first chapter in this section describes the gradual weakening of the synthesis of faith and reason worked out by geniuses such as St Thomas in the thirteenth century, as well as the progressive unravelling of this synthesis. Our world is largely the product of science and its child, technology. The advent of this science is an event that outshines in importance all the events of the past millennium.

From the point of view of faith, the culture we live in reduces doctrine to probable opinions at most, and revelation to religious experience and intuition. Only science is rigorous in its methods: so runs the argument. Faith has but a tenuous connection to rigorous reason; it prefers intuition and the dubious signs of miracles and holiness.

The second chapter deals with the charge that faith is grounded upon such 'weak reason', and not upon 'strong reason' which is the prerogative of science. This chapter expounds the wisdom of three seminal thinkers who respond to this state of affairs. They are John Henry Newman, Eric Voegelin, and Bernard Lonergan representing Anglican, Lutheran and Catholic worlds, respectively. They recover the more inclusive sense of reason and its methods for the human, ethical and theological realms of inquiry. However, they do so *in dialogue with the unfolding wonder of a science and technology advancing on all fronts.*

The third chapter considers the relationships that divine revelation sets up with our humanity, particularly in respect of human rationality and its quest for first principles. Far from being a red light to thinking, this revelation stimulates thought. The result is theology: faith and hope and love all seek understanding. Not only, but such seeking corresponds to an earlier seeking that archaeology, anthropology and the history of thought show to lie at the core of our very humanity. All the ancient religions and cultures in fact witness to this search. Taking our cue from John Paul's encyclical, *Fides et ratio*, we outline the access to truth, both that provided by revelation and that attained by the natural light of reason, as well as their fascinating intersection. After all, does not the Christ who reveals the Father to men and women (Mt 11:27) not also reveal human beings to themselves?[16] There is no authentic theology without philosophy, and no authentic philosophy without openness to the possibility of encounter with divinity.

Part Two: *Don't Presuppose Faith, Propose it Afresh!*

The second section of this theological dialogue sets out to tell the faith in the context and the circumstances of our times. It is never enough to presuppose the faith, it is always necessary to propose it afresh. Perhaps the new challenges we have been describing are measures allowed by Christ, the Lord and Omega point of history, to stimulate us to unpack the riches of revelation, which are unfathomable (Eph 3:8). This is in any case a primary concern of this work: to listen with sympathy to the concerns of our contemporaries in order to initiate the 'dialogue of salvation' (Pope John Paul II). But what is this faith? What is the good news? It is the wonder of humankind risen in and with the resurrection of Christ as the victory of God without which 'our preaching is in vain ... and we are the most unfortunate of all people' (1Cor 15:14, 19).[17] In the words of Leo the Great, 'In whatever part of the world a man is regenerated in Christ, with his ancient sinfulness destroyed, he passes over into a new man by a rebirth ...' (See Brev, 31 Jan). The author of First Timothy puts it like this:

> Christ was made visible in the flesh,
> attested by the Spirit,
> seen by angels,
> proclaimed to the pagans,
> believed in by the world,
> taken up in glory. (1Tim 3:16)

Christianity is a large thing: you cannot take it up in a teacup.

The first chapter here presents the revelation which God made to Israel. In a history which is both 'scenic and almost supernatural', God begins to tell us who he is by showing us what he does! There results the unfolding history of Israel, word and deed combining. It is the history of God's search for humankind. In it one sees both the commitment of God to the way of history as well as the forging of the categories of promise for humanity's future with God. The emerging categories, however, are not capable of easy harmonisation. How can one harmonise, to take but one example, the category of the 'Messiah' with that of the 'Suffering Servant'? The first must live, the second has to die. Of course the movements played out in the course of Israel's exceptional history are not the only preparation for the new and eternal covenant that is coming. In the words of Søren Kierkegaard, 'Preparation for becoming attentive to Christianity does not consist in reading books or in making surveys of world history, but in *deeper immersion in existence*'.[18] This in fact was the primary purpose of the last chapter that focused on the intersection of divine and human search in the drama of human existence. No one finds who has not first been seeking.

Hidden in the First Covenant, the New Covenant becomes manifest as the Mystery of Christ, to borrow St Paul's language. However, that manifestation is not obvious. How could it be? That the Infinite should bond with the finite, that the Eternal should unite with the temporal, pulverises all our categories. It is the utterly Unexpected that enters in Jesus of Nazareth. What do we see in him? 'Heaven on earth, earth in heaven; man in God, God in man; heaven on earth and earth in heaven; and him whom the whole universe cannot contain, confined in a tiny body.'[19] This fifth chapter focuses on Jesus' bringing of the Kingdom of God as the very life of his homeland in the Trinity. At the core of the Kingdom is the art shown in the deeds and words of Jesus.

This art is an art of loving, together with its subtle, albeit incisive, movements. The chapter takes us into the practical import of the gospel of Jesus' person, words and deeds. The revelation occurring in him is above all else practical. St Bonaventure in the thirteenth century saw Jesus as the very art of the Blessed Three brought into history. Jesus manifests this art of his homeland on earth. His task in fact was to radiate in the world the splendour of the love of his homeland. Later the Apostle to the Gentiles will exhort the new believers at Ephesus, 'Walk in love *as* Christ loved us and gave himself up for us', having *first* reminded them of their deepest identity as 'God's work of art, created in Christ Jesus to live the good life as from the beginning he had meant us to live it' (Eph 5:1; 2:10).

There follows the sixth chapter on the summit moment of Jesus' passion, the experience of his crucifixion and forsakenness by his Father

(Mk 15:34; Mt 27:46). The history of the last century is a history of suffering on a scale unprecedented in previous history. This fact made Christians in the decades after World War II read these primary texts of revelation with new eyes. In particular, their eyes turned towards the cry of abandonment on the Cross. The fact that both Mark and Matthew place only one logion on the lips of the suffering Christ (Mk 15:34; Mt 27:46) should have alerted Christians much earlier to the central emphasis of these evangelists. The Jesus of St Mark in fact seems to marginalise the role of his miracles and teaching (Mk 2) as he sets his face towards Jerusalem and rejection and crucifixion in spite of the remonstrations of Peter (8:27-33). The world will always want to live and rise without dying, but this Jesus chooses to die so that all of us can live beyond death in the 'space' he opens up between himself and his eternal Father. Jesus as the Son of God made man, reaches men and women in their greatest distance from God, yes, in their very God-forsakenness.

Had not the Old Testament already perceived the real meaning of death by crucifixion when it announced, 'Cursed be every one who hangs on a tree' (Dt 21:23)? In spite of this principle the Son of God sets his face from the beginning towards Jerusalem and the cross (Mk 8:27-33). ' ... now God speaks his final word: his Son takes over in suffering the role of those who say "no" and carries it through to his inconceivable abandonment by God ... Whoever removes himself even an inch from this self-interpretation of God ... is no longer a Christian.'[20] In Jesus forsaken one sees a distance from God which the Son himself had to experience, who, being Love that is beyond all knowing (Eph 3:19), becomes one with us to the point of the cry of our God-forsakenness. 'In Jesus forsaken we glimpse in God the greatest deprivation of his own being God, to the point of being the "last" human being, of even becoming "sin and accursed". Because of this becoming one with us, every suffering face of humanity is his own, every face of sacrificed innocence is his.'[21]

The experience behind the whole of the New Testament begins to peep out. This is the theme of the seventh chapter. The texts composing the New Testament, in fact, are the articulation of the primitive communities' experience of the in-breaking of absolute love

into the world (1Jn 1:1). It is with this engendering experience that this chapter grapples. It notices that the three great building blocks of the New Testament, namely, the synoptic gospels, the Pauline literature and the Johannine, each ask themselves one and the same great question, who is this Jesus who dies and is alive? Progressively more *differentiated* answers emerge. These answers move from the categories of the Old Testament being applied to Jesus in the synoptics to the Pauline insight that God is 'the Father of our Lord Jesus Christ' while Jesus is 'the Son of this Father'. As for John, the differentiation is most explicit: God is '*the* Father' and Jesus is '*the* Son'. The philology leads to the theology: God is 'the Father' and the same One is 'the Son' and the same One is also 'the Spirit'. The challenge is to expand our minds to the measure of revelation! In doing so we learn that Trinity is the only hypothesis that covers the data of the New Testament.

Not only our minds, but also our hearts need expansion, for, as we have been stressing, revelation is eminently *practical*. As Newman loved to stress, 'the whole duty and work of a Christian is made up of these two parts, faith and obedience; "looking unto Jesus", the divine object as well as author of our faith, and acting according to his will'.[22] The Son enfleshed in our flesh 'teaches men how God really is and since he is himself a man, astonishingly he teaches them to imitate this God'.[23] It begins to dawn on us that the crucified and raised Son has 're-located' us human beings where 'no eye has seen, nor ear heard, nor the heart of any person imagined' (1Cor 2:9; Is 64:3; Jer 3:16). Relationship is the first key even to an elementary reading of our 'place'. 'On that day, you will understand that I am in my Father *and* you in me *and* I in you' (Jn 14:20). The three relations that constitute the mystery of faith stand out in this one verse. They are the relationships of the Son to the Father, of Christ to us, and of Christian to fellow-Christian. The paschal Christ is speaking in order to tell us *where we are* in the drama of what the God of Jesus Christ is showing, giving and communicating!

The seventh chapter sets out the key relationships among believers resulting from this wonderful locating brought about by the self-communication of the Blessed Trinity. This is what 'the eyes of the heart' (Eph 1:18) must begin to see. Christ has re-located us! The result, that there is, in fact, an entirely new way of saying 'I', 'You', 'S/He' and 'We'. Each time one utters a particular pronoun, one thinks of the other-in-relationship, since each pronoun involves relationship. The apartness of the person understood as 'individual substance' (Boethius) is corrected and enriched by the dimension of communion that overcomes aloneness while protecting irreducibility. Our amazing 're-location' through Christ, however, must include not only the being of substance but also the being of consciousness (Lonergan). As Percy Walker has noted, 'consciousness involves two relations, that of knowing and the relation of with. To live the truth of their dignity, Christians must find both relations'.[24] Otherwise the revelation given in Christ is not appropriated by believers. The realisation of our presence in the *milieu trinitaire* can inspire our lives and pre-empt a certain subtle islamisation of 'the faith given once for all to the saints' (Jude 3).

And yet in spite of a revelation so extraordinary, many Christians seem not to view the life of faith in a manner radically different to that of other monotheistic religions. Tragically, there has been an 'exile of the blessed Trinity', not that we would refuse to confess our access to the Father through the Son and in the Holy Spirit (Eph 2:18), but that this has little practical meaning and so little relevance to everyday living. The gravity of this loss consists in the fact that we may be quite unable to appreciate that the Blessed Trinity is the form of our life with God *and with one another*. Along with such practical nominalism, flattening out as it does the revealed order of divinity, there is perhaps no realisation at all that the Trinity is the infinite source of communion and so of society or a world reconciled. Chapter eight studies this 'exiling' of the Trinity. However, it also points towards its remarkable return, particularly since the Council, to the extent that it is now the very grammar of theology. For the Council defined the Church, following the Fathers, as 'a people made up from the unity of the Father, the Son and the Holy Spirit'.[25] The Church becomes the created home of the Trinity while the Trinity stands forth as the uncreated home of the Church.[26]

Notes

1. Henri de Lubac, *The Drama of Atheist Humanism*, San Francisco 1995, 14.
2. Tatiana Goricheva, *Talking about God is Dangerous*, London 1986, 12.
3. Alexander Solzhenitsyn (1922–) won the Nobel Prize for Literature in 1970 and was deported the same year from the U.S.S.R. See Olivier Clément, *The Spirit of Solzhenitsyn*, London 1976, for his philosophical, theological and spiritual insight.
4. Joseph Ratzinger. 'Introduction to Christianity: *Yesterday, Today, and Tomorrow*', in *Communio*, 31(2004), 482–483.
5. *Gaudium et spes*, 1.
6. Eric Voegelin, *The New Science of Politics*, Chicago & London 1952, especially 112-121.
7. Emmanuel Levinas, *Unforeseen History*, translator Nidra Poller, Chicago 2004, 128.
8. Second Vatican Council, Dogmatic Constitution on Divine Revelation *Dei Verbum*, 2.
9. Pope Benedict XVI, Encyclical *Deus caritas est*, Rome 2006, 18.
10. F. Dostoievsky, *Raskolnikov's Diary*, ed. Fülop-Miller 1928, 417.
11. This is the English title of Andre Glucksmann's, *La troisieme morte de Dieu*, Paris 2004.
12. Pope John Paul II, *L'Osservatore Romano*, 7 October 1982: translation my own.
13. Giuseppe Zanghí, 'Una chiave di lettura dell'ateismo dell'Europa' in *Nuova Umanitç*, XXVII (2005/5), 646.
14. Bruno Forte, *Trinità come storia*, Milano 1985, 13–14: translation my own.
15. Theodore Besterman (ed.), *Voltaire's Notebooks*, Toronto 1952, I, 231.
16. *Gaudium et spes*, 22.
17. N.T. Wright, *Jesus the Victory of God*, London 1996.
18. S. Kierkegaard, *Post-scriptum*, Paris 1941, 378.
19. St Peter Chrysologus, *Sermo 160: Roman Breviary*, vol. I, 331.

20. Hans Urs von Balthasar, 'God is his own Exegete' in *Communio*, XIII, 4(1986), 283.

21. G.M. Zanghí, 'Towards a Theology of Jesus Forsaken', in *Being One*, 5(1996), 57.

22. John Henry Newman, *Parochial and Plain Sermons*, I, London 1868, 153.

23. Hans Urs von Balthasar, ibid., 283.

24. Walker Percy, *Signposts in a Strange Land*, New York 1991, 124.

25. Second Vatican Council, Dogmatic Constitution on the Church *Lumen gentium*, 4.

26. See Anne Hunt, *Trinity*, Washington 2005, for both a stimulating survey of Trinitarian theology and a personal deployment of the method of the '*nexus mysteriorum*' in the search for the 'most fruitful understanding' of the mystery.

Part 1

Thinking and Reasoning Today

Chapter I

Alienation and the Search for Home

> The decisive question for men and peoples is whether they
> have succeeded in filling themselves with the eternal, or (to
> put it more humbly) whether they have allowed the eternal
> to be operative within them.[1]

Our times are in movement again. The West moved forward with
new vigour when, after the fall of the communist Wall dividing
Europe in 1989, new horizons opened up for travel, trade and the
exchange of the spiritual goods of education and learning. The most
public expression of this is the expanding European Union, now
encompassing the nations from Russia to the Atlantic. The ideal of a
united Europe had been born immediately after the war, rising in
fact like a phoenix from the ruins of a war-devastated continent. The
truth is that it was Christian politicians such as De Gaspari and
Giordani in Italy, Schumann in France, Adenauer in Germany, to
name but a few, who, though the real alternatives to megalomaniacs
who triggered and forced the Second World War, were destined not
to don the robes of high office. But just as those Christians built
upon the very ruins and rubble of a pulverised Europe, so now that
vision which inspired such heroic recovery is perhaps slipping again
from view. Why this oscillation? Why could the West turn to the
Christian view of things for reconstruction in the immediate post-
war years, and then forget both the wisdom of these innovators and
the actual reconstruction of Europe? Was it simply a case of any port
being good enough in a storm?

Perhaps the answer lies deeper. There is a fault-line in the history
and thought of Europe that slips and slides as soon as sufficient weight

is made to bear upon it. In the nineteenth century Cardinal Newman predicted the imminent arrival of this state of affairs. He foresaw a time when the consensus about God as the essential and indispensable reference point of human existence would be denied. Such a denial would pose for believers a challenge that the whole history of the world before them had never known or even imagined. 'You will find, certainly in the future, nay more, *even now, even now*, that the writers and thinkers of the day do not even believe there is a God ... Christianity has never yet had experience of a world simply irreligious ... Even among the sceptics of Athens, St Paul could appeal to the unknown God.'[2]

Friedrich Nietzsche, Newman's contemporary, wrote of this wilting in typically vigorous terms: 'We Europeans find ourselves confronted with an immense world of ruins; some things still tower aloft while other objects stand mouldering and dismal, but most things are already lying on the ground, picturesque enough. Where were there ever finer ruins?'[3] What Nietzsche described was the beginning of post-modernity. A term that is as elusive as flying clouds, it tries to catch up in one word the climate of our times.

This is the kind of challenge and scenario that is now with us. It has certain characteristics, however, that add greatly to its intriguing perplexity. The first of these is the fact that it did not arise outside of Europe but rather within Christian Europe. Pope John Paul II put it in these terms when speaking to the European Synod of Bishops in 1982, 'The crises of European man are the crises of the Christian. The crises of European culture are the crises of Christian culture. Still more profoundly can we affirm that these trials, these temptations and this result of the European drama not only question Christianity from outside as a difficulty or an external obstacle, but in a certain sense, they occur within Christianity and within the Church? In this light, Christianity can discover in the adventure of the European spirit the temptations, the unfaithfulness and the risks that belong to man in his essential relationship with God in Christ'.[4] There is a kind of epochal and collective 'Dark Night' that has overtaken the West. It is as if the sun had set imperceptibly upon our culture, and the resulting darkness had overcome the light (Jn 1:7). For two millennia the Gospel was successfully transmitted from one generation to the next and from one culture to another. Why has this communication apparently broken down today? An examination of some of the characteristic traits of our times may provide a clue to the answer.

Our World

Our world is the fruit of an extraordinary development unprecedented in human history, namely, the scientific and technological revolution. This revolution 'outshines everything since the rise of Christianity and reduces the Renaissance and the Reformation to the rank of mere episodes, mere internal displacements, within the system of medieval Christianity'.[5] This world has its typical images and its own icons. But they are images and icons that are quite different from the images and the icons of our bi-millennial faith. The result is that the Church and society do not easily recognise each other. The Gospel and the men and women of today speak in different languages. The result is a serious breakdown in our dialogue. 'In our highly technical world, faith is without images and images are without faith'.[6] And even if Malraux is correct in predicting that 'the next century [the twenty-first] will be religious, or else it will not be at all', the emerging religiosity is far from the Christian message of the Incarnation, the paschal event, and the Trinity. It is a kind of wild religiosity.

Secondly, there has been an interruption of the flow of tradition. If tradition was that universally recognised ensemble of beliefs, practices and attitudes expressing the principles and criteria for personal and social living, and contributing to the polity's self-identity as much as memory contributes to the identity and well-being of the individual person, that same tradition claimed both divine authority and age-old legitimation. Tradition ensured that the essential meanings and truths and values were handed down from generation to generation, and from century to century. The process of tradition provided the source of unity and of meaning for individuals and communities. And because that tradition was guaranteed and supported by authority and institution, there is now a resistance to all three, to tradition, authority and institution. 'Man liberates himself from pre-established authority and tradition. He wants to see, judge and decide for himself.'[7] Emancipation is the word that captures the spirit of our times. With this aspiration towards untrammelled freedom there goes a resentment against 'everything given, even his own existence, the very fact that he is not the creator of the universe and himself'.[8]

In so far as the modern world finds a unity at all, it founds it on a predominantly functional basis of technical communication and co-operation. Unfettered freedom has now become the norm, not trust in, and acceptance of, tradition or institution or authority. Tradition, as G.K. Chesterton plainly saw, was the democracy of the dead, the refusal to forget our forbears and, with them, what was great and noble and good. Today, however, tradition has been reduced to a caricature of its true self as 'the way things were once done'. It can be at home in the museum, but it has no place in the marketplace.

Thirdly, there is a consequent unitary culture in our world. This unitary culture is dominated by a technical uniformity from which a new poverty emerges. There is an increasing sameness about the multiplicity of cultural goods. How will this culture provide unity for life, both individual and collective? How will it provide the goals for truly human existence, and the ideals by which people can live in a manner appropriate to their true dignity? The first Christians saw in Jesus Christ the norm of life, 'For me to live is Christ' (Phil 1:21). The event of Christ threw down the dividing walls separating Jew and Greek (Eph 2:14). Christ provided the incomparable focus of unity for all of humankind with God and within itself. This is what the *Letter to the Ephesians* enthusiastically proclaims to all and sundry. Henri de Lubac makes the point in his epoch-making youthful work, *Catholicism: The Social Aspects of Dogma*, when he writes that 'fundamentally the Gospel is obsessed with the idea of the unity of human society'.[9] Today, however, the Gospel and faith are no longer understood as the unifying point of reality, the magnetic centre of the world, and the key to the thrust of the history of the world. More seriously still, those who would seek such a focus of unity and meaning do not even look towards the Gospel in this respect. The tragic implications of this are realised when one sees that the world is going towards a unity *of some sorts* in spite of obvious contradictions and obstacles.

When the medieval church had to hand on the faith and the Gospel to those who could neither read nor write, she turned to pictorial representation. In the splendour of the medieval cathedrals, with their stained glass, and in the whole panoply of painting and sculpture one can see how the Church developed a magnificent world of images to communicate the Gospel to the crowds. (It is enough to think of Fra Angelico or Giotto, or the splendid sculptures of the Crucified that have come down to us in Ireland.) Very appositely, this pictorial representation has been called the *Biblia Pauperum*, the Bible of the poor. In this century a new *Biblia Pauperum* is necessary, because the inherited set of images is unintelligible to our contemporaries. And just as the medieval *Biblia Pauperum* was strikingly original then, so the new *Biblia Pauperum* for today will have to bring out the one Gospel with a vigour that is fresh and a beauty that attracts the men and women of this new millennium.

The Home we had

We are indebted to the historians, the archaeologists, the palaeontologists and the anthropologists for an enormous expansion of our temporal horisons. In particular, we owe them the knowledge we have of *homo sapiens* who appeared about 50,000 years ago. They concur in identifying an explosion of symbolic expressions signifying a search for a communion with the ultimate Source of our existence. This search, in fact, is the constant in each and every civilisation whose remains and heritages have been catalogued by the various sciences, whether it is the cave-painters of Lascaux and Altamira, or the philosophers among the Greeks. That search constitutes the heart of culture and pinpoints that which is the specifically human feature of *homo sapiens*.

While all peoples witness to this search for the Ultimate Source, only one People knew that it was that Ultimate Source that sought out humanity. We humans only seek because God has first sought us out! Beginning with Abraham, and going down through Moses and all the Prophets, the People of Israel knew that God was in search of them. 'When Israel was a child I loved him, and I called my son out of Egypt' (Hosea 11:1), and 'I have loved you with an everlasting love, and therefore I am constant in my affection for you' (Jer 31:3), articulate Israel's experience of God's search for communion with humankind.

'In the fullness of time', to quote the recurring phrase of the Scriptures (Rom 8:15; Gal 4:4; Mk 1:15), the two great searches encounter and cross each other. 'And the Word became Flesh, and made his home among us, and we saw his glory, the glory that is his as the only Son of God, full of loving kindness and rocklike fidelity.' Or as T.S. Eliot puts it,

> Here the impossible union of spheres of existence
> Is actual. Here past and future are reconciled and overcome.[10]

In Jesus, then, human search and divine search intersect. In Jesus Christ, human search and divine Answer are one. This means that he is the unsurpassable synthesis of Culture and Revelation, God become flesh, and human flesh raised to heights beyond the Angels, indeed divinised (Heb 1:3-4). The words of St Augustine put it well, 'This is the greatest gift which God could give to men: he made his Word, through whom he created all things, head over them and joined them to him as his members, so that he might be Son of God and son of man, one God with the Father, one man with men'.[11] The synthesis of Revelation and Culture that is Christ occurred again and again wherever Christianity took root in the cultures of the ancient world. The early Church Fathers spoke of finding in these cultures 'seeds of the *Logos*'. St Justin, to take but one instance, is convinced that the 'gospel and philosophy do not face the believer with a choice of alternatives, nor are they complementary aspects of truth which the thinker would have to weld into the complete truth; in his conception, the Logos of the Gospel is rather the same word of the same God as the *logos spermatikos* of philosophy, but at a later stage of its manifestation in history'.[12]

The Fathers quite simply recognised in the human cultures around them quests or anticipations of the Incarnate Word. In fact, the encounter between the Christian Culture of the Gospel and the Greek, Latin, Celtic, Germanic and Slavic cultures resulted in a flowering of new and beautiful cultural syntheses, in which each of these cultures became more or less completely penetrated by the Gospel.

The result of this inculturation of the one Gospel in the many cultures was the marvellous medieval synthesis which was like a great Cathedral of Faith and Culture. This cathedral became the living space, the *Lebensraum*, in which European men and women were to live for centuries. The cathedral was decorated, as we have seen, with a magnificent panoply of pictorial representation which constituted the *Biblia Pauperum* in which the men and women of the time could read the elements of the Faith given once for all to the saints. This Faith is proclaimed in creed and the doctrine of the Church, celebrated in the sacramental life, lived out in the lives of Christians, and prayed in the sincere prayers and devotions of true believers.

The Loss of this Home

For reasons that would take an inappropriately long time to unravel, the synthesis of the Gospel and what we can call European culture began to come apart at the seems about 1400 a.d. The fault lay in the foundation and so was not obvious for a long time. Faultlines, in fact, are only detected through their eventual impact and, as the world of geology well knows, that may include the catastrophe of the earthquake, the volcano or even the tsunami. At the political level, the European nation states began to feel the need to be completely independent of any spiritual authority, at least in so far as that interfered with their temporal power. At the intellectual level there developed, gradually but relentlessly, the notion of autonomy – a subject not addressed formally and sympathetically by the Church until the Second Vatican Council and *Gaudium et spes* in 1964–5. In art, there was the elaboration of a more secular music, architecture, painting, sculpture, and so on. Moving on some centuries there were the American, French and Russian revolutions, with their more or less violent assertion of the rights first of the middle classes against aristocracy, and then of the rights of the proletariat against the middle classes as well as against aristocracy.

Western culture, then, came to be viewed as a struggle for the autonomy of the human spirit against an earlier Christian culture that had come to be seen as blocking its emergence as a genuinely secular experience. Consequently, its path came to be considered as a necessary exodus from the Church, with the Renaissance, the Reformation and the Enlightenment as the key stages in that exodus. 'The successive waves of secular and atheistic thought which have emerged in modern Western culture must be interpreted in the light of the singular gifts received through revelation. The varieties of unbelief and rejection of God are the "temptations", "risks" and even "perversions" of individuals and peoples who have been exposed to biblical revelation and experienced the concomitant liberation of human reason.'[13] However, since the synthesis of medieval Christendom had taken into itself the earlier, pre-Christian quest for the Absolute that had been the mark of *all* the great pre-Christian cultures, the gradual rejection of Christianity left the 'new culture' searching for its own Absolutes.

Inevitably an aspect or part of the Totality was then invested with ultimate meaning, whether it was Nature, or Race or Class, or History, or the Economy/Capital, or Progress, or Science/Technology, or Sexuality, or Evolution or whatever. 'Ideology in all its theoretical forms, as also in all its practical realisations, is the very expression of this hunger and thirst for totality. Emancipation is turned into totalitarianism.'[14] This quest for new absolutes, which are such only in appearance, led to what may be called the prophetic disappointments of philosophers like Nietzsche, poets like Baudelaire, writers like Kafka or Beckett, painters like Francis Bacon. As Philip McShane, an Irish philosopher once remarked, three great books of the twentieth century, Heidegger's *Being and Time*, Marcel's *Being and Having* and

Sartre's *Being and Nothingness*, could all be summed up in one title, Being and Loneliness, since in different ways each expressed modern humanity's loneliness for God.

Giuseppe Zanghí, an Italian philosopher, has brilliantly analysed the contemporary impact of such a development. A definite crisis now exists originating in the anthropological leap at the beginning of the modern era. 'From Descartes onwards, men and women emphasise the discovery of themselves as subjects and they underline progressively the reality of self-awareness and of reason as the centre of the person. Slowly this idea increasingly acquired, also thanks to Kant, a transcendental, if not a metaphysical, solidity. But precisely this absolutising of self-awareness and reason leads into a crisis that flows from the claim of such reason.'[15] There is with time a loss of the Transcendent, which is negated as negating the human, a loss of the movement towards the other and towards history once seen as the great domains of freedom for humanity, and, finally, a loss of the subject himself, his very deconstruction. Paul Ricoeur speaks of a 'wounded *cogito*', a '*cogito* which places itself, but does not possess itself, a *cogito* which grasps its own original truth only within, and by means of, the admission of inadequacy, illusion, the deception of its own immediate consciousness'.[16] The arc of modernity leads, paradoxically, to the absence of transcendence, to rampant individualism, the eclipse of the other, and ultimately to the deconstruction of the self.

Now all this only accentuates the question which man is to himself, his mystery. It highlights the search that refuses to go away, and cannot be banished for as long as the sun shines and the earth spins and the tides ebb and flow. That search abides even if contemporary men and women no longer believe in 'strong reason', and a Pope has to entreat them not to lose hope in the power of that very reason and its capacity to search for and discover the essential truth. The dialogue may not be easy, since there are assumptions now powerfully driving this determined type of modern culture.

The Way Home

'Whoever has ears to hear, let him listen to what the Spirit is saying to the Churches' (Rev 2:7, 11). Only the Holy Spirit is capable of making heard the call of God to conversion, to discernment and to prophetical witness in that interior extended space that is the believing community. His voice reaches us in the joys and the sorrows, the hopes and the cries of the men and the women who walk with us on the journey of time towards the fatherland (GS 1). This attitude of faith, of hope and of love characterised the event of the Council, which is the gift of the Holy Spirit to the Church in our times (Pope John Paul II).

It is enough to read the opening of the *Dogmatic Constitution on Divine Revelation* to be convinced of this attitude. 'This sacred Synod wishes to set before the minds of the faithful sound teaching about divine revelation, so that by hearing it, they may believe, by believing hope, and by hoping love.' The Council was called as a pastoral audit designed to unpack 'new things and old' from the household of divine revelation for the flock 'for whom Christ died' (ICor 8:11; Acts 20:28). Here and in other places in its sixteen documents, it strikes the keynote of the need for freshness and vividness in the exposition of the Faith of the Apostles.

It might have been expected that, given the mutual incomprehension that had grown between the Church and Modern Culture, the Council would have adopted a defensive posture. Perhaps a fresh formulating of an apologetics defending her position, a building up of her bastions against the surrounding infidelity, and a calling on the world to re-enter a renewed Christendom, such as was there during 'the ages of faith', might feature centrally on her agenda. This in fact had tended to happen in recent centuries, though of course it needs to be said that the situation varied considerably from country to country.

Nothing of the kind happened at Vatican II. Instead, the Council sought out an original and incisive form of evangelisation, though the word itself was not used during the Council and only gained currency after Paul VI's great Apostolic Letter, *Evangelii nuntiandi*. It did so according to two hermeneutical principles: first, it set out from what is most original in the Gospel, and, second, it aimed at what is most pressing on the stage of the history we are living and in the demands of the culture that challenges everywhere. The Council wished to speak from the heart of God to the heart of the modern world so that modern men and women 'by hearing might believe, by believing might hope, by hoping might love'![17] In the words of a Council expert, 'This is precisely what the Second Vatican Council had intended: to endow Christianity once more with the power to shape history ... Christianity – at least from the viewpoint of the Catholic Church – was trying to emerge again from the ghetto to which it had been relegated since the nineteenth century and to become involved once more in the world at large.'[18] *Cor ad cor loquitur* (heart speaks to heart).

This conciliar agenda inevitably means the doctrine of the God of Jesus Christ, namely, the Blessed Trinity. It also means the doctrine of Christ as 'the One of the Trinity' who came to locate the life of the Trinity in the midst of the world through the agency of his Cross, Resurrection and the sending of the Holy Spirit. Thirdly, it requires the doctrine of the Church understood in the light of the Trinity and the Cross. Finally, it means the doctrine of the woman who was the Mother of God and who 'let all God's glory through'.[19] The urgency of this doctrinal perspective may not be obvious, and in this lies a major aspect of the drama of the Church at this time. Karl Rahner, for example, claims that if the doctrine of the Trinity were to be dropped from the Church's profession of faith, the majority would not notice its omission, and, what is sadder, would have little or no adjustment to make to their faith-life.[20] An emptying out of substantial elements of 'the Faith given once for all to the saints' (Jude 3) seems to have stolen imperceptibly over the faith of many. Now if what is most original about Christianity is the God of Christianity, then the question could be asked, 'Is the God of Christians a Christian God?'[21]

The genius of the Second Vatican Council lies perhaps in the fact that it elaborated these mysteries in the context of the mystery of the Church thus producing its masterpiece, *Lumen gentium*. Its ecclesiology is focused in three keywords, *mystery, communion* and *mission*. The life of the Trinity, which is *the* mystery of faith, is brought down to earth to be the form, shape and life of the community born out of the death and resurrection of Christ, namely, the Church. The Church is therefore 'the people made one from the unity of the Father, the Son and the Holy Spirit'(4). She is the icon of the Holy Trinity, the mystery of communion and the sacrament of unity. She is this communion spread out both synchronically and diachronically and whose mission it is 'to gather into unity the scattered children of God' (Jn 11:51f) until the Lord returns (ICor 11:26). The *Instrumentum Loboris* for the recent European Synod of Bishops lamented the fact that, while the threefold of mystery, communion and mission are essential to the understanding of the Church, they are lived only by a few while many continue to see the Church as nothing but a hierarchical organisation!

An illustration in explanation of this most original ecclesiology of the Council may be useful. An emigrant leaving his homeland and going to another land has to perform two operations. First, he has to adapt to his new surrounds and its culture. This is essential if he is to find his feet and communicate with the many people he now encounters. Next, he brings inevitably from his own country the life that he lived there, at least in its more treasured aspects and most intimate dimensions. The life of his homeland becomes vividly present to him both as fond memory and present identity. In fact, it is notorious how fond of their homelands exiles frequently become the moment they leave them behind.

Now at the heart of the Great Mystery of our religion (ITim 3:16) there is an emigration and an immigration. 'One of the Three' leaves his homeland, the divine Trinity, as it were, and becomes flesh in our history, fulfilling the centuries of the First Covenant in a new and eternal Covenant (Jer 31:31; I Cor 11:24). On coming into our world he adapts himself perfectly to our condition, being found in human form and being humbler yet (Phil 2:8). This is an amazing *kenosis* for him (Phil 2:7). However, he also brought with him the life of his homeland, as the life of mutual love among divine and distinct Persons, the Father, the Son and the Holy Spirit. And he intended to recompose the human scenario according to this model. This is because the whole human family, from Adam and Eve 'til the last man and woman who will stand on this earth, is to be remade 'in the image and the likeness' of its trinitarian prototype. The Church is the created home of the Trinity, while the Trinity is the uncreated home of the Church. This is a recurring theme in the Fathers of the Church, the great Scholastics, and is now vibrantly recovered by theologians such as Yves Congar and Henri de Lubac.

The so-called 'ecclesiology of communion' is a breakthrough with incalculable practical consequences for the Church's mission to the society and the culture of our times, where many live on the street as it were, because they are homeless (Paul VI). First of all, it overcomes inherited ways of thinking that are dichotomies, such as 'the teaching Church versus the learning Church', 'the Church as institution versus the Church as charismatic', 'ministerial priesthood versus royal priesthood', and so on. It overcomes these dichotomies precisely because it identifies something earlier, more vital and more foundational of the Church, namely, the Church as a communion of created persons caught up in the communion of the Father, the Son and the Holy Spirit. Next, for the first time the Church is beginning to take the relationships between the divine Persons as the model of the relationships to be established at every level in the Church, and indeed in the whole of society. They are to obtain between Christian and Christian, between man and woman, at the heart of every family whether natural or religious, among bishops, among priests, between priests and bishops, between the hierarchy and the faithful. If the history of the Church shows how the mystery of the Trinity was lived in a vertical fashion, Christ giving us access to the Father in the Holy Spirit (Eph 2:18), the flow of history and the Council and the specific religious situation of our age have all indicated the necessity of supplementing the vertical by the addition of the horizontal unity of Christians.

St Teresa of Avila gave us the wonderful symbol in the sixteenth century of the 'Interior Castle' as an understanding of that vertical communion with the Divine Persons. Today, however, the Interior Castle must be added to by the constructing of the 'Exterior Castle'.

For did not Jesus pray on the night before he suffered, 'May they all be one. Father, may they be one in us, *as you are in me and I am in you*'. 'One in Us': the horizontal communion of believers is a communion 'in' the Father, the Son, and (by implication) the Holy Spirit. The final phrase is, alas, often overlooked. Finally, did he not also indicate the means to that unity, namely, the new commandment to love one another as he has loved us (Jn 13:34; 15:12)? That very commandment he described as his 'own' and as 'new'. On this mutual love depends the entire credibility of the enterprise he was launching. In the words of Pope John Paul II, '... the communion among the members of the Church is the primary and the principal sign the Church offers so that the world may believe in Christ'.

Now this brings relationship to the centre of the mystery of the Church. Walter Kasper vigorously puts forward this principle when he writes that today 'we are witnessing a revolution in the way of understanding being. The ultimate and supreme reality is not substance, but relation'. For Aristotle, however, relation was one of the weakest of the accidents. Kasper stresses that 'because God presented himself as the God of the Covenant and dialogue, the God for us and with us, relation does not come after substance, but before; ... the meaning of being therefore is not substance in itself but the love that communicates itself'.[22] This means that persons and their relationships must enjoy clear precedence over both programmes and structures.

Not only does the mystery of God consist in the trinitarian relationships (each divine Person is, in fact, a subsisting relation, as St Thomas Aquinas shows), but Christians are called to live by these relationships. By living them, they participate in the life of the Blessed Trinity and become the credible followers of Christ. For divine revelation is given to us, not to satisfy human curiosity, but to make us live. It is given to us as 'the initial and essential idea of Christianity',[23] not that we should know more but that we should do better! And it is from that Source alone that the Church can draw the vision and the energy to meet the challenges of our particular time.

Becoming Home Makers

At length a tripartite way begins to emerge. It suggests the combination of a method, a source and a perspective. We will look at each briefly. The first has to do with listening to and living the Word of God, the second with Christian lifestyle or spirituality, the last with the issue of truth and modern culture. And with these we can become home builders, for as Henri de Lubac perceptively saw, 'although the Church rests on eternal foundations, it is in a continual state of rebuilding'.[24]

First, there is a *method*. The Council, following Scripture, stressed obedience to the Word of God, both written and handed on in the life of the Church. Thus the whole Church is to listen devoutly to the Word, pondering it faithfully. The Magisterium itself is not above the word of God but serves it, albeit with the sure charism of truth.[25] The whole Church has to grow in the Marian art of 'treasuring', 'storing' and 'pondering' (Lk 2:19, 52) the living Word of God (DV 8). This will enable us to *be* the Church in the way Jesus wants his Church to be. It will prevent the task of implementing the great Council, which is Herculean in any case, descending into a form of 'religious business'. It will protect it as a Gospel-driven adventure. In a particular way, such obedience to the Word will teach us to look out for 'the greatest of the ways' which is always charity (ICor 12:31). As Pascal so acutely observed, 'the truth without charity is not of God'. The way of Charity will guide us to treasure especially his dying wish and the pearl of the whole Gospel, namely, the New Commandment. We will also discover that the measure of that mutual love is his measure, that is, the measure that is without measure, 'Love one another *as I have loved you*'. This leads us to the mystery of Jesus crucified and abandoned, who is the Word of God summed up and fully unfolded, the one who, lifted up on the Cross, draws all to himself and gathers together the scattered children of God (Jn 12:32; 11:52). It is this Christ whom Paul described as 'the power and the wisdom of God' (ICor 1:24), and who was Paul's key 'method' as an apostle of Jesus Christ (ICor 12:31).

Then there is a *Source*. This consists in a spirituality which is the motor-force to drive this method and give it soul. Without a sound spirituality of communion, the method will remain barren, for the Word of God will not be lived. Naturally, such a spirituality should strongly mirror the discovery of the Church as mystery, communion and mission. In the pages of the Gospel it is possible to discern the form of a spirituality for this life of communion which is the key to the mystery of the God who built this unique communion with us and for us, 'giving himself up in our place as a fragrant offering and a sacrifice to God' (Eph 5:2-3). This is the way of building that communion which he desires above everything else. With that art of loving, Christians can together build the family of God on earth, a family that answers to the prayer of the Head of the Church, 'Father, may they be one in us ... so that the world may believe it was you who sent me' (Jn 17:21).

Some of these steps can be easily identified and so mentioned at once. They include the following. First, as Christ loved all and died for all, Christians are under the divine imperative to *love all*. 'If you love those who love you, what right have you to claim any credit'(Mt 5:46)? Next, 'God loved us first' (I Jn 4:19), and 'Christ died for us while we were still sinners' (Rom 5:8). Christians can never love God first, but they can be *the first to love each neighbour* they encounter. The truth is that they should aim at this primacy of being the first to love. God's initiative in loving us first would thus gain a certain social visibility.

Third, Christ loved by serving even to the point of giving his life for his disciples on the wood of the Cross (Mk 10:45). This was, in fact, the very programme of his ministry (Lk 4:14-18; Mk 8:27-33). Christians need to *aim at serving*: each person I meet is my master and I am his servant, or rather, the servant of Christ in him! If only a few of his followers were genuine servants of him in their brothers and sisters, the world would soon belong to Christ! Fourth, Christ loved us by *making himself one with us*, first in the incarnation and finally in his death on the Cross. He not only took on our humanity out of love for us, he also took on the human condition, as ancient authors loved to repeat. Paul understood this step in the art of loving with special clarity – it became in fact a key plank in his method of evangelising. 'I made myself a Jew to the Jews ... For the weak I made myself weak. I made myself all things to all men ... I still do this, for the sake of the Gospel, to have a share in its blessings' (ICor 9:20, 22-23). Whoever, then, would draw from this source of life and love must learn the Christian and apostolic art of *making himself one* in everything except sin with each brother and sister he meets.

These four steps, then, indicate an 'art of loving', which is spelled out in the New Testament and which energises the whole adventure of living the Church as a communion of distinct but equal persons. These four steps, however, flow into a fifth and concluding step which acts as the crowning of a spirituality of communion or unity: where two or more people live this way something wonderful happens *among them*: Jesus begins to live among them. This is clearly spelled out for us in St Matthew's Gospel: 'Where two or three are gathered together in my name, I shall be in their midst' (18:20). Encapsulating as it does the ecclesiology of St Matthew, this sentence was among the most quoted texts of the New Testament whenever the Fathers of the Church thought about the mystery of the Church. Such a spirituality flows from the pure Gospel, it creates a collective or communitarian life among believers, and that enables them to witness and to evangelise, for they do first and only later teach and speak (Acts 1:1). This is the style of evangelisation needed for our times, for, in the memorable words of Paul VI, 'modern men and women listen to witnesses more easily than they listen to teachers, and if they do listen to teachers it is because they are first witnesses'.[26]

An Italian theologian has noted the many benefits of such a spirituality. It places the accent on the life of the Church as one of communion and so involves the definitive exit from an anxious pastoral method of conservation. It involves a more prophetical pastoral method of witness: one must do before teaching (Acts 1:1). It will underline the reality, not only of the ordained priesthood, but also that of the royal priesthood received in baptism as a call to bear fruit in the world. It will highlight the four great dialogues which the Council has opened to the Church and so make manifest the authentic face of the Church for the third millennium. It will sow seeds of a new sociality based on the principles of the Gospel. It will translate the gospel of life into concrete witness.[27]

Finally, there is a *perspective*. This consists in the great question of truth in the context of contemporary culture. The truth we are referring to here is not only the truth discoverable by the natural sciences but above all moral, spiritual and religious truth. As already hinted, this is a major issue today, since the movement of history has brought us to a point of surrender as to the very discoverability of truth in the fields of metaphysics, morality and religion. Today 'there is a philosophy, an attitude of principle towards reality, that tells us, "It is nonsense to ask ourselves what it is; we can only ask ourselves what we can do with things"'.[28] And without truth can we live anywhere but in a fool's paradise, doing, it is true, wonderful things in a world bursting with energy, but without any ultimate vision? Not only is there nothing to be known, but we are largely incapable of knowing it! And this in all the areas that matter, such as the meaning of our existence, the mystery of death, the difference between good and evil, the true path to happiness if that is not a chimera, the ultimate purpose of the universe. Not only does such a culture not have the answers to these questions, questions that are constitutive of humankind, it does not have the inescapable questions at the forefront of its mind.

The paradigm of modern society in the West is that of the plurality of opinions. There is no single Truth, not even the many truths. There are only the many *opinions*. The result is a radical and rugged individualism. Man is intensely self-made, but from what and for what purpose? These questions are so unanswerable that they ought not to be asked, as Auguste Comte famously claimed. The net impact of such a state of affairs is vividly to be seen in the majority of the democracies of the West, where opinions both clashing and contradictory are facilitated in the laws of the land. A striking instance of this is perhaps that of bioethics where medical progress has brought forward possibilities of such Frankensteinian magnitude that many sensitive and perceptive people shiver at the prospects. What is wrong, in the final analysis, with the prospect of human cloning if the human person is not a unique individual made in the image and likeness of God, a Thou in relationship to infinity and in training for future glory? Can human beings, human society and human history be anything but a cruel farce if we cannot know the meaning, indeed the ultimate meaning, of our existence?

The upshot of all this is a crisis in the West in the very concept of truth.[29] This crisis, however, is also perhaps an opportunity, as the Greek roots of the word, 'crisis', suggest. The opportunity consists in the necessity of rethinking the very concept of truth. Going beyond a rather conceptual and intellectual notion of truth, there are emerging today some precious emphases. The truth is acquiring at its core the dimensions of history, of dialogue, of the link with life and praxis, and of openness to the future. What is needed therefore is a living model of the truth which includes necessarily the dimension of dialogue. The pluralism of today does not have to degenerate into a tolerant indifference, even if this is the danger and the tendency. Instead, it could open out towards a model of communion and of relationship where, through the acceptance of the other and of his truth, the way could be opened to explore together *the* Truth and then to live the Truth together.

This is a most urgent task, for the challenge of pluralism tends to undermine both Christian faith and Christian life. Pluralism, in fact, proposes the ideal of tolerance. However, such tolerance finds it impossible to tolerate *any claim to truth*. 'Tolerance does not tolerate truth, though that was once its purpose.'[30] Now in the Christian scheme of things, the Truth, far from being only a collection of moral and doctrinal truths, is a Person, Jesus the Christ. According to the classical formulae of faith, he is both 'the fullness of humanity and the fullness of divinity', linked in the relationship that is called the 'hypostatic union'. And one could make a strong argument that that Union has 'personalised' the family of humankind more than any other, and promises to do the very same even more in the future.

In *Veritatis splendor*, Pope John Paul underlines this fact as follows: 'Christ crucified reveals the authentic sense of freedom, he lives it fully in the total gift of himself, and calls the disciples to share in his freedom'(85). This full self-gift reveals that the truth, which is Christ in the event of his death and resurrection, is the truth of the Father himself. It is love. So that men and women can make this encounter with the event of Christ, God has desired his Church. If her dimension of communion is lived between Christians, then Christ lives in 'that space of grace' (Mt 18:20), where our non-believing brothers and sisters can enter and find the fullness of life, not as a theory, but as an experience, not as a burden but as a gift, not as a law but as an adventure. 'By this love you have for one another all will know you are my disciples' (Jn 13:35).

Now the truth of Christ as event, as an event lived, attracts, spreads and makes news. This event gives in the process not only the truth of the Christ Event, but also its goodness and its beauty. And as the classical world saw, and Aquinas stressed and a theologian such as Hans Urs von Balthasar shows again in our times, beauty places crowns upon both truth and goodness, since it adds persuasion to the truth and attraction to the good. Thus the event of Christ attracts and persuades. In the process it radiates the light of the glory of God, the glory shining on the face of his Son crucified and glorified (2Cor 4:6), as 'our hope of glory' (Col 1:24). In that way the Event of Christ converts, energises and sends out on mission, for it is unthinkable that someone should have heard the Gospel and still not want to tell the Gospel.[31]

The Woman whom God Placed at the Centre of his 'Home'

In God's most wise design there is a woman at the centre of his plan, that plan which, though existing in the Heart of the Blessed Trinity from all eternity (1Cor 2:7; Eph 3:10; Col 2:2-3), has only now been communicated to humanity. It is a plan to unite all things in heaven and on earth, so that the mystery shall become a communion on earth that moves outwards in space and time to 'all of creation' (Mk 16:15). This plan fascinated the early Church. St Irenaeus of Lyons, himself the royal door to patristic theology, sees in the notion of 'recapitulation' (Eph 1:10) the organising and unifying dimension of divine revelation. Just as a sonata in music begins with an exposition, advances to a development and concludes with a recapitulation, so too God's most wise 'design that stands for ever' (Ps 33:11) is summed up in the eternal Word becoming flesh in order to re-found and restore the whole of creation. Now this summit suggests the real historical woman in whom eternity and time rhymed, so that heaven came on earth even as earth entered heaven. In this woman, recapitulation received historical anchorage. As Henri de Lubac puts it, 'The central fact is the revelation of the plan realised by God in humanity: this plan is an organic whole with a progressive development in history'.[32] In part two of this study we shall have occasion to develop vital dimensions of the divine plan.

Mary has this one task: to enable the Church to become herself as the 'charity of unity' (St Augustine) and the home where mutual love is both the life and the law. Writing in the thirteenth century, St Bonaventure defines the Church as 'the place where people love each other mutually'.[33] Now this could appear to be an impossible task were it not for the fact that God has placed a woman at the centre of his Church! And not any woman but she who

> gave God's infinity
> Dwindled to infancy
> Welcome in womb and breast
> ...
> And makes, O marvellous!
> New Nazareths in us.34

She has lived with God-made-man here on earth, and in the inspired pages of the New Testament one may detect in her a style of loving by which she shows a concrete way of bringing about that communion of which she is the first witness and the permanent reminder.

Our times, in fact, need to look to her with particular attention, not in order to see what we want to see, but rather to see the great things

God has done to her, to understand why 'all ages will call her blessed' (Lk 1:48-49), and to learn to live by that love that builds up (ICor 8:1) the household of the faith. Hans Urs von Balthasar is well within the mark when he writes that 'without Mariology Christianity threatens to become functionalistic, soulless, a hectic enterprise'.[35] We need to look today to where Christianity shines out, not as laboriously repeated doctrine, but as a breathtaking adventure.

In Mary one discerns a principle that crosses the whole of history and of divine revelation. In a particular way, it emerges during the history of the Church. This principle has been formulated by Klaus Hemmerle with these words, 'What comes down from heaven must also grow up from the earth'.[36] Fruit is the gift of heaven, and yet it grows from below, from the earth. Without sunshine from above and without the good soil beneath, the tree cannot grow and there will be no fruit. Still, the fruit is more than the addition of sun and earth: it is something new. In Mary one sees the very personification of this principle and pattern. When 'in the fullness of time' (Gal 4:4; Rom 8:15) God gave his Son to humankind, this woman received him and conceived him in purest love *as the representative of Israel and of humankind*. St Thomas perceived this with typical insight, 'By means of the annunciation the consent of the Virgin was sought *in the place of the whole of humankind*'.[37]

The Father offered his Son to humankind and this Mother conceived him by the overshadowing of the Holy Spirit so that he became bone of her bone and flesh of her flesh. The Father gave his Son to humankind, and this woman gave him his flesh and blood. The 'yes' which Mary spoke in Nazareth will be spoken again by her on Calvary and yet again in the Upper Room when 'the Spirit descending … discloses the one discharge from sin and error'. In each constitutive moment of divine revelation, the same pattern is visible: what falls from heaven must grow up from the earth! In all of this one sees the 'final concordance reached in Mary between the descending grace which calls to her and the ascending grace in her which answers the call'.[38] Mary thereby guards the principle that, though revelation is the initiative of God, his gift, he deals with human persons in a dialogue that is salvation history.

As the carrier of the cause of Christ, the Church has an immaculate core in the Virgin of Nazareth, Calvary and the Upper Room. 'The Church is henceforth what was created on the Cross: the gathering of believers around those endowed with (hierarchical) ministry and with Mary in their midst.'[39] That is why innumerable medieval representations of Pentecost portray Mary as the centre and focus of the Spirit-enlightened Church. Appointed from the Cross as the Woman-Mother of the Church that is born from the wounded side of the Redeemer, Mary 'from that moment is taken by the disciple to his own' (Jn 19:27). Her mission as the Queen of Apostles rises before us, without her claiming any of the apostolic powers or authority.

In this post-modern age, the Marian principle of the Church has been rediscovered. As co-essential with the Petrine principle, Mary highlights vital dimensions of the Church for today. This is the significance of the fact that the *magna charta* of the Council, *Lumen gentium*, when seeking to highlight something of the mystery of the Church, could not omit her. Correcting the imbalance of post-Reformation theology which had set out to highlight the Petrine principle on its own, the Council reached towards Mary and her place in the mystery of Christ and his Church. Mary shows the way of life, the renewal, which the Spirit is indicating to the Church for our times and in our times. She personifies this way because she is the perfect disciple of the Lord and, after her Son, the greatest protagonist of his Way. Gregory of Nyssa does not hesitate to say that Mary taught John the Evangelist the authentic theology of Jesus, while St Ambrose stresses that Mary oriented him upwards towards the mystery of the Trinity as the infinite fountainhead of that communion that is the Church.[40] As she once saved the infant Christ.

Notes

1. Reinhold Schneider, *Der Inselreich. Gesetz und Grösse der britischen Macht*, Leipzig 1936, 14; as quoted in Hans Urs von Balthasar, *Tragedy under Grace, Reinhold Schneider on the Experience of the West*, San Francisco 1997, 97.

2. John Henry Newman, *Catholic Sermons*, London 1957, 123: the italics are Newman's.

3. Friedrich Nietzsche, *The Gay Science*, 358, as translated in Hans Urs von Balthasar, *The Office of Peter and the Structure of the Church*, San Francisco 1986, 38.

4. Pope John Paul II, as quoted by Giuseppe Zanghí, 'A Reflection on Postmodernity' in *Being One*, 7(1998), 80–81.

5. Herbert Butterfield, *The Origins of Modern Science, 1300–1800*, 2nd ed., New York 1966, 7.

6. Klaus Hemmerle, 'The Hour of the new Beginning' in *Being One* 1(1992), 4.

7. Walter Kasper, *An Introduction to Christian Faith*, London 1980, 5.

8. Hannah Arendt, *The Burden of our Time*, London 1951, 438.

9. Henri de Lubac, *Catholicism*, London 1950, xv.

10. T.S. Eliot, *Four Quartets*, Dry Salvages, V.

11. St Augustine, *Commentary on the Psalm* 85, 1.

12. Eric Voegelin, 'The Gospel and History', in *Published Essays 1966–1985*, Baton Rouge 1990, 173.

13. Gerald Hanratty, *Light from Paris. Cardinal Lustiger on Faith and contemporary Culture*, Dublin 1995, 15.

14. Bruno Forte, *Dove va il cristianesimo?*, Brescia 2000, 91; see also his 'Faith and Reason: the interpretative Key to the Principal Encyclicals of Pope John Paul II' in James McEvoy, *The Challenge of Truth. Fides et Ratio*, Dublin 2002, 203–218.

15. Giuseppe Zanghí, 'Pluralismo e verità morale. Sfida per il Cristianesimo', in *Nuova Umanità*, XVI(1994), 10.

16. Paul Ricoeur, *Il conflitto delle interpretazioni*, Milano 1986, 258.

17. *Dei Verbum*, 1.

18. Joseph Cardinal Ratzinger, 'Introduction to Christianity: *Yesterday,*

Today, and Tomorrow' in *Communio*, xxxi (2004), 482–483.

19. G.M. Hopkins, 'The Blessed Virgin compared to the Air we Breathe' in *Poems and Prose*, London 1986, 55.

20. See Karl Rahner, *Il Dio Trino come fondamento originario e trascendente della storia della salvezza*, in *Mysterium Salutis 3*, Brescia 1969, 404.

21. Bruno Forte, *Trinità come storia*, Milano 1988, 13: translation my own.

22. Walter Kasper, *The God of Jesus Christ*, London 1984, 156.

23. John Henry Newman, Preface to the Third Edition of the *Via Media*, London 1878, xlvii.

24. Henri de Lubac, *Catholicism*, 321–322.

25. See *Dei Verbum* 1; 10.

26. Pope Paul VI, Apostolic Letter *Evangelii nuntiandi*, 41.

27. See Piero Coda, 'Chiesa per il terzo millennio' in *Gen's. Rivista di vita ecclesiale*, XXXI, 4(2001), 108–112.

28. Joseph Ratzinger, *Faith, Truth and Culture. Reflections on the Encyclical, Fides et ratio*, 8.

29. Pope John Paul II, Encyclical *Veritatis splendor*, 32.

30. James V. Schall, S.J., '"The Whole Risk for a Human Being": On the Insufficiency of Apollo' in *Logos. A Journal of Catholic Thought and Culture*, 7(2004), 22.

31. See Pope Paul VI, *Evangelii nuntiandi*, 24.

32. Henri de Lubac, *Catholicism*, 320.

33. St Bonaventure, *Hexameron* I, 4.

34. Gerard Manley Hopkins, ibid., 55, 56.

35. Hans Urs von Balthasar, *Elucidations*, London 1975, 72.

36. Klaus Hemmerle, *Brücken zum Credo*, Freiburg im Breisgau 1984, 20.

37. St Thomas, *Summa*, III, q.30, a.1.

38. Hans Urs von Balthasar, *The Glory of the Lord*, vol. I, Edinburgh 1982, 363.

39. *Idem, Der dreifache Kranz*, 73.

40. Gregory of Nyssa, PG 10:984–988; *Ambrose, De Institutione Virginum*, 7, 50: PL 16, 319.

Chapter II

The Losing and the Finding of 'Strong Reason'

In the opening chapter we had occasion to describe both the great Cathedral that the Church built as a home for humanity, as well as the collapse and consequent loss of this same home. Our concern was to understand the phenomenon of the 'epochal dark night of the soul' (John Paul II) that is now upon us, at least in Europe and in the West generally. Now it is our task to analyse more closely the emptying out of the substance of revelation in the case of peoples once at home in the *Lebensraum* of the Faith.

What is the principal characteristic of our world? Can we arrive at an accurate understanding of our contemporaries? Understanding is not only a value in itself, it also puts one on the road to deep dialogue. Understanding may even open a door to fresh discovery and new horizons in our own assimilation of the divine revelation which has been given to us but whose length and depth, height and width exceed our wildest imaginings and will always do so (Eph 3:18-9). According to the philosopher of history, Eric Voegelin, 'we do not live in a post-Christian, or "post-philosophical", or "neopagan" age, or in the age of a "new myth", or of "utopianism", but plainly in a period of massive deculturation through the deformation of reason'.[1] And if the faculty for knowing the true and the good is diseased, how great will the resulting darkness have to be?

The religion of Christ puts itself forth as truth, in fact, as the final truth about God, man and the world.[2] The unknown genius who, as early as the second decade of the second century, wrote the *Letter to Diognetus* put it like this: 'The Almighty Himself, the Creator of the Universe, the God whom no eye can discern, has sent down His own very truth from heaven, His own holy and incomprehensible Word to plant it among men and ground it in their hearts.'³ The Founder himself made a simple equation between truth and himself, 'I am the Truth' (Jn 14:6). It is the claim to truth, to truth that is ultimate and everlasting, which has characterised Christianity from the very beginning.

Thinking of this and similar texts, Cardinal Newman makes the point with customary clarity: 'The very idea of Christianity in its profession and history ... is a definite message from God to man distinctly conveyed by his chosen instruments, and to be received as such a message; and therefore to be positively acknowledged, embraced and maintained as true, on the ground of its being divine, not as true on intrinsic grounds, not as probably true, but as absolutely certain knowledge, certain in a sense in which nothing else can be certain, because it comes from him who can neither deceive nor be deceived.'⁴ Jesus Christ in fact is '[T]he only man in the history of the world who dared make a claim how God had established him in the Old Testament; who for that reason was looked upon as crazy and possessed (Mk 3:20-21) and was crucified. For modesty is becoming to a wise man, and it is becoming for a prophet to say "Word of the Lord", not "but I say to you"'.⁵

This is both the glory and the 'scandal' of the faith that was given once for all to the saints (Jude 3). 'On this claim is founded the missionary tendency of the faith: only when the Christian faith is truth, does it regard all men: when it is simply a cultural variant of man's religious experience closed up in a symbolic key and never intended to be deciphered, then it must remain in its own culture and leave the others in their own.'⁶ But what happens if a culture announces that we cannot access moral, spiritual and revealed truth because we do not have the capacity to do so? Our reason, it is claimed, lacks the ability to know, and our mind the ability to access, the vital higher echelons of reality. Such a culture has to pronounce all claims to know the truth about God, about man and about the world and history as illusory if not actually arrogant. Tolerance will then become the highest ideal of such a culture. Such a tolerance, however, is one that presupposes a paradoxical and strange inconsistency: it 'does not tolerate truth, though that was once its purpose'.⁷

There was a time when reason and mind did not think of themselves in that fashion. The history of the formation and the deformation of reason now beckon. This beckoning requires us to address the true nature of reason. To do so demands a quick look at reason in the ancient world of Greece and Rome. It was there that, in the discovery of philosophy by the Ionians, reason (*nous*) was clearly articulated as *the* constituent of our humanity. And it was there that the first preaching and inculturation of the divine revelation that had descended on the soil of Israel took place. As the encyclical *Fides et ratio* notes, this is a fact that has a providential significance in the Christian scheme of things.[8]

'Reason is the constituent of humanity at all times', while 'its differentiation and articulation through language symbols is an historical event'.[9] The articulation of reason occurs with particular clarity in the emergence of *philosophy* in ancient Greece. These philosophers saw in reason the distinctive component of humanity. Reason consisted in the tension towards the ground of reality. As such it constituted the very structure of humanity. Aristotle characterised man as the *zoon noun echon*, as 'the living being that possesses *nous*'.[10]

Now it does not do justice to the insight of these lovers of wisdom and searchers for truth to see in *nous* a merely intellectual faculty in the modern sense. Pascal contrasted famously '*la raison*' and '*le coeur*'. For its part the Greek differentiation of human existence as *nous* combines 'heart' and 'reason': *nous* is the depth dimension of the person, the universal organising constant of society, and the concrete existential thrust of existence beyond itself towards the mystery that envelops human existence. As such, it is 'a persuasive force of order through the stark light it lets fall on the phenomena of personal and social disorder'.[11]

It is true that the phrase *zoon noetikon* translates as *animal rationale* and that this translation became standard. However, the characterisation of man as a rational animal developed into something like a word definition. 'The philosopher, however, was not interested in word definitions but in the analysis of reality.' This interest led to the discovery that reality flowed between two poles, the subjective and the objective. Aristotle characterised these poles as *seeking* and *drawing*. 'The terms *seeking (zetein)* and *drawing (helkein)* do not denote two different movements but symbolise the dynamics in the tension of existence between its human and divine poles. In the one movement there is experienced a seeking from the human, a being drawn from the divine pole.'[12] Every human being lives in an in-between, the result of this tension. However, as if to increase the drama of human existence, there is also a magnetic field of pulls and counter pulls surrounding each person. This involves the necessity of choosing between pull and counter pull. In turn this opens up the drama of human existence. Plato tells the Parable of the Cave where the man who is fettered with his face to the wall is dragged (*helkein*) by force to the light.[13] One of the achievements of this articulation of reason is that it allowed Plato to personify the truth of his articulation in the person of Socrates. This is the central contention of *The Apology*: Socrates is killed for being truly obedient to the pull towards the good of justice and truth, and can say to his Athenian executioners as he is led out to drink the hemlock, 'Now it is time that we were going, I to die and you to live; but which of us has the happier prospect is unknown to anyone but God'.[14]

An heir to this legacy of philosophy in the early second century after Christ is Justin Martyr. His case provides a splendid illustration of the principles that the philosophers have been mentioning. An accomplished philosopher at the time of his conversion to Christianity, Justin clearly understood that 'the Gospel did not reject all philosophy but rather absorbed the life of the mind into the overflowing *pleroma* of the revelation of the infinite Word of God'.[15] He realises that 'the Gospel and philosophy do not face the believer with a choice of alternatives, nor are they complementary aspects of truth which the thinker would have to weld into the complete truth: in his conception, the Logos of the Gospel is rather the same word of the same God as the *logos spermatikos* of philosophy, but at a later state of its manifestation in history'. So perfect was this dovetailing that for philosophers such as Justin 'Christianity is not an alternative to philosophy, it is philosophy itself in its state of perfection'.[16]

It is more than interesting that the first preachers of the Gospel did not set out in the first instance to dialogue with the religions. Rather, they appealed to reason and asserted the truth that was beyond all reason. And so they turned to philosophy and the philosophers, while of course realising that the mystery of Christ's Cross 'could not be expressed in philosophy' (ICor 1:17) without a huge enlargement of the latter's horizons. The episode of Paul entering Athens in the *Acts of the Apostles* and proclaiming the Gospel to the heirs of the great philosophers makes the point dramatically. Jerusalem and Athens are not in opposition: rather, they are allies. This is the message of the Apostle of the Gentiles both as a Roman citizen and as a convert to the fullness of the revelation given to the people of Israel in Christ.

The Unravelling of the Synthesis between Faith and Reason

From the beginning of the fourteenth century a number of religious, political and social currents began to flow in Europe. These were the renaissance, the reformation and, finally, the enlightenment. Though unfolding in that order, they exerted a cumulative and converging impact on the great synthesis effected in Patristic and Scholastic theology, notably that of Thomas Aquinas who had made of Aristotle 'a hewer of wood and a drawer of water' in the service of Faith. The outcome of that impact was a real falling behind in Christian thinking and in the culture of Europe. The first tremors, in fact, of the resulting earthquake were felt towards the end of the seventeenth century. The year 1680 was to be a year of destiny in this respect.

In that year three phenomena occurred. 'Then it was that Herbert Butterfield placed the origins of modern science, then that Paul Hazard placed the beginning of the Enlightenment, then that Yves Congar placed the beginning of dogmatic theology.'[17] Butterfield explained that while many of the discoveries that properly belong to modern science had been taking place since 1300, the dominant context was Aristotelian. These new ideas did not sit easily with the old ideas. It took until the end of the seventeenth century to formulate accurately the new methods and principles involved in the new science. The new science, however, 'outshines everything since the rise of Christianity and reduces the Renaissance and the Reformation to the rank of mere episodes, mere internal displacements, within the system of medieval Christendom'.[18]

As to the Enlightenment, it was in full swing by 1680. It exhibited a full-blown assault on Christianity from all quarters. It was appalled at the spectacle of the great religious wars fought among Christians. It therefore moved from the God of Abraham to the God of the *philosophes*. The unity of Europe, indeed of Christendom, could no longer be rooted and grounded in Christianity; the legacy of Christianity in fact was the source and the cause of the wars of religion! If the Christians of Europe had divided and torn each other apart for almost two centuries in the name of their dogmas, how could Europe look to that foundation for its future unity? Europe decided to replace the God of Revelation by the God of the philosophers.

Now these two movements – the rise of modern science and the emergence of the Enlightenment – were a source of great perplexity for the theologians. One can sympathise with their plight as they perceived an undermining of the revealed truth of God and their own authority. They had inherited the Augustinian and Thomistic idea and practice of Theology as 'Faith (hope, charity) seeking understanding'. The Reformation, however, had placed at the top of its agenda the issue of the *precise location* of the authority of revelation. Theologians read this programme as a possible undermining of the truths of the faith. They decided to act to defend the endangered dogmas of faith. The implications of this dramatic change were tragic.

Their theological style now 'replaced the inquiry of the *quaestio* by the pedagogy of the thesis. It demoted the quest of faith for understanding to a desirable, but secondary, and indeed, optional goal. It gave basic and central significance to the certitudes of faith, their presuppositions and their consequences ... the new dogmatic theology not only proved its theses, but also was supported by the teaching authority and the sanctions of the Church'.[19] The Good News did not require the terms of philosophy, which are in any case incapable of expressing the crucifixion of Christ (1Cor 1:17). Rationality that had once been the mark of the faith was now seen as the very enemy of the same faith. Theology gradually withdrew from conversation with the emerging culture, and this culture moved away increasingly from contact with revelation. The divorce of revelation and reason was under way.

The Emergence of 'Weak Reason'

Faith had jettisoned Reason, then. And having lost Reason, faith had also lost its reasonableness. Faith was reasonable in the measure in which it could do without reason! The cry of Tertullian from the third century rang out across Europe with increasing clarity, 'What does Athens have in common with Jerusalem? The Academy with the Church?'.[20] Reason for its part gradually lost interest in Faith. This was strange in the extreme, for from time immemorial reason had found a welcome in the house built by divine revelation. The life of reason, in fact, had been welcomed by the descending truth of God in Christ. The *pleroma* of revelation called forth in turn the unrealisable potencies of reason, whether individual, societal or historical. This led to a flowering of each culture evangelised by the Faith.

And theology under the handling of great geniuses such as Athanasius, Augustine and Aquinas defined itself as the thinking that happens within the life of faith so that faith can seek ever deeper understanding. As with faith, so also with hope and love: hope seeks understanding and love seeks understanding, in fact the understanding for which it has new eyes (Eph 1:18). But throughout the eighteenth century reason turns away. It has found new terrain. It turns towards the fields of the newborn natural and human sciences as its proper object, in fact, its *only object and concern*. What it starts to discover yields new fields of knowledge with the promise of even greater discovery.

Reason, then, having lost its citizenship in the House of God, sees the House of God as the realm belonging to faith exclusively. It must follow that faith is left without reason, and reason is not only without faith but is also the *rival of, if not the actual alternative to, faith.* The thinking of believers and of theologians is without reason or at best is based on 'weak reason'. In 'the common opinion of men ..., though they contrast faith and reason, [they] consider *faith to be weak reason*'.[21] With typical perceptiveness, John Henry Newman had diagnosed the outcome of the divorce of faith and reason. Thus faith is 'unscientific' and unverifiable and ultimately without evidences. The glory of the New Science is that it is grounded on 'strong reason'. In the new worlds opening up by means of the natural sciences great crowds now decide to walk by sight and not by faith (2Cor 5:7).

Perhaps a glowing example of someone who discerned clearly the new world emerging from such a radical first principle was John Henry Newman. His life spans most of the nineteenth century (1801–1890) and expresses the tone of England and mainland Europe. As early as 1839 he uses the term 'weak reason'.[22] The great march-of-mind of the Enlightenment had been underway over the previous century. In England, the Reformation had determined not only the place of the Church under the monarchy, it had also changed the religious landscape from Catholicism to Anglicanism as the ideal *Via Media* between an unreformed Catholicism and an exaggerated Reformation.

Newman tells us the 'popular sense' of faith and reason in his own day. 'Faith involves easiness, and Reason slowness in accepting the claims of Religion ... Faith is conversant with conjectures or presumptions, Reason with proofs.'[23] Thus the opponents of faith easily bring 'the charge of weak reasoning' against the work and arguments of the Fathers of the Church and the work of theologians generally.[24] This view is unpacked further in an address given in Dublin during his term as Rector of the fledgling Catholic University. 'You may have opinions in religion, you may have theories, you may have arguments, you may have probabilities; you may have anything but demonstration, and therefore you cannot have science.'[25] This statement is not only an undermining of faith and revelation – they are only the opinions that certain groups of people happen to hold – it is also a clear formulation of the model of knowing at the heart of the *New Science* that now crosses the sky like Phaeton in his chariot. But the most radical aspect of the New Science is its claim to be the one and only way of knowledge, the one and only method by which we encounter and find truth. This is 'strong reason' in full flight.

The conclusion becomes inevitable: 'Christianity has been the bane of true knowledge, for it has turned the intellect away from what it can know, and occupied it in what it cannot ... Truth has been sought in the wrong direction, and the attainable has been put aside for the visionary ... The world has lost two thousand years.'[26] Newman sees and understands the disgust that the protagonists of this view of knowledge will feel towards those who see the dogmatic principle as essential to revealed religion. The protagonists of the New Science were in possession of one and only expression of reason – albeit a new one – which they unwittingly erected to be *the very nature* of reason. One deployment of mind became *the nature of mind*. They did not advert to the fact that the mind is greater than all its acts since it is their source. One expression of rationality was scarcely the only rationality. This constituted both the dramatic strength and the narrowness of their claim.

The implications, however, for revealed truth were appalling in prospect and devastating in the event. The central Christian truths were only opinions, since no one could believe what he did not understand, nor could anyone believe what he could not prove.[27] Newman called this pervasive and floating attitude 'religious liberalism'. He defined it as the view that 'there is no positive truth in religion, but that one creed is as good as another ... It is inconsistent with any recognition of any religion, as *true* ... Revealed religion is not a truth, but a sentiment and a taste: not an objective fact, not miraculous; and it is the right of each individual to make it say just what strikes his fancy'.[28] In this state of things, emancipation from the shackles of religion and its replacement by the fruits of the New Science became the goal of enlightened humanity. Man's future and problems could be dealt with by reason, if not at once, at least inevitably. This confidence in strong reason will claim increasingly a comprehensive overview of reality. The search for totality will become totalitarian inexorably. We are at the dawn of the great ideologies that have unleashed the apocalyptic wars and violence of the last century.

Newman was not alone at this time. In another milieu entirely, in the Catholic School of Tübingen, thinkers like Möhler and Drey[29] and Hirscher were working out similar methods in theology. 'Their theology is happily free of purely negative polemics and nervous apologetics. It tries to find a way to the opponent's real strength and thus to learn from him.'[30] This stands out in their insistence that the method of theology, though different from that of the New Science, is still parallel to it. The difference is dictated by the fact of different subject matter, while the parallel character emerges from the operation of one and the same reason in scientist and theologian even if different modalities of rationality are employed.[31]

The Regaining of 'Strong Reason' for the Faith

Newman's analysis of the 'destruction of reason' in its classical sense, occurring as it does in the nineteenth century on foot of the first flowering of that march of mind called the Enlightenment, hopefully serves to capture something both of the tone and the tenets of the New Science, as well as of the resulting situation of the Faith in Europe in the nineteenth century.

Newman saw it as an age when 'love was cold'.[32] No new revelation could be given. No new revelation had to be given. The difficulty lay rather in the new culture, more particularly in the roots of that culture. Those roots ran well below the surface level of the soil. They constituted an axiom for the followers of the new march of mind: the one and only layer of reality accessible to humanity was that which the New Science, and it alone, accessed. Since this science was empirical and concrete, knowledge of the invisible and the mysterious was impossible, their pursuit like the chasing of chimeras in the desert, and their systematic elaboration a waste of time and resources.

However, '[T]his closure in self, this reduction of reason, cannot be the criterion of philosophy, and the whole of science cannot end up being unable to pose the questions proper to man, without itself becoming an empty and ultimately dangerous occupation'.[33] The dogmatism of the New Science made dialogue difficult, indeed.

However, it also challenged the Church and her thinkers to develop an appropriate *organon investigandi*. How can we give 'an account of the hope that is within us' to our contemporaries (1Pet 3:15)? Can we know the truth? That is the question, the abiding question, indeed, the ultimate question. In answer to this key question, I propose to follow an historical order advancing a sequence of recent Christian thinkers representative of the Anglican, Protestant and Catholic worlds. These are, respectively, John Henry Newman, Eric Voegelin and Bernard Lonergan.

I. John Henry Newman (1801–1890)

What Newman undertook to craft from early youth was an epistemology of faith. In notes written in 1860, one reads, 'How can one make use of reason where faith is concerned? How can one claim one has made use of one's intellect honestly and respectfully with regard to one's Creator? If a religion is open to *reason* and at the same time to *all,* there ought to be sufficient available reasons for rationally convincing each individual'.[34] From the *Oxford University Sermons* (1826–1843) all the way to the *Grammar of Assent* (1870) he set out to provide the true and real way to understand the relationship between revelation and reason. In doing so he wished to justify the faith of all: of the devout who have no time to study, of children who cannot study, and of the masses of believers who have neither the time nor the interest to study.[35]

Not only is the New Science not the only way to truth, its very method has a certain similarity with the way in which one comes to know faith and theology. What is this way? 'There is a faculty in the mind which I think I have called the inductive sense, which, when properly cultivated and used, answers to Aristotle's *phronesis*, its province being, not virtue, but the *"inquisitio veri"*, which decides for us, beyond any technical rules, when, how, etc. to pass from inference to assent, and when and under what circumstances etc. etc. not.'[36] He likes to contrast that true and real route to moral, spiritual and revealed truth with what he calls 'the rude operation of syllogistic treatment'.[37]

Newman, who always felt himself 'unreal' when planning to write a treatise, lived a life-long friendship with the accomplished scientist, William Froude. Their extensive correspondence has a concreteness and intensity that still impress.[38] In Froude, he recognised the quintessential scientist of the day who could write, 'More strongly than I believe anything else I believe this. That on no subject whatever … is my mind (or as far as I can tell the mind of any human being), capable of arriving at an absolutely certain conclusion … Our "doubts" in fact, appear to me as *sacred*, and I think deserve to be cherished as *sacredly* as our beliefs'.[39] It would be difficult to find a clearer statement of the New Science then advancing like a tide in full flow.

In his reply Newman makes a distinction between 'scientific inquiry' and 'personal inquiry'. Froude responded by asking him to 'really and truly work out this question'.[40] The request acted like a goad. Newman pointed to three kinds of inference: formal, informal and natural.[41] He then contrasted these with assent or judgement. That contrast turns on two differences between inference and assent. While the conclusion is necessary in the case of formal inference, its truth is *conditional upon the truthfulness of the premises*. In the case of judgement, however, the conclusion is simply *unconditional*. In fact, 'assent preserves its essential characteristic of being unconditional'.[42]

The second difference is that in formal inference one need not understand or 'apprehend' the terms of the premises; an assent such an 'apprehension' is necessary. The fact is that 'it is the mind that reasons, and that controls its own reasonings, not any technical apparatus of words and propositions'.[43] Just as many different streams may flow out from one and the same Alpine lake, so too the mind is the source of the different modalities of reason as evident in the sciences, whether natural or human, and in theology and philosophy. The mind is more versatile and vigorous than any of its works.

Newman stresses the fact that Aristotle saw the distinction between the different sciences long ago.[44] Newman, in fact, struggled for the broadening of 'the concept of intelligence too narrowly defined by classical rationalism', as Maurice Nedoncelle perceptively remarks.[45]

What, then, is the way by which we reason and come to know in faith and theology? Newman answers with vigour, 'It is the cumulation of probabilities, independent of each other, arising out of the nature and circumstances of the particular case ... probabilities too fine to avail separately, too subtle and circuitous to be convertible into syllogisms, too numerous and various for such conversion, even were they convertible'.[46] This is the way people normally reason in fact. However, it is not a privileged access to reality, since it 'does not supersede the logical form of inference, but is one and the same with it'.[47]

There are some wonderful analogies mentioned by Newman in illustration of this form of reasoning in the concrete. He likens it to the image of a polygon inscribed in a circle gradually expanding to become one with the circle as its limit. In fact, 'a proof is the limit of converging probabilities'.[48] Other analogies compare the 'cumulation of probabilities' to 'a *cable* which is made up of a number of separate threads, each feeble, yet together as sufficient as an iron rod', which 'represents mathematical or strict demonstration'.[49]

This real and universal way of reasoning has two further characteristics. It is the reasoning of the whole person, not of an isolated faculty of reason. He loved to quote the dictum of St Ambrose, *Non in dialectica complacuit Deo salvum facere populum suum* [God did not decide to save his people by means of logic].[50] His conviction was that 'it is the concrete being that reasons'.[51] Closely allied to this fact is a second: the preponderance of moral and spiritual factors in accessing what is true and good and loveable. 'Truth there is, and attainable it is, but ... its rays stream in upon us through the medium of our moral as well as our intellectual being.'[52] It follows that 'a good and a bad man will think very different things probable'.[53]

Here one touches the famous teaching of Newman on conscience. And there he locates the beginning of the way towards both the religious truth that frees and the revealed love that uplifts.

Conscience is not only a moral judgement but also a moral imperative. As a moral imperative or dictate, it is a Voice that speaks to us in nature and in revelation, and is therefore a 'connecting principle between the creature and his Creator'.[54] The result is that we know ourselves to be addressed. Conscience which is as real as memory, intellect, will or the sense of the beautiful, plays a major role in our accessing spiritual and moral reality. In fact, conscience yields the most 'real' and 'imaginative' apprehension of, and assent to, spiritual and divine realities. Obedience to this dimension of conscience transforms the subject to enable him to perceive spiritual realities.[55]

II. Eric Voegelin (1901–1985)

Eric Voegelin stands out among a school of philosophers who analysed the descent into hell of ideological cultures and their politico-apocalyptic wars during the last century. This school includes thinkers as seemingly unconnected as Dostoievsky, Camus and Solzhenitsyn.[56] Voegelin's particular focus as a philosopher was on the history of man's search for order and meaning. In pursuit of that history he studied the great matrices of human self-understanding in mythology, the philosophy of Greece, the Revelation given to Israel, as well as the whole of western history and philosophy. His abiding concern was to understand both the roots of the present disorder and the source of that remediative order so badly needed in our time. This is the key to his great four-volume work, *Order and History*. There he explores the structure of the originating experiences and their symbolisation in the sequence of myth, philosophy and revelation.

His extensive study of ancient, Greek and biblical texts led him to the discovery of a constant pattern in all cultures. All cultures are born from an originating experience which shapes, guides and inspires that culture along the roads of its subsequent history. The originating or founding experience exists as a wellspring of meaning that is both articulated and lived by the society or culture in question. Voegelin speaks of this articulation as 'symbolisation'. This includes basic texts, key rituals and ordering structures which are intended to hand on the originating experience to the later generations.

Now the key to the symbols, whether doctrinal, ritual or structural, is their participation in the experience that engendered them. 'The symbols ... intend to convey a truth experienced.'[57] This is particularly the case with respect to revelation and faith. Since 'faith is the substance of things hoped for, and the evidence of things unseen' (Heb 11:1), the doctrines and sacraments symbolising the experience of revelation suffer from a unique disability. 'For, in the first place, the symbols are not concepts referring to objects existing in time and space but carriers of a truth about nonexistent (transcendent) reality. Moreover, the mode of non-existence pertains also to the experience itself, in as much as it is nothing but a consciousness of participating in nonexistent reality.'[58] It has to follow that when the experience engendering the symbols is no longer present in a man or woman, the reality from which the symbols derive their meaning has disappeared.

The meaning of the symbols presupposes the living by the community of the experience from which they originated. Now this living is existentially costly. To love God with all one's heart and soul and mind, to love one's neighbour as oneself, and to seek first the Kingdom of heaven and its justice, require a level of religious and moral engagement that is not to be easily presumed. But such an engagement, individually, socially and historically on the part of the community, is simply indispensable if the originating experience is to remain as the matrix whence the faith-life of the community is to be appreciated and realised. If this does not happen, Voegelin sees two reactions as inevitable.

The first is the routine recitation of the symbols of faith. While things may continue for a time, this decline leads sooner or later to a shallow piosity. 'This people honours me only with lip-service, while their hearts are far from me' (Mk 7:6; Is 29:13). They are a people without roots, hollow men and women. The second reaction is scepticism: the experience of every priest and teacher is rich in encounter with 'the smart idiot questions of 'How do you know?' and

'How can you prove it?' Such questions betray minds untouched by the realities behind, within and engendering the doctrines and sacraments of faith.

In that way, then, Voegelin 'tried to suggest the phenomena of original account, dogmatic exposition, and sceptical argument as a sequence that can attach itself to every experience of nonexistent reality *when it becomes articulate and, through its symbols, enters society as an ordering force'.*[59] He suggests two instances of this sequence, the first occurring in ancient Greece when the legacy of the wisdom gained in the heroic endeavours of Plato and Aristotle melted down into the dogmatic philosophy of the Schools and the sceptical reaction of the next century. The second occurred in historical Christianity in the High Middle Ages. Voegelin's account of the second bears remarkable similarity with the account we have already seen in this chapter.

Voegelin's diagnosis of our times in the light of his account of the true order of history has immediate and dramatic value for our understanding of reason and revelation. The life of reason is manifest in the search and in the questions posed by the search, while the drama of revelation challenges reason to still greater searching. 'Question and answer are held together, and related to one another, by the event of the search ... The answer will not help the man who has lost the question; and the predicament of the present age is characterised by the loss of the question rather than of the answer.'[60] The curious by-product of the Enlightenment was the loss of the deeper questions. However, the kind of descent into hell endured by modern men and women during 'the difficult past century' (John Paul II), when more human beings were murdered in concentration camps than died in the great wars, has become a catharsis, assisting the recovery of the abiding and more fundamental questions.[61]

Since Voegelin's analysis of order and disorder in our modern world places greater emphasis on the philosophical than on revelation, it is rich in relevance for the recovery of strong reason. That is why he uses as the epigram of *Order and History* St Augustine's principle, 'In the study of creatures one should not exercise a vain and perishing curiosity, but ascend towards what is immortal and everlasting'.[62] He discerns the dead end of modernity: the closure of the soul and the mind against God and his revelation in Christ, and the consequent release of apocalyptic wars over the earth. But he also sees the beginnings of the opening of the soul and the rediscovery of the search for the order that can save and heal. He discerns the centrality of divine revelation and faith in that project: reason in fact is made for revelation and finds there its unlimited freedom in the peace of truth and goodness. 'There is no answer to the Question other than the Mystery as it becomes luminous in the acts of questioning'.[63]

The analysis of Voegelin throws light furthermore on the true nature of inspired Scripture. Scripture is the expression of the experience of those first eye-witnesses and others in the earliest Christian communities who wished to communicate what they had seen with their eyes, and looked upon, and touched with their hands (1Jn 1:1). That communication had initially engendered a remarkable response: by hearing they believed, by believing they hoped, and by hoping they loved.[64] Christianity became a heroic adventure of the soul.

Scripture symbolises the experience of the in-breaking of Absolute Love into the world of the Apostles and the first disciples. It is therefore the articulation of that which is beyond all knowing (Eph 3:18), the divine love in Christ 'greater than which nothing can be thought' (*id quo nihil maius cogitari nequit*). This requires that its exegesis respect its true nature, and search for the infinite Word enfleshed in Christ. The original faith had declined into dogma and doctrine divorced from the original sense of participation in God, and this declined in turn into a moralism. 'Nietzsche's criticism can be reduced to one proposition: modern man has been trying to preserve Biblical morality while abandoning Biblical faith. That is impossible. If the Biblical faith goes, Biblical morality must go too, and a radically different morality must be accepted. The term which Nietzsche uses is "the will to power".'[65] Voegelin gets to the root of this diagnosis first by recovering the true nature of reason as transcendentally open to the Beyond and attracted by the Beyond, and then by recovering the various matrices of experience in Philosophy and Revelation.

Finally, while Voegelin is critical of the role of dogma in the general scheme of revelation and its symbolisation, some of that criticism may in fact be due to his worry lest the formulae blunt the *élan* of reason or try to dominate the God they intend to serve. Here is the Achilles tendon of his thought. The fact is that dogma achieves an essential unpacking of revelation, but in no way exhausts revelation as expressed in scripture and tradition. 'Without the increasing precision of dogma, the content of faith and experience is forever in danger of distortion and evaporation.'[66] Instead, all dogmas unfold from the revelation and must always be enfolded by the same revelation. Or to put it in the words of Hans Urs von Balthasar, 'The great need is to bathe again all dogmas in the one great love Mystery revealed in Christ'.[67]

III. Bernard Lonergan (1904–1984)

As in the Christian life, so also in the intellectual order: self-knowledge is very difficult to attain. This is the conviction of Bernard Lonergan. What are we doing when we are knowing? Why is this activity knowing? What do we know when we perform this activity? The three questions are as clear as they are difficult to answer. But one thing is certain: they may not be ignored, as Immanuel Kant has memorably shown by means of his three great questions.[68] Bernard Lonergan is the thinker who, more than any other in the last century, has pursued these questions. He did so in order to recover the true meaning of human rationality. It was his conviction that:

> [t]he specific drive of our nature is to understand, and indeed to understand everything, neither confusing the trees with the forest nor content to contemplate the forest without seeing all the trees. For the spirit of inquiry within us never calls a halt, never can be satisfied, until our intellects, united to God as body to soul, know ipsum intelligere and through that vision, though then knowing aught else is a trifle, contemplate the universe as well.[69]

The quest of Lonergan, then, was a quest for knowledge of knowledge or human rationality. The human spirit is constituted as exigence, the exigence to know. In this exigence the spirit of wonder is present and operative. He invites his readers to discover their own sense of wonder, and, more particularly, the operations of intelligence they perform both habitually and unconsciously and which manifest this very same wonder. To become conscious of our own hunger to understand, and to discover personally what one is doing when knowing, is to enter upon the way of self-discovery and of the human person's insatiable desire for what is true, good, beautiful and eternal.

This rationality, however, has been heavily overlain by whole schools of philosophy who have taken up positions on the subject. It is not the rationality of the empiricists who limit it to what is immediately given to the senses. For the empiricist, 'understanding and conceiving, judging and believing are merely subjective activities'.[70] Neither is it the rationality of the rationalists who limit it to our concepts. Nor is it the rationality of the idealists who limit it to our *a priori* ideas. Even the practitioners of the theology which Lonergan saw around him in Canada, England and Rome were often caught within the deductive rationalism of a conceptualism that masqueraded as true theological science. 'His chief adversaries are the conceptualists who, if not "rationalist" in the scholastic world, are strongly deductivist ... They began with concepts, then combined concepts into propositions, and thirdly joined proposition to proposition to construct a syllogism.'[71] The problem – and it is a major one indeed – with this procedure is that it overlooks two major factors. The first concerns the source of our concepts, the second concerns the adequate grounds for judgement or certainty.

Lonergan had already seen this in Newman's *Grammar of Assent* which he read six times as a young philosopher at Heythrop and considered to be the classic in the field of epistemology.[72] Newman had differentiated 'formal inference' and judgement in terms of two factors: the first was that one did not need to understand the terms of the propositions constituting formal inference, whereas this was of the essence in coming to judgement. The second was that the truth of formal inference is *always* conditional upon the truth of its component propositions. However, the truth of a judgement is simply unconditional. Judgement, in fact, affirms that which simply *is*. Newman had famously and at heroic lengths[73] shown this in terms of what he had called the 'illative sense'. The mind reaches judgement by the accumulation and the convergence of evidences, and not by the rude operation of syllogistic method.

With his competence in science as well as in philosophy and classical literature, Lonergan passionately studied human knowing. The study took him through the whole anthology of the West. He began with Hegel and Marx whose philosophy of history engaged his attention, went on to Newman, Augustine, Plato and Aristotle, before discovering Aquinas. For eleven years he struggled to 'reach up to the mind of Aquinas'.[74] That reaching profoundly changed him. Since the theme of this chapter is the recovery of strong reason, we must now turn to Lonergan's account of how we reason and how we avoid the deformation of reason.

From the very outset Lonergan 'contends that basic philosophical questions frequently are disputed not because their solution is intrinsically complicated but because key data and their implications often are overlooked'. The key data of consciousness are in fact overlooked. Lonergan begins from these data, from 'what more generally is sometimes termed "the foundational primacy of the subject", where "subject" means the concrete conscious individual that is you or me'. He is convinced that long before the advent of modern philosophy, with its methodical turn to the subject, one may 'discern a methodical priority of introspective rational psychology – what today we might call "phenomenology" – over metaphysics in the writings of Aquinas ... Aquinas' skill at the study of objects, including human souls, was shaped in no small way by his skill at the study of human subjects, especially the concrete human subject that was Thomas Aquinas'.[75] Still, neither Aristotle nor Aquinas formally attended to this method: '... if Aristotle and Aquinas used introspection and did so brilliantly, it remains that they did not thematise their use, did not elevate it into a reflectively elaborated technique, did not work out a proper method of psychology'.[76] Now this is what Lonergan sets out to do, particularly in his great philosophical treatise, *Insight. A Study of Human Understanding*.

Human knowing is the expression of wonder. This wonder manifests itself as the detached, disinterested and unrestricted desire to know and to do. 'By the desire to know is meant the dynamic orientation manifested in questions for intelligence and reflection ... The desire to know ... is simply the inquiring and critical spirit of man.'[77] By his method of careful introspection Lonergan detects the unfolding of this wonder-driven desire to know. The result is a definite and dynamically recurring cognitional structure. That structure has definite stages which can be briefly described, even if they can be appropriated *only* through very painstaking self- discovery.

Human knowing begins with the experience of data which I naturally wish to understand. Understanding begins with what-questions which lead to a direct insight into that set of data. One finds in it an intelligible unity that makes sense of the data. This unity makes the data into an intelligible whole and a thing. This direct insight then proceeds to formulate a concept of the thing and to forge a notion of what it is. In that way one arrives at an answer to the What-question which spontaneously arose from the desire to know when this desire encountered the data of experience.

The goal of knowing, however, is not yet attained. My answer to the What-question could be wrong. This appears immediately in the fact that one's desire to know immediately throws up a further and unavoidable question. It is the question, 'Is it real? Is it that thing?' This Is-question follows naturally upon the answer to my What-question. My rationality simply, but insatiably, desires to put my insight-understanding beyond all possible error. This makes me reflect again on the process by which I arrived at my insight into the data. I realise that I have paid attention to all the relevant sensible data, that my direct insight does justice to those data, and that my concept definition does justice to my direct insight. I now begin to realise that I have enough evidence to support a positive judgement. Moved by this reflective insight I can make the positive judgement. I affirm the thing and in that way arrive at an answer to the *Is*-question. Now I know the thing as real, as existing, as true and as being. The detached, disinterested and unrestricted desire to know will not stop until it knows being, which 'is the object of the pure desire to know'.[78]

It is easy to give an example of the process. I am travelling in Michigan State in the month of November. Being a little fatigued by the day's travel, I decide to retire early. Sleep falls quickly until I am awakened abruptly by short, rapid and repeating sounds. I wonder to myself, *What is it?* A few possibilities suggest themselves. Perhaps it is someone firing a rifle or a handgun. Or perhaps it is police and criminals in a shootout. Or my hotel room is located very near a shooting range. As I listen further, I think to myself, *But it is rather late for some individual to be firing a gun.* As to the second hypothesis, I realise that a shootout between criminals and the police would hardly last as long. The third hypothesis is least likely since a shooting range would scarcely be open at such a late hour and within a built-up area. I listen further, and as I do so I realise that the discharges are ongoing, are widespread as if to take in the whole town, and seem to illumine the room slightly. Oh, yes, this is November and November is Thanksgiving and this is Thursday. 'It's Thanksgiving and Fireworks!' *But is it?* I decide to get out of bed to verify my hypothesis. I cross the still dark room and, careful not to trip, I reach the window and pull the curtain only to see a sea of flashes, reports and unending canopies of coloured light bending earthwards. *Now I know* what was making that noise.

The Answer to Kant

Immanuel Kant famously studied the *a priori* conditions of possibility of knowledge and of science.[79] His three *Kritiks* have set the parameters of the debate in philosophy ever since. He contends that our concepts and definitions yield our categories. However, these are *a priori* in that they exist in the subject antecedent to the encounter with the sensible data or phenomena. They are then applied in the encounter with the data. But it may not be assumed that they reach the thing-itself, the *noumenon*. They exist prior to the thing itself: they are *a* priori. This is the origin of his principle of 'synthetic *a priori* propositions'. Kant is therefore the prophet of an intellectual agnosticism.

This is where Lonergan enters the struggle and challenges Kant. 'Kantian theory has no room for a consciousness of the generative principles of the categories.'[80] What gives rise to the categories? But there is more. Knowing in the Kantian scheme stops at *Verstand* or understanding which is considered to be the equivalent of judgement. In the process it separates the phenomenal and the noumenal, the thing-for-us and the thing-itself. There is no room for judgement, the level of reflective rationality where knowing attains the unconditional and reaches being as that which simply *is*. Inspired by Newman and guided by Aquinas, Lonergan identifies the distinct role of judgement in cognitional structure. The strength of his epistemology resides in its methodical introspection by which he attends to the actual data of consciousness, detecting the actual cognitional journey or structure, and inviting others to do the same in order to know that greatest of strangers, oneself, and one's recurring structured knowing of truth and goodness and reality.

Knowing and then Doing

The human subject, however, is not only a knower but also a doer. The distinction occasions what Lonergan scholars now call the 'early' and the 'later' Lonergan. If the early Lonergan quite deliberately challenged all to respond to the Oracle of Delphi by knowing themselves, the later Lonergan 'advances to a more holistic analysis of the human subject, where the volitional and the affective aspects of the person are being integrated into the total picture'.[81] Once again Lonergan appropriates what one is doing when one is acting. '[W]e will be satisfied if we bring you here to grasp in your own decisions and doings a recurrence of the three levels already discussed, but now in a new context or with the addition of a new dimension.'[82] After the question, What-is-to-be-done?, there arises the question, Is-it-to-be-done? This brings us very close to the level of decision.

One notices at once a similarity of pattern, an isomorphism, between knowing and doing. Corresponding to the cognitional threefold of experiencing, understanding and judging, there is the ethical threefold of moral experiencing, the understanding of what is to be done, and finally the judgement of value that this particular good is actually to be done. And just as the two questions – the What question? and the Is it so question? – in the structure of cognition move experience to understanding and understanding to judging, so too there are two questions in the structure of doing. These are, first, the 'what's to be done' kind of question, the second, 'is it to be done' kind of question. Once the second question is answered, then decision can follow. Of course I may fail to decide and to act. That failure is a failure in reasonableness: '… one can be a rational knower without an act of willing', but 'one cannot be a rational doer without an act of willing'.[83] There is, however, a radical difference between the rationality of judgement and the rationality of decision. 'Judgment is an act of rational consciousness, but decision is an act of rational self-consciousness' emerging 'if in fact a reasonable decision occurs'.[84]

Conversion: The Implication of these Structures

It has to be stressed that this account of our permanently recurring cognitional and ethical structures is not abstract but concrete and personal. It is all too easy to read on and so miss the point. And the point is that you are that knower and you are that doer, but that you need to attend to your knowing and doing in order to appropriate *what you are actually doing when you know and when you do*. Now this self-attention is most demanding in the event. The result is that many people are perfect strangers to themselves. However, to attend to our knowing and doing is to discover the rationality of our strange-structured and unfolding wonder. Lonergan describes this self-attending and consequent self-appropriation as 'intellectual conversion' in the area of our knowing and as 'moral conversion' in the area of our deliberating and acting.

He sees intellectual conversion as 'a radical clarification and, consequently, the elimination of an exceedingly stubborn and misleading myth concerning reality, objectivity, and human knowledge. The myth is that human knowing is like looking, that objectivity is seeing what is there to be seen and not seeing what is not there, and that the real is what is out there now to be looked at'.[85] The purpose Lonergan has in mind in *Insight* is to help each person to appropriate the true nature of our knowing and to 'discover the self-transcendence proper to the human process of coming to know'.[86] Besides intellectual conversion, there is also moral conversion. Like the former, it emerges in the dynamic self-appropriation of our ethical or doing structure as the demand for consistency between knowing the good and doing the good. This conversion 'changes the criterion of one's decisions and choices from satisfactions to values'.[87]

In intellectual conversion one attains to the truth of one's knowing. Since this attainment is true knowing, it is the knowing of what is real and objective. In moral conversion one attains to the truth and the good of one's ethical and moral being. There is yet a third conversion, that of religious conversion which results from God's love flooding our hearts through the gift of the Holy Spirit which has been given to us (Rom 5:5). Lonergan notes that, since the days of St Augustine, love or grace has been seen as operative and co-operative: the former changes the heart of stone into a heart of flesh, while the latter is the heart of flesh becoming effective in good works through human co-operation. This conversion enjoys a primacy over the other two. Here Lonergan joins hands with Augustine for whom, in the sentence beloved of Heidegger, 'only through love does one enter into truth'.

Authentic Rationality as the Door to Self-Transcendence

It is part of the genius of Lonergan to have articulated the conscious intentionality of our knowing. The detached, disinterested and unrestricted desire to know manifests and expresses that very intentionality. However, as has perhaps been suggested, the authentic performance of knowing and doing throws up the 'the transcendental precepts' that emerge in our intentionality. These are 'Be attentive, Be intelligent, Be reasonable, Be responsible'.[88] These 'precepts', however, are under threat from many quarters. In fact, they can only be fulfilled by means of a self-transcendence that leads to conversion.

There are various levels of such conversion. There is intellectual conversion. It 'is a radical clarification and, consequently, the elimination of an exceedingly stubborn and misleading myth concerning reality, objectivity, and human knowledge'. Of this level of conversion Lonergan is the great analyst. Then there is moral conversion by which one 'changes the criterion of one's decisions and choices from satisfactions to values'. Finally, there is religious conversion which 'is other-worldly falling in love. It is total and permanent self-surrender without conditions, qualifications, reservations'.[89]

Now these conversions are both laborious in attainment and precarious in possession. So much is this the case that the existential order of their occurrence is the very reverse of the order just listed.

> Though religious conversion sublates moral, and moral conversion sublates intellectual, one is not to infer that intellectual comes first and then moral and finally religious. On the contrary, from a causal viewpoint, one would say that first there is God's gift of his love. Next, the eye of this love reveals values in their splendor, while the strength of this love brings about their realisation, and that is moral conversion. Finally, among the values discerned by the eye of love is the value of believing the truths taught by the religious tradition, and in such tradition and belief are the seeds of intellectual conversion.[90]

Here one notices the powerful presence of the thought of St Augustine. He articulated, particularly in the *Confessions*, the actual order of these conversions without perhaps doing the systematic self-appropriation that Lonergan has done.[91] It was Augustine's own dramatic struggle to be free from slavery to immoral satisfaction that enabled the Doctor of Charity to appropriate personally the necessity of grace to do what is right. 'By Your gift [of grace] I had come totally not to will what I willed but to will what You willed.'[92] Religious conversion sublates moral conversion. Newman valiantly set about the same project in the nineteenth century, highlighting the role of the various conversions in the journey to faith.[93] However, it was Lonergan's years of reaching up to the mind of Aquinas that enabled him to achieve the self-appropriation of his own subjectivity to the point where he shows that true objectivity is the fruit of authentic subjectivity.

In Conclusion

The Enlightenment began with the affirmation of 'strong reason'. 'Hence enlightenment was a process of emancipation. Man liberates himself from pre-established authority and tradition.'[94] Typical of this confidence in 'strong reason' is the statement of Immanuel Kant who proclaimed 'man's emergence from the immaturity for which he himself is responsible. Immaturity is the inability to use one's understanding without the help of another ... *Sapere aude!* Have the courage to make use of your own understanding! is therefore the motto of the Enlightenment'.[95] In this decision, however, there is a conscious and firm option not to reach beyond or higher. Rather, here we encounter the decision to remain within a world that is co-extensive with human concepts and human reason only. Of these very words an Italian philosopher writes, 'Words such as these were once for me an invitation to reflection as the goal to be reached. I did not notice the extent to which they took me away from that which Plato called philosophy. In fact, where is Eros here, Eros which is thrust and ecstasy and longing?'[96] This is the death of reason as discovered by the Greeks and as presupposed in Revelation. And it is the opponent of reason as understood by Pascal who, as we have seen at the outset of this chapter, combined and contrasted heart and reason. In that way he identified the authentic knowledge that is born of love.

The early morning light of the presumed 'strong reason' of the enlightenment quickly faded into the night of 'weak reason'. Once it was proclaimed that beyond the worlds accessed by empirical and 'scientific' reason there was none other, the worlds opened to humankind by Philosophy and by Revelation were pronounced either inaccessible or illusionary. Interest in them was therefore wasteful of time, ability and energy. An aspect of totality will now be made to stand for the totality. Thus either the will-to-power (Nietzsche) or the proletariat (Marx) or the sexual urge (Freud) or economics is invested with ultimate significance. 'The dream of totality becomes ultimately totalitarian.'[97] This is the immediate genesis of the great apocalyptic wars of the last century and the descent into hell that is most appallingly expressed in Hitler's concentration camps and Stalin's Gulags. The process is described by Max Horkheimer and Theodor W. Adorno through a powerful metaphor at the beginning of their *Dialectic of Enlightenment*: 'The fully enlightened earth radiates disaster triumphant.'[98]

Great Christian thinkers, however, diagnosed the scene and proposed positive responses. We looked at a sample of these. Newman in eighteenth-century England worked out a psychology and epistemology of faith that re-connected, albeit at great and heroic lengths, faith and reason. 'Truth there is, and attainable it is, but its rays stream in upon us through the medium of our moral as well as our intellectual being; and that in consequence that perception of its first principles which is natural to us is enfeebled, obstructed, perverted, by allurements of sense and the supremacy of self, and, on the other hand, quickened by aspirations after the supernatural.'[99]

Eric Voegelin as philosopher of history and exegete of the great matrices of experience in myth, philosophy and revelation established the principle of experience and its manifold symbolisation. He also proposed the hermeneutical principle of the reciprocity of mystery and search as constitutive of the drama of humankind. He detected a sequence of originating experience, adequate symbolisation, and the existential verification in daily living of the originating experiences or else their gradual betrayal. The strength of his investigation is that it looked out for the daily living out of such symbolised experience. In that way he was able to correlate experience, text and reason, and to show how the 'destruction of reason' came about.

Bernard Lonergan, finally, was fascinated by the isomorphism of Thomist and scientific thought. He laid out the parallel structures of knowing in both areas, particularly in *Insight*. In that way he invited scientists to reflect on the permanent structure of method, and philosophers and theologians to attend to the acts of understanding and judgement they perform. One and the same reason or mind operates in scientist and theologian, but in different fields of inquiry. Lonergan saves the rationality of faith and theology by bringing theologians and scientists into dialogue, while he signals the danger of totalitarian ambition on the part of modern science. 'Thoroughly understand what is to understand, and not only will you understand the broad lines of all there is to be understood but also you will possess a fixed base, an invariant pattern, opening upon all further developments of understanding.'[100]

Notes

1. Eric Voegelin, 'The Gospel and Culture', in *Published Essays 1966–1985*, Baton Rouge and London 1990, 178.
2. Second Vatican Council, *Decree on the Formation of Priests*, 15.
3. *Epistle to Diognetus*, in Maxwell Staniforth (ed.), *Early Christian Writers*, London 1968, 178.
4. John Henry Newman, *A Grammar of Assent*, London 1890, 386–387.
5. Hans Urs von Balthasar, 'Wer ist Jesus Christus – für mich?' in Medard Kehl and Werner Löser (eds), *The von Balthasar Reader*, Edinburgh 1982, 113.
6. Joseph Ratzinger, 'Faith, Truth, and Culture', Reflections on the Encyclical *Fides et ratio*, 6.
7. James V. Schall, 'The Whole Risk for a Human Being: On the Insufficiency of Apollo' in *Logos. A Journal of Catholic Thought and Culture*, 7(2004), 22; see previous Chapter, n. 30.
8. *Fides et ratio*, 72.
9. Eric Voegelin, 'Reason: the Classic Experience', ibid., 265.
10. Ibid., 267.
11. Ibid.
12. Ibid., 183.
13. Plato, *The Republic*, 515e.
14. Plato, *Apologia*, conclusion as translated in *Plato. The Last Days of Sacrates*, London 1979, 76.
15. Thomas Norris, 'The Theological Formation of Seminarians' in *Irish Theological Quarterly*, 64(1999), 399.
16. Eric Voegelin, ibid., 173
17. Bernard Lonergan, 'Theology in its new Context' in *A Second Collection*, London 1974, 55.
18. Ibid., 56.
19. Ibid., 57; see Yves Congar, 'Théologie' in *DTC* 29, 432f.
20. Tertullian, *De Praescriptione Haereticorum*, VII, 9: *SC* 46, 98.
21. J.H. Newman, *Oxford University Sermons*, London 1900, 202; italics added. The date is 13 January 1839. This may be the very

first reference anywhere to the idea of 'weak/strong reason'; see Brúno Forte, 'Faith and Reason: The Interpretative Key to the Principal Encyclicals of Pope John Paul II' in James McEvoy (ed.), *The Challenge of Truth. Fides et ratio*, Dublin 2002, 203–218.

22. Ibid.

23. Ibid., x.

24. Ibid., 334.

25. J.H. Newman, *The Idea of a University*, London 1907, 387.

26. Ibid., 389, 390.

27. J.H. Newman, *Apologia pro vita sua*, Note B, 'On Liberalism'.

28. Wilfrid Ward, *Life of Cardinal Newman*, II, London 1913, 460–461.

29. Johann Sebastian Drey, *Brief Introduction to the Study of Theology. With Reference to the Catholic Standpoint and the Catholic System*, Notre Dame and London 1994.

30. W. Kasper, op. cit., 10.

31. Fascinating in this respect is the correspondence carried on in the 1840s and 1850s between Newman and the scientist, William Froude. See G.H. Harper, *Cardinal Newman and William Froude, F.R.S., A Correspondence*, Baltimore, 1933. Nicholas Lash criticises Harper's critique of the exchange because Harper 'took for granted just that restricted, monochrome notion of human rationality which, in the *Grammar* as in the *University Sermons*, sought to undercut': Introduction, *A Grammar of Assent*, Notre Dame and London: University of Notre Dame Press, 1979, 3.

32. J.H. Newman, *Oxford University Sermons*, 198.

33. Joseph Ratzinger, ibid., 12–13.

34. Text quoted in Latourelle and Fisichella (eds), *Dictionary of Fundamental Theology*, New York 1994, 734.

35. *Letters and Diaries*, XIX, 294; *Oxford University Sermons*, 231–232; 253–254.

36. Wilfrid Ward, *Life*, vol. II, London 1912, 589.

37. J.H. Newman, *Grammar*, London 1913, 288.

38. G.H. Harper, *Cardinal Newman and William Froude, F.R.S., A*

Correspondence, Baltimore 1933. Nicholas Lash is critical of Harper's understanding of reason because Harper 'took for granted just that restricted, monochrome notion of human rationality which, in the *Grammar* as in the *University Sermons*, Newman sought to undercut', Introduction, *A Grammar of Assent*, Notre Dame and London: University of Notre Dame Press, 1979, 3.

39. J.H. Newman, *Letters and Diaries*, London , XIX, 294.

40. Ibid., 283.

41. *Grammar*, chapter VIII, 259–342.

42. Ibid., 38.

43. Ibid., 353.

44. Ibid.,353–359.

45. M. Nedoncelle, 'Le Drame de la Foi et de la Raison dans les Sermons Universitaires de J. H. Newman', in *Etudes*, 247(1945), 75.

46. *Grammar*, 288.

47. Ibid., 292.

48. Ibid., 321.

49. *Letters and Diaries*, XXI, 146.

50. *Apologia pro vita sua*, 225. This text reappears as the epigram of the *Grammar*.

51. Ibid., 225.

52. *Grammar*, 311.

53. *Oxford University Sermons*, 191.

54. *Grammar*, 117.

55. See Bernard Lonergan, *Method in Theology*, London 1970, 338, where he refers to Newman's recurring *principle* that 'logic makes but a sorry rhetoric with the multitude', quoting the *Grammar* at pages 94–97.

56. See David Walsh, *After Ideology. Recovering the Spiritual Foundations of Freedom*, San Francisco 1990, especially 45–58.

57. E. Voegelin, 'Immortality: Reality and Experience', in *Published Essays 1966–1985*, Baton Rouge and London 1990, 52.

58. Voegelin, ibid., 54.
59. Ibid., 54; 'nonexistent' here indicates that which is not empirical or merely sensate.
60. 'The Gospel and Culture', in *Published Essays 1966–1985*, Baton Rouge and London 1990, 175.
61. A. Solzhenitsyn, *Cancer Ward*, New York 1968, 160 where there is a striking debate about the avoidance of the unavoidable questions concerning human existence.
62. St Augustine, *De Vera Religione*, XIX, 52.
63. *Order and History*, IV, 330.
64. See Dogmatic Constitution on Divine Revelation, *Dei Verbum*, 1, quoting St Augustine, *De catechizandibus rudibus*, IV, 8: PL 40, 316.
65. Leo Strauss, 'Progress or Return?' in Thomas L. Pangle, *The Rebirth of Classical Political Rationalism*, Chicago 1989, 240.
66. David Walsh, ibid.
67. Hans Urs von Balthasar, *Convergences. To the Source of the Christian Mystery*, San Francisco 1983, *passim*.
68. These questions are, What can I know? What must I do? What can I hope for? See Cahal Cardinal Daly, 'Faith and Reason: 'Diatribe or Dialogue? A Reflection on *Fides et Ratio*' in *The Challenge of Truth. Reflections on* Fides et Ratio', ed. James McEvoy, Dublin 2002, 219–239.
69. Bernard Lonergan, *Verbum.Word and Idea in Aquinas*, London 1968, 53.
70. *Idem, Method in Theology*, London 1972, 238.
71. Frederick E. Crowe, S.J., *Lonergan*, London 1992, 49.
72. For a recent study of Newman's influence on Lonergan, see Michael Paul Gallagher, S.J., 'Lonergan's Newman: Appropriated Affinities', in *Gregorianum* 85, 4(2004), 735–756.
73. David Tracy, *The Achievement of Bernard Lonergan, S.J.*, New York 1970, 127.
74. Bernard Lonergan, *Insight. A Study of Human Understanding*, London 1955, 748.

75. Michael Vertin, 'The Two Modes of Human Love: Thomas Aquinas as interpreted by Frederick Crowe', in I.T.Q, 69(2004), 31–45, here 31–32, 33.

76. Bernard Lonergan, *Verbum*, Foreward to the 1967 book edition, p.x.

77. *Idem, Insight*, London and New York 1957, 348.

78. Ibid., 348.

79. For an analytical study of Lonergan and Kant on human knowledge, see Giovanni B. Sala, *Lonergan and Kant: Five Essays on Human Knowledge*, translated from the Italian by Joseph Spoerl and edited by Robert M. Doran, Toronto Buffalo London 1994.

80. Ibid., 341.

81. Declan Marmion and Raymond Moloney, 'Rahner and Lonergan' in *The Furrow*, 55(2004), September, 489.

82. Garrett Barden and Philip McShane, *Towards Self-Meaning*, Dublin 1969, 55.

83. Lonergan, *Insight*, 615.

84. Ibid., 613.

85. Lonergan, *Method in Theology*, 238.

86. Ibid., 239.

87. Ibid., 240.

88. Ibid., 231.

89. Ibid., 240.

90. Ibid., 243.

91. See *Confessions*, III, 4; VIII, 5; 8; 11; 12; IX, 1; X, 27.

92. St Augustine, *Confessions*, IX, 1.

93. See my *The Theological Method of John Henry Newman*, Brill 1977, chapter 'Theology and its Methodical Foundations', 84–111.

94. Walter Kasper, *An Introduction to Christian Faith*, London 1980, 5.

95. Immanuel Kant, 'Beantwortung der Frage: Was ist Aufklärung?' in *Werke* (ed.), W. Weischedel, VI Darmstadt 1964, 53.

96. See G.M. Zanghí, 'La terza navigazione. Preghiera di un

filosofo', in *Nuova Umanità*, xxvii(2005), 43–56, here 46–47.

97. Bruno Forte, 'Faith and Reason: the Interpretative Key to the Principal Encyclicals of Pope John Paul II' in James McEvoy, *The Challenge of Truth. Fides et Ratio*, Dublin 2002, 205.

98. Max Horkheimer and Theodor Adorno, *Dialectics of Enlightenment*, New York 1969, 3.

99. See n. 52.

100. Bernard Longeran, ibid., 748.

Chapter III

Revelation in Relation to Reason

> The depth of man will never be understood if it is not
> enlightened by a ray from the unfathomable brightness of
> the Trinitarian life.[1]

We have been looking at the drama of the struggle to recover 'strong
reason'. The three figures we studied, John Henry Newman, Eric
Voegelin and Bernard Lonergan, representative as they are of three
principal component layers of the Western tradition of faith and
culture, all set out to retrieve the original sense of human reason from
its practical eclipse by scientific and instrumental reason. Their work
has set up a context in which the first rays of 'the dawn of an open and
questioning reason'[2] appear. This provides an exciting, indeed
dramatic, setting for a reading of Pope John Paul's encyclical on faith
and reason, *Fides et ratio*. The encyclical is both a dialogue with the
children of the enlightenment and, perhaps more specifically, *an
invitation to believe again in the power and the range of reason*. If the
enlightenment began as the movement to emancipate reason from
faith, now faith in the person of a pope asks the children of that
enlightenment to believe again in reason!

At the beginning of St Luke's Gospel there is an episode that sets in
dynamic relationship revelation, theology and philosophy. As such it
provides a paradigm for the subject of this chapter. The episode is that of
the annunciation to Our Lady. St Luke (1:26-38) underlines the dramatic
dialogue at the core of the encounter as well as the significance of the
event for the history of salvation.[3] The angel Gabriel makes known to
Mary that God has an eternal Son and that she has been chosen by the
Father to welcome that Son into the world on behalf of Israel and of

humanity. Furthermore, the enfleshment of the Son of the Most High in Mary's flesh will occur through the agency of the Holy Spirit. Here one has a clear statement of the fact of the revelation that both fulfils Old Testament revelation and provides the content and substance of the new and eternal Covenant. That content is nothing less than the very 'Son of the Most High' (1:32) now offered to Mary to become her Son also, and the gift of the Holy Spirit who 'will come upon Mary'. (1:35) The two arms of the Father, to use the language of St Irenaeus,[4] are extended to Mary as the sign of the Father's election and of his eternal merciful love that would embrace the world through Mary at this summit moment of revelation. And Mary says, 'I am the handmaid of the Lord, let it be done to me according to your word' (1:38). Mary's faith, by which she 'gave God's infinity dwindled to infancy welcome',[5] is the perfect correlative of the revelation now culminating at this vital stage of the dialogue of the God of 'the House of Jacob' (1:33). with Israel and with humanity as represented by, and personified in, Mary.

Now what is truly fascinating in Luke's account is that 'Mary's faith did not end in a mere acquiescence in divine ... revelations'. Luke highlights the fact that Mary 'treasured all these things and pondered them in her heart' (2:19), and concludes that she 'stored up all these things in her heart' (2:52). 'She does not think it enough to accept, she dwells upon it; not enough to possess, she uses it; not enough to assent, she developes it; not enough to submit the Reason, she reasons upon it.'[6] Revelation and faith had led immediately into theology and, by implication, into the activity of reasoning that we call philosophy. 'And thus she symbolisises to us, not only the faith of the unlearned, but of the doctors of the Church also, who have to investigate, and weigh, and define; ... to anticipate or remedy the various aberrations of wrong reason.' Mary, then, is 'an example [in] the use of Reason, in investigating the doctrines of faith'.[7] And by implication she is also an 'example' in philosophy which is the product of reason, being reason in its orderly and investigative operation. And so at the very beginning of the New Testament as event we find a living paradigm for the subject matter of Pope John Paul's encyclical, *Fides et ratio* (FR).

Humankind is an enigma.[8] The fact stands out the moment one looks at the story of the search of *homo sapiens* for the meaning of human existence. This is where the encyclical begins: 'In both East and West, we may trace a journey which has led humanity down the centuries to meet and engage truth more and more deeply ... A cursory glance at ancient history shows clearly how in different parts of the world, with their different cultures, there arise at the same time the fundamental questions which pervade human life: *Who am I? Where have I come from and where am I going? Why is there evil? What is there after this life?'*[9]

Now this strongly suggests that it is legitimate to see in the religious story of humankind a kaleidoscope of responses to this quest which largely defines the human being. These responses are also capable of classification, according to a hermeneutic of orientation based on the essential structure of each one. Such a classification might then enable us to grasp, by means of comparison and contrast, the divine freshness and originality that live deep down in Christian Revelation.

To begin with, there is the way of the primitive religions. Under the double impact of death and evil, on the one hand, and the luminosity of the cosmos, on the other, these religions sought communion with the divine as perceived in the more lasting strata of the cosmos. There are certain key elements in these religions. First, they are polytheistic, since their gods 'always represent some aspect of human need, the need for protection from the perils of nature, the need for defense in battle, the need for love. The gods are always gods in service of man'.[10] A second aspect of these religions is that of mythology. Mythology is important for its view of time as primeval time and for its use of imagery taken from our spatio-temporal world.

Next, there is the way of the great religions and of philosophy. The moment the human being became aware of the inadequacy of the religions was a moment of breakthrough to a new and better way towards the Divine. God is not any part of the cosmos. In fact, he is beyond the cosmos. The greatness of this tradition and breakthrough is that it purified man's age-old quest and desire, and pointed out the way to succeed in the quest for the Beyond or the Beginning. There cannot be many gods, in fact only one, and this One is unlike all of the things around us. This transcendent God of the philosophers is 'the God who can be sought only by the way of radical negation, in which the self in an ultimate act of abandonment cuts itself loose from everything finite and loses itself in the infinite abyss of the nameless one'.[11]

Unquestionably, such abandonment enjoys great nobility, as is obvious both in the great religions of Asia and in classical philosophy. According to many theologians and philosophers, such as Eric Voegelin[12] and von Balthasar[13], however, these religions founder for two reasons. First, the individual person has to abandon his original intuition of his own worthwhileness and lovableness. Secondly, the One discovered by Philosophy and the Great Religions is impersonal and faceless. 'It is not possible to love a faceless Infinite. Here once again the original intuition of love is denied. And so it would seem that man's original search ends in an *aporia*.'[14]

Is there any way beyond this dilemma in which the search for the Divine requires the negation of the I, as well as the rejection of the world and of the many, since all are incompatible with the One, the Divine? The nation of Israel, however, made the breathtaking discovery that it is not we who seek God primarily, but it is God who seeks us out. In the tension between the human and divine poles of existence, the divine pole is the prime mover. This is the germ idea in the election of Abraham and in the unfolding of his mission: 'in you I will bless all the nations of the earth' (Gen 12:3).[15] The history of the children of Abraham introduces a movement that is the complete reverse of the basic impulse of the primitive religions, the Great Religions, and Philosophy: 'For here, it is no longer the man Abraham who starts out in search of God. It is God himself who speaks to man, who leads him, not to religious meditation on the Absolute but to a way of simple obedience to the divine will.'[16] They discover his love for them both collectively and individually in the saga and the vicissitudes of their history as the Chosen People to whom the God of Abraham gives the gift of covenants, the blessing of the Law, and the guidance of the Prophets.

The Way of Judaism, however, is the way of God seeking an ever deeper communion with his people, a communion which they find increasingly difficult and beyond their capacities. Their traumatic discovery is that they are not capable of living in the divine-human *Lebensraum* opened up for them by the God of Abraham, Isaac and Jacob.[17] Accordingly, the God of Israel promises a fulfilment within history at a time to be decided by God in the future. Thus Israel looks towards an historical future, 'a vanishing point, an *omega*, when the ever imperfect, again-and-again broken covenant becomes finalised, the messianic time arrives, the lines of God and people cross each other in a final event'.[18] The notion of the future time, the messianic time, is thus central in Israel.

These two religious approaches, *that of Israel towards a future where God will bring his fullness in a way that will inaugurate 'the fullness of time', and that of the great religions, Philosophy and the primitive religions where the divine is in the Beyond, are irreconcilable.* They are 'like the vertical and the horizontal. One cannot be a Zen Buddhist and a Communist at the same time. One cannot devote one's life for the furtherance of world progress and at the same time withdraw from the world'.[19] Here, then, we are faced with a deepening of the dilemma. Can this vertical as it were of the primitive and the non-Christian religions, with their impersonal faceless Divinity, together with the negation of the world and our humanity as the only way to the Divine, ever be reconciled with the horizontal of Judaic futurism and hope? That is the question.

> But what is irreconcilable in the world (the vertical and the horizontal) forms a cross, an empty cross that cannot be occupied by anyone. Jesus Christ alone can fill this empty space, because he is the fulfilment both of pagan human longing *and* of Jewish hopeful faith. He is the Word of God for all mankind.[20]

For in Christ the divine search of the God of Abraham, Isaac and Jacob for all humankind expressed through his instrument, Israel, has intersected with the age-old search of humankind for the Beyond and the meaning of human and historical existence. His cross in fact effectively symbolises this synthesis. In the elegant words of T.S. Eliot, 'Here the impossible union of spheres of existence is actual'.[21]

He effectively overcomes the dilemma in the search from below where the divinity is faceless, and so not the love fulfilling humankind's primordial intuition that reality is love. Christ also overcomes the rejection of the other and of the world, since his incarnation and cross affirm both the infinite value of each person as 'the brother for whom Christ died' (ICor 8:11), and the preciousness of each moment of time because the moment the Timeless entered time, every moment of time has entered Eternity. 'We saw his glory, the glory that is his as the only Son of God, full of loving kindness and rocklike fidelity' (Jn 1:14). The very Ground of Being smiles on us in the Incarnation and on the Cross, as a parent smiles on a child.

Brief overview of the Faith–Reason Relationship in the Time of the Church

The Marian paradigm with which we began vigorously indicated that the fullness of revelation and the faith that is correlative to it, far from rendering obsolete the philosophical and theological quests, only served to heighten their liveliness. The woman who 'let all God's glory through'[22] is the very model of that devout and searching reasoning that faith presupposes, stimulates and guides. Now indeed there was an unending abundance of life and light in the eternal Word made flesh for the good reason that in him 'all the fullness of God was pleased to dwell' (Col 1:19 RSV). The Marian 'pondering', 'storing' and 'treasuring' would perpetuate itself in the time of the Church, and issue in the form of theology and philosophy mutually refining each other yet balancing delicately in the harmony of revealed Faith and searching Reason.

The drama of that perpetuation during the Christian centuries deserves some little attention at this juncture. Joseph Ratzinger describes the interaction of Revelation and Philosophy and Theology in a temporal sequence of unity, distinction, opposition and new relationship.[23] It is not the only reading of the interfacing of Faith and Reason that is possible. It is, however, appropriate for our immediate concerns.

In the earliest times the unity of theology and philosophy is the norm. A vivid instance is Justin Martyr who was a professional philosopher who became a Christian in the middle of the second century for the reason that he found in revelation not an alternative to philosophy but its fulfilment. Christianity for Justin was 'the only true and profitable philosophy'.[24] According to Eric Voegelin, Justin is convinced that 'gospel and philosophy do not face the believer with a choice of alternatives, nor are they complementary aspects of truth which the thinker would have to weld into the complete truth; in his conception, the Logos of the gospel is rather the same Word of the same God as the *logos spermatikos* of philosophy, but at a later stage of its manifestation in history'.[25] It was precisely this unity that allowed the Fathers of the Church to detect in the cultures of the nations the 'seeds of the Word'. This allowed for an inculturation of the Gospel that led to a new flowering of the culture being evangelised, as its particular *logoi spermatikoi* germinated in the encounter with revelation.

A fascinating corroboration of this fact is to be found in the earliest Christian art. Original research shows that 'in its earliest beginnings Christian art arose out of the quest for the true philosophy', a fact that dashes the idea that the relationship between faith and philosophy is quite abstract. 'It was philosophy which enabled the first plastic expressions of the faith ... the shepherd, the *orans* and the philosopher.' The philosopher image represents the true person of wisdom, the one who is the 'prototype of the *homo christianus* who has received the revelation of the true paradise through the Gospel'. Besides, 'the figure of the philosopher now becomes the image of Christ himself'. For Christ alone has the answer to the universal problem of death. And the most penetrating question, the question stinging and piercing the side of each and every man and woman, is the question of death. 'Philosophy, the search for meaning in the face of death, is now represented as the search for Christ': he is the 'one philosopher who gives an effectual answer by changing death and, therefore, changing life itself.'[26]

The earlier phase of unity between Reason and Philosophy was to be followed by their distinction. This distinguishing was in a unique way the work of St Thomas. 'In his thinking, the demands of reason and the power of faith found the most elevated synthesis ever attained by human thought, for he could defend the radical newness introduced by Revelation without ever demeaning the venture proper to reason' (78). The lines of demarcation between them were drawn in the following manner. Philosophy is the search of unaided reason for answers to the ultimate questions about reality. Philosophical knowledge comprises exclusively that sort of knowledge which reason as such can gain by itself, without the guidance of revelation ... Theology in contrast, is rational reflection upon God's revelation; it is faith seeking understanding. It does not, therefore, discover its contents by itself but rather receives them from revelation, in order then to understand them in their inner coherence and intelligibility'. It was an easy step from this to the insight that the domains of inquiry belonging to philosophy and theology could be distinguished as the natural and supernatural orders, respectively. This distinction effectively distinguished revelation and philosophy, faith and reason, grace and nature.

Distinction, however, quickly led to separation and even opposition. '... since the late Middle Ages, philosophy has been paired with pure reason while theology has been coupled with faith and that this distinction has moulded the image of the one as well as the other.'[27] Mutuality now leads to mutual rejection or at least mutual distrust. As FR puts it, 'what for Patristic and Medieval thought was in both theory and practice a profound unity, producing knowledge capable of reaching the highest forms of speculation, was destroyed by systems which espoused the cause of rational knowledge sundered from faith and meant to take the place of faith' (45). Thus today the world of philosophy is often suspicious of any kind of dialogue between revelation and reason, faith and philosophy. Philosophers such as Heidegger and Jaspers, to mention just two of recent philosophers, stress that philosophy is by its very nature questioning. It follows that whoever believes he already knows the answers is no longer capable of philosophising. For Jaspers, whoever supposes himself in possession of the answers has failed as a philosopher: the open movement of transcendence is interrupted in favour of an imagined ultimate certainty. Of course, Jaspers is categorically opposed to the very idea of revelation. The reason is that 'God for him is not a personal being but a mere cipher of transcendence, and thus God cannot be expected to speak and act in history except in a mythological sense'.[28] In that instance one would have to speak of the rejection of revelation and faith, and not only the separation of them from philosophy and reason.

But if philosophy separated from, and then opposed, revelation, the reverse also happened: revelation and theology entered into the rejection of, and opposition to, philosophy. The first seeds of this opposition go back to Tertullian, who is famous for the adage, '*Credo quia absurdum*'! But it flamed up again and again in the Middle Ages. The opposition of Luther is famous, and has been reactivated again in the last century by Karl Barth who saw the idea of *analogia entis* as a kind of Trojan horse welcomed into the household of faith. Here he saw the ontological option of Catholic Theology condensed in a formula that bonded the *philosophical idea of being and the biblical notion of God*. Famously, Barth sets his face totally against any kind of continuity or unity between Revelation and Philosophy, and proposes paradox instead.

This brings matters, it seems, to an impasse. 'On the one hand, philosophy defends itself against the prior given which faith implies for thinking; it feels that such a given inhibits the purity and freedom of its reflection. Theology, on the other hand, defends itself against the prior given of philosophical knowledge as a threat to the purity and novelty of faith.'[29]

A Context for Understanding the Church's Interventions

Now this sequence sets up the context for understanding the Church's interventions in the great debate. These interventions are described in the happy phrase *'the diakonia of the truth'* (2). The impasse arrived at shows the need for intervention, not because the 'Church has a philosophy of her own' (49), but because she is convinced that Faith and Reason are in harmony since both are gifts of the one God of truth. They are after all 'the two wings on which the human spirit rises to the contemplation of the truth'(1). Furthermore, she is convinced of the multiple injuries which the antithesis of Faith and Reason causes to both. These injuries affect the true meaning of Reason and Philosophy, as well as, logically, of revelation and theology. 'The censures were delivered even-handedly: on the one hand, *fideism* and *radical traditionalism,* for their distrust of reason's natural capacities, and, on the other, *rationalism* and *ontologism* because they attributed to natural reason a knowledge which only the light of faith could confer'(52). Eventually the impasse was picked up at the First Vatican Council where 'for the first time an Ecumenical Council … pronounced solemnly on the relationship between reason and faith' (52). What was the core of that teaching? *Dei filius* provides a core summary as follows, 'There are two orders of knowledge, distinct not only in their point of departure, but also in their object'.[30]

The Situation Today

The encyclical is quite fortright in its assessment of the situation at the end of the second millennium. Surveying the situation today, we see that the problems of other times have returned, but in a new key. The most striking aspect here is the phenomenon of the deep seated distrust of reason which has surfaced in the most recent developments of much of philosophical research. Here we are face to face with what has come to be aptly called 'weak reason'.

The *significance* of this phenomenon should not be missed. The result of reason's opposition to, and rejection of, faith was initially autonomous reason. From the French Enlightenment onwards, philosophy tried to eclipse faith altogether. It was no longer a case of opposing the claims of revealed religion, but rather of replacing them. The protagonists of the Enlightenment saw the whole history of the West as leading to a 'dogmatic slumber'. Immanuel Kant, in many ways the synthesiser and the catalyst of the Enlightenment, articulates the central thrust of the Enlightenment. As we saw in the last chapter, Kant highlighted 'man's emergence from the immaturity for which he himself is responsible. Immaturity is the inability to use one's understanding without the help of another ... *Sapere aude*! Have the courage to make use of your own understanding! is therefore the motto of the Enlightenment'.[31]

The fruits of that experiment over the past two centuries are obvious in the apocalyptic ideologies that have traversed the globe. And now a Pope has to plead with the modern world to believe in reason, its dignity and its power to reach the truth in its own domain! The irony of that plea should not be overlooked!

Philosophy must believe in the capacity of reason to reach truth. Failure to undertake that project leads to a crisis of the truth itself: moral and spiritual reality is beyond us. Even if it exists, it cannot be known. A defeatist attitude in this vital area means that philosophy must rest content 'with more modest tasks such as the simple interpretation of facts or an enquiry into restricted fields of human knowing or its structures'(55). And there is talk at times of 'the end of metaphysics'.[32]

Theology, too, is being revisited by 'the temptations of other times'. They appear in the guise of 'a certain *rationalism*'(55) where an uncritical acceptance is offered to certain philosophical opinions. This allows them the scope of being norms which either approve or reject areas of revealed truth! Philosophy becomes the measure of revelation!

Corresponding to this rationalism, 'there are also signs of a resurgence of *fideism*' (55). The encyclical mentions a number of symptoms of such a malaise. First, there is the failure to recognise the 'importance of rational knowledge and philosophical discourse for the understanding of faith, indeed for the very possibility of belief in

God'. Such a failure, of course, departs from the explicit teaching of *Dei filius*[33] which highlighted the unity in distinction of philosophy and theology as the perfect antidote to both rationalism and fideism, a point reiterated strongly in FR when it claims that 'the relationship between theology and philosophy is best construed as a circle'(73).

A further sign of fideism is a 'Biblicism' which 'tends to make the reading and exegesis of Sacred Scripture the sole criterion of truth'(55). This view and practice is in direct conflict with the balanced teaching of *Dei Verbum* where it is a case of Scripture and Tradition combining to 'comprise a single sacred deposit of the Word of God entrusted to the Church'.[34] The truth is that 'the supreme rule of faith'[35] 'derives from the unity which the Spirit has created between Sacred Tradition, Sacred Scripture and the Magisterium of the Church in a reciprocity which means that none of the three can survive without the others' (55).[36]

Finally, there is the symptom of fideism that is apparent in 'the scant consideration accorded to speculative theology, and in the disdain for the classical philosophy from which the terms of both the understanding of faith and the actual formulation of dogma have been drawn' (55). These specific complaints of the encyclical constitute a challenging examination of conscience for Catholic theologians, and also for all theologians who would wish to relate dynamically divine revelation and the unceasing quest for answers to the questions that are ineradicable from the human spirit.

The Wisdom of the Cross or the Wisdom of the World? A Proposal

According to the New Testament, Jesus Christ crucified and risen is the summit of divine revelation. He is therefore the Word of God fully unfolded and communicated to humankind. Perhaps Nicholas of Cusa puts it most vividly:

> This one voice of [Jesus] proclaims that there is no other life except life in the Word, and that the world, proceeding from

> the Word, is sustained in its existence by the Word and
> guided back to its origin ... After this mighty voice had
> grown continually louder through centuries up to John, the
> voice of one crying in the wilderness, it finally assumed
> human form and after a long succession of modulations of
> teachings and miracles which were to show us that of all
> frightful things the most frightful had to be chosen by love,
> namely death, it gave out a great cry and died.[37]

What is the relation between this revelation and that universal search
for truth that is expressed in philosophy? What is the relation between
'the wisdom of the Cross' and the philosophy of being? This question
is of central and abiding significance. For the truth is that 'the
preaching of Christ crucified and risen is the reef upon which the link
between faith and philosophy can break up, but it is also the reef
beyond which the two can set forth upon the boundless ocean of
truth' (23).

In one of the earliest texts of the New Testament, the First Letter
of Paul to the Corinthians, these great questions are addressed. For
Paul saw clearly that 'the depth of revealed wisdom disrupts the cycle
of our habitual patterns of thought, which are in no way able to
express that wisdom in its fullness ... The crucified Son of God is the
historic event upon which every attempt of the mind to construct an
adequate explanation of the meaning of existence upon merely
human argumentation comes to grief. The true key-point, which
challenges every philosophy, is Jesus Christ's death on the Cross' (23).

Paul saw the crucified Christ as the way in which God chose to
reveal himself, *to say who he is*, and *to tell us who we are*. The cross is not
the way in which we would travel in order to find the truth, but it *is*
the way in which God travels towards us in order to communicate the
final truth of his being and also the truth of our being. Furthermore
and most importantly, it is 'the word of the Cross' (1:18) that shows us
the wisdom of God.

Paul, however, notices how this revealed wisdom of the Cross is
under attack from the wisdom of the world of his time. In fact, he

names two versions of that wisdom: '... while the Jews demand miracles and the Greeks look for wisdom, here are we preaching a crucified Christ; to the Jews an obstacle that they cannot get over, to the pagans madness, but to those who have been called, whether they are Jews or Greeks, a Christ who is the power and the wisdom of God' (1:22-4). Paul identifies here two standard attitudes which the German exegete, Ernst Käsemann, describes as 'egocentrisms'.[38] The one is a religious 'egocentrism'. It is typified by certain followers who demand of God a manner of acting and of speaking in conformity with what they adjudicate to be appropriate. They look for a God who will show his *dynamis* by the way of miracles, and not through the mercy and the seeming weakness of the Cross. Their mindset is truly set against any other way for the God of the Old Covenant to act. In a word, they think and act in such a manner as to tell God how to be God, and so claim for themselves the role of being the measure of the truth of God, of his interventions and even of his very nature!

The other 'egocentrism' is the specifically intellectual or philosophical one, being that of the Greeks who are bold enough to presume that by the energy and the light of speculative thought they can plumb the depths of God. Little wonder that they would dismiss the claimed wisdom of a crucified Christ: it is 'madness'! No true philosophy could accept this message for its sheer irrationality! Both 'egocentrisms' set up horizons that are absolutely closed to what God can and has done, and to the manner in which he has done it, a manner which shows 'a Christ who is the power and the wisdom of God' (1:25). The encyclical points out that for both 'egocentrisms' 'what is required is a decisive step towards welcoming something radically new', since 'in order to express the gratuitous nature of the love revealed in the Cross of Christ, the Apostle is not afraid to use the most radical language of the philosophers in their thinking about God', for 'Christ is the power and the wisdom of God'! What is necessary is to enter into 'the logic of the Cross' (1:18). In that way the crucified Christ acts as the 'demystifier' of the man or woman who is falsely religious or intellectual and who wishes to set himself up as the measure of the depths of God himself. At this point FR makes a comment that is most insightful and germane to the central theme of the encyclical: 'Reason cannot eliminate the mystery of love which the Cross represents, while the Cross can give to reason the ultimate answer which it seeks' (23).

The fact is that the core of Christian revelation as manifest in the shock of the Cross, 'the un-Word at the core of the Word',[39] far from being the enemy of reason and of philosophy, is their authentic friend and ally. However, for philosophy to reap this great benefit, it must go through a deep *metanoia*. It is necessary, in fact, that human intelligence should take on the very form of the Crucified in its activity and in the dynamism of searching. In FR 76 the theme is approached where the issue of a so-called 'Christian philosophy' is broached. The term indicates 'a way of philosophising, a philosophical speculation conceived in dynamic union with faith'.[40]

It involves two aspects that determine its identity. The first is subjective and consists in the fact that faith purifies reason. 'If faith, as we have seen, consists essentially in accepting the wisdom of the cross revealed in the event of the Crucified and Risen Lord, it is obvious that reason itself will be profoundly touched by the grafting of this event on to the heart of the person. Reason itself will be redeemed by the Pasch of Christ.'[41] This means that reason must plunge into the death and the resurrection of Christ in order to rise with Christ (see Rom 6:3-11).

The pope mentions two ways by which this purification of human reason and so of philosophy can be done. The first consists in the fact that 'faith liberates reason from presumption, the typical temptation of the philosophy'. It is this presumption that is the object of St Paul's vigorous inveighing against philosophy in I Corinthians, as well as the censures of the Fathers, while closer to our own times 'philosophers such as Pascal and Kierkegaard reproached such presumption'. The second way of purification consists in the courage to tackle questions which are difficult to resolve if the data of revelation are ignored. Revelation 'stirs philosophy to explore unexpected paths and warns it against false trails'.[42] Among these questions are 'the problem of evil and suffering, the personal nature of God and the question of the meaning of life or, more directly, the radical metaphysical question, "Why is there something rather than nothing?"' (76).

The second aspect of the influence of faith on reason is objective since it has to do with content. The central truths of divine Revelation could never have been known by unaided reason. As well as these core truths, however, 'Revelation clearly proposes certain truths which might never have been discovered by reason unaided, although they are not of themselves inaccessible to reason'. Among these truths is the notion of a free and personal God who is the Creator of the world, the notion of sin as it appears in the light of faith, which helps to shape an adequate philosophical formulation of the problem of evil; the dignity, freedom and equality of human beings; and the meaning of history as event.

When one combines these two aspects, namely, the purification of reason and the thrust of reason towards the ultimate depth of the truth revealed by God, we could say that human intelligence is not only called to open itself to the abyss of the wisdom of the Cross, welcoming it into itself, but also to make its own the dynamism of dying to itself and of rising with Christ. Here is reason's very law of life! 'Human knowing, in other words, is freely called to accept a certain "crucifixion" in order to be redeemed and recreated by the Spirit of the Risen Lord who freely leads it to penetrate into the mystery of God which is fully revealed in Christ. In this dynamism, reason is not denatured but becomes progressively and fully itself according to the full stature of the plan of God for the human creature.'

Some Concluding Comments

1. The relationship between revelation, theology and philosophy is seen by FR against a horizon of history. This means that it looks at this key relationship on the broad canvas of the human story of *homo sapiens* and the incoming history of divine revelation which makes its own specific, though not separate, history, the history of 'God with us', what one might call 'the Immanuel History'. The encyclical begins

with the assertion that 'in both East and West, we may trace a journey which has led humanity down the centuries to meet and engage truth more and more deeply'. However, it also highlights the fact that 'the Church is no stranger to this journey of discovery – she has made her pilgrim way along the paths of the world' (1).

2. If FR looks at its theme along a historical horizon, it still concentrates principally on the situation of faith and reason today. In fact this is its focus. Broadly speaking, it notices both a decrease of faith in Divine Revelation, as well as a decrease of faith in reason, 'faith' in the second instance denoting confidence in the capacity of reason to find the truth in the vital areas of the meaning of human existence, the existence of God, the problem of evil, the way to happiness, the truths of the moral order, and the immortality of the soul. This is the phenomenon described today as 'weak reason'.

3. For our world this is like a drama where the plot has been tragically lost, so that we live in a civilisation bursting with energy and activity, but without any idea whatsoever of the goal or the purpose of such activity.[43] This is, in fact, the insinuation of the poetic opening words of FR, 'Faith and reason are like two wings on which the human spirit rises to the contemplation of truth: and God has placed in the human heart the desire to know the truth – in a word, to know himself'. It is logical, in the light of this drama, that the encyclical should address the vital issue of the re-integration of Revelation and Philosophy. Its theme, therefore, is not faith on its own, nor philosophy on its own, but faith and philosophy in dynamic tension with each other. The encyclical is a pressing appeal for philosophy and faith to 'recover their profound unity which allows them to stand in harmony with their nature without compromising their mutual autonomy'(48).

4. A measure of the seriousness of this breakdown in relationship is to be seen in the fact of an Ecumenical Council picking up the subject in the nineteenth century in a particularly formal and extensive fashion. A historical analogy suggests itself at once and perhaps provides a view. The great debates of the fourth to the eighth centuries on the truth of Christ and of the mystery of God, debates entirely driven by the sting of various heresies, were the context and cause of the first

Ecumenical Councils where the foundational dogmas of the faith were struck off one by one. I do not think that fact is without significance for the intervention of the First Vatican Council in the context of the struggle then raging in the wake of the French Revolution between the claims of faith and the claims of enlightened reason. The First Vatican Council in giving such central importance to the issue as to put it high up on its agenda bears witness to the seriousness of the issue and to the ripeness of discussion and insight necessary to make an adequate statement on the unity in distinction of faith and reason.

5. Perhaps the best analogy of all for the relationship between faith and reason is that of the relationship between the two natures of Christ. As Chalcedon teaches, these two are related 'without confusion and without separation' in the one Person of the eternal Word of the Father. In a similar way, Christian wisdom involves a synthesis of philosophy and theology, which is not a mixing of the two nor a situation where theology denies philosophy its proper autonomy in relation to methods and field, and philosophy denies theology its distinct source and methods.

6. We began this paper with the event of the Annunciation where we detected a paradigm for the interrelating of revelation, faith and reason. The pope concludes his encyclical with a Marian analogy: 'Just as the Virgin was called to offer herself entirely as human being and as woman that God's Word might take flesh and come among us, so too philosophy is called to offer its rational and critical resources that theology, as the understanding of faith, may be fruitful and creative. And just as in giving her assent to Gabriel's word, Mary lost nothing of her true humanity and her freedom, so too when philosophy heeds the summons of the Gospel's truth its autonomy is in no way impaired'(108). The encyclical ends with the delightful quotation that Mary is 'the table at which faith sits in thought'.[44]

7. The Encyclical avoids staying on the high plateau of principles: it descends in fact to the plane of particulars and the demands of detail. In the course of this chapter I highlighted one such

particular, namely, that of the historical event that is the summit of the whole of divine revelation, the Event of Christ Crucified (23, 76, 97). I did so for two purposes: first, to focus attention on the final bonding of God's self-revelation with the philosophical search for the ultimate answer to the mystery of human existence as this mystery is made acute in the mystery of death, 'a metaphysical thorn lodged in man's being'.[45] The second reason was to highlight the propensity of faith and reason to register mutual disdain, philosophy accusing revelation of foolishness or fancifulness, and revelation refusing to give the apostolic account of the hope that is provided by revelation, a hope that precisely because it is universal in its claim, must give an account of itself at the bar of reason. In this way the pope's desire that 'the *parrhesia* of faith must be matched by the boldness of reason' (48) can be attained. Indeed, there is almost nowhere that we need a more courageous faith and bolder reason than in the opposition between 'the wisdom of the world' and 'the wisdom of God', which St Paul sets before the Corinthians in his first letter.

8. The encyclical not only addresses particular issues, but also throws down very specific challenges to theology and to philosophy. For example, in 93 there is the challenge to consider the *kenosis* of God, 'a grand and mysterious truth for the human mind'. The challenge here is to think out the true meaning of this wonder of the faith in the light of the mysteries of the Incarnation and the Blessed Trinity. This means that the *kenosis* of God in Christ is the revelation of the inner life of God who is the Holy Trinity. This leads furthermore to the challenge to think out a new understanding of created being in the light of the revealed nature of Uncreated Being. Thus there comes into view what Klaus Hemmerle calls a 'Trinitarian ontology'.[46] Perhaps here is where one could locate concretely an aspect of 'the reef beyond which faith and philosophy can set forth on the boundless ocean of truth. Here we see not only the border between reason and faith, but also the space where the two may meet' (23). This very subject shall return in chapter six.

Notes

1. Henri de Lubac, *Théologies d'occasion*, Paris 1984, 107.

2. Bruno Forte, 'The Interpretative Key to the Principal Encyclicals of Pope John Paul II' in James McEvoy (ed.), *The Challenge of Truth*, Dublin 2002, 206.

3. See Feargus O Fearghail, *The Literary Forms of Lk 1,5-25 and 1,26-38*, Marianum (Rome), xliii(1981), 321–344; Robert J. Karris, The Gospel According to Luke, in *The New Jerome Biblical Commentary*, London 1993, 680–681 for useful exegetical comments; and Hans Urs von Balthasar, 'Mary – Exemplar of the Church', from *Pneuma und Institution*, as translated in Medard Kehl and Werner Löser (eds), *The von Balthasar Reader*, Edinburgh 1982, 218–220 for helpful theological comments.

4. See St Irenaeus, *Adversus Haereses*, IV, pr. 4; IV, 7,4; IV, 20,1; V, 1,3; V, 5, 1; V, 6,1; V, 28,4; *Demonstratio Apostolica*, 11.

5. In the poem 'The Blessed Virgin compared to the Air we Breathe', in Gerard Manley Hopkins, *Poems and Prose Poems*, selected and edited by W.H. Gardner, London 1986, 55.

6. John Henry Newman, *Oxford University Sermons*, London 1900, 313.

7. Ibid., 313, 314.

8. See the perceptive treatment of this subject in Walter Kasper, *An Introduction to Christian Faith*, London 1980, 13–36; Angelo Scola, *Questioni di Antroplogia Teologica*, Roma 1997, 33–36.

9. *Fides et ratio* (henceforth FR), 1: English translation by Veritas Publications, Dublin, 1998.

10. John O'Donnell, 'Hans Urs von Balthasar: The Form of his Theology', *Communio*, XVI 3(1989), 459.

11. Ibid., 460.

12. Eric Voegelin, 'The Gospel and Culture', chapter in *Published Essays 1966–1985*, volume 12 of The Collected Works, Baton Rouge and London, 1989, 172–212; for an exposition of the key themes of Voegelin's thinking see Maurice P. Hogan, *The Biblical Vision of the Human Person. Implications for a Philosophical Anthropology*, Frankfurt am Main, 1994.

13. See Hans Urs von Balthasar, *Spirius Creator: Skizzen zur Theologie III*, Einsiedeln 1967, 20–25; an English translation of this text is available in Medard Kehl and Werner Löser (eds), *The von Balthasar Reader*, Edinburgh 1982, 99–102.

14. John O'Donnell, ibid., *460*.

15. In the Septuagint, 'In you all the nations shall be blessed', repeated in Sir 44:21 and in Gen 18:18; 22:18; 26:4; 28:14.

16. Hans Urs von Balthasar, 'Catholicism and the Religions', *Communio*, 1(1978), 8.

17. *Idem, Herrlichkeit. Eine theologische Aesthetik. Alter Bund*, Einsiedeln 1967, 'Die Geschichte des Bundes aber erwies, dass das erwahlte Volk nicht fähig war, im Bereich der absoluten Liebe zu existieren', 383.

18. 'Theology and the Aesthetic', *Communio*, VIII (1981), 69.

19. Ibid., *69–70*.

20. Ibid., *70*.

21. T.S. Eliot, *Four Quartets: The Dry Salvages*, V.

22. Gerard Manley Hopkins, ibid., *55*.

23. Joseph Ratzinger, *The Nature and Mission of Theology*, San Francisco 1995. The title of the German original is *Wesen und Auftrag der Theologie: Versuch zu ihrer Ortsbestimmung im Disput der Gegenwart*, Einsiedeln 1993.

24. Justin Martyr, *Dialogue with Trypho*, 8,1.

25. Eric Voegelin, 'The Gospel and Culture', in *Published Essays 1966–1985*, Baton Rouge and London 1989, 173.

26. J. Ratzinger, ibid., 13–14.

27. Ibid., 16–17

28. A. Dulles, *Models of Revelation*, Dublin 1983, 10.

29. J. Ratzinger, ibid., 19.

30. DS 3015; *Gaudium et spes*, 59 quotes the text.

31. Immanuel Kant, *'Beantwortung der Frage: Was ist Aufklärung?'*, in *Werke*, W. Weischedel (ed.), VI, Darmstadt 1964, 53.

32. Klaus Hemmerle, *Thesen zu einer trinitarischen Ontologie*, Einsiedeln 1976, 7f.

33. See B.J. Lonergan, *Method in Theology*, London 1972, 337, '... the separation (of philosophy and theology) weakened both natural theology and systematic theology. It weakened natural theology for abstruse philosophic concepts lose nothing of their validity and can gain enormously in acceptability when they are associated with their religious equivalents. It weakened systematic theology for the separation prevents the presentation of systematics as the Christian prolongation of what man can begin to know by his native powers'.
34. Dogmatic Constitution on Divine Revelation *Dei Verbum*, 10.
35. Ibid., 21.
36. The radical reciprocity of Scripture and Tradition and Magisterium has clear Trinitarian overtones. It also provides an interesting hermeneutic of the different positions generally associated with the Churches and Ecclesial Communities emanating from the Reformation, as well as the reductionism inevitably visited upon the written Word of God when unaccompanied by the witness of Tradition and the *diakonia* of Magisterium.
37. Nicholas of Cusa, *Excitationes*, I, 3, opera Basel 1565, 411–412.
38. Ernst Käsemann, 'Il valore salvifico della morte di Gesù in Paolo', *passim*, in *Prospettive paoline,* Italian translation, Brescia, 1972; see also Piero Coda, *Evento pasquale, Trinità e storia*, Roma 1984, for an extended treatment of the Paschal Mystery and the Trinity.
39. See Hans Urs von Balthasar, *The Glory of the Lord*, I, Edinburgh 1989, 77–89.
40. For an interesting treatment of this topic, see A. Dulles, 'Can Philosophy be Christian?', in *First Things,* 102 (April 2000), 24–30.
41. Piero Coda, 'Sapienza della croce, e astuzia della ragione', Conference given at the Pontifical Lateran University, Rome, 3 March 1999.
42. A. Dulles, 'Can philosophy be Christian?', *First Things*, 102 (April 2000), 29.

43. See Eric Voegelin, 'The Gospel and Culture', ibid., 172–212, *passim*.

44. Pseudo-Epiphanius, *Homily in Praise of Holy Mary Mother of God*, PG 43, 493.

45. J. Ratzinger, ibid., San Francisco 1995, 23.

46. Klaus Hemmerle, *Thesen zu einer trinitariseben Ontologie*, Einsiedeln, 1976.

Part 2

Don't Presuppose Faith, Propose it Afresh!

Chapter IV

The Drama of Israel: The Categories of the Promise

The Jewish theologian, Abraham Heschel (1907–1972), sees the whole of the Old Testament as the search of God for humankind. God goes out in search of men and women.[1] It is not men and women who go in search of God. Rather it is the God of Abraham, of Isaac and of Jacob who seeks out the children of Israel. That seeking is the *leitmotiv* of the drama unfolding throughout the whole of the First Covenant, the catalyst of Israel's history. The great drama of Israel is the search in fact for the perfect convergence of the clearly proclaimed will and word of God, on the one hand, and, on the other, the welcoming and accepting word of Israel. One may read the whole history from Abraham to Jesus of Nazareth, a period of some, 2,000 years, as the search for this convergence. Thus the Psalmist strives to recall the wonder of the devout Israelite who reflects on his dramatic history:

> What is man that you should think of him,
> Mortal man that you should care for him? (Ps 8:4)

There are key moments in this experience of Israel. Those moments are the matrices that constitute the originating experience of the People of God. They push it forward relentlessly towards ever broader horizons, and set the stage for a final mysterious encounter between humankind and the God of Abraham, Isaac and Jacob, 'the name by which God is to be known for all generations' (Ex 3:15). We will look at a sample of them in order to grasp something of Israel's experience of revelation. Then, at the appropriate moment, we will tease out the concepts or figures that encapsulate or emerge from Israel's experiences. We will begin by looking at the vocation of Abram of the

Chaldees to be the 'Father of the Nation', the central experience of Moses in his calling and in the setting up of the Covenant, then the experience of the prophets as exemplified in that of Hosea, and finally the experience inspiring the text of Second Isaiah (Isaiah 40-55).

1. The Experience of Abraham

First, then, we turn to the experience of Abram. The text expressing his calling is in Genesis 12:1-3. He is called to leave behind his own people, his clan, his own house and his own land. He is invited to go into the land that God will show him and give him. More significantly still, he is promised an eternal descent: 'I will make you a great nation … In you all the nations of the earth shall be blessed' (v. 2).[2] Already here in this foundational experience of Israel – the 'children of Israel' are also called 'the children of Abraham' – one can clearly detect vital dimensions of the experience of Israel. These include the experience of vocation, election and of promise. Here, then, one notices the germ of the idea of Israel as a 'chosen People', and as 'the People of the Promise'. When Saul of Tarsus will come to describe this People – his people – he will simply list these dimensions of their historical experience (Gal 3:8-29).

By the very fact of that call, the God of Abraham distinguishes himself strikingly from man, society, the world. He is not a polytheistic God immersed in the visible order of things. Rather, he is distinct from Abraham, from his clan and from his world. On the other hand, however, he is deeply involved with Abraham and promises through that same unfolding involvement to generate a history of 'God with us'. The God of Abraham is both personal and different from all the surrounding divinities of the ancient near East. In these cultures the divinity is consubstantial with the cosmos, permeating it with his presence. The peoples of ancient Egypt, Assyria and of Canaan compacted together the divine and the cosmic. They lived with what philosophers of religion and historians of philosophy like to call 'cosmological consciousness' where the consubstantiality of the divinity with the cosmos of man, society and world has precedence over any differentiation of the divine from the other 'components of reality'.[3]

What happens in the case of Abraham is that the divine differentiates from the other components of the cosmos. In an act of free and personal choice, God identifies himself to Abraham and calls him to be the agent of his designs for Abraham's own descendants and, through them, for the whole of humankind and the world. This will involve on Abraham's side a trusting in God and obedience to his Word and will. Faith thus makes its appearance. It is the correlative of vocation, word and promise. The faithful and mysterious God opens himself towards Abraham, while Abraham is called, not only to believe, but also to entrust himself to this God. Thus there emerges an in-between differentiating, while bonding, the God of Abraham and the children of Abraham. It is in this space that revelation will gradually and dramatically unfold over the centuries following Abraham.

2. The Experience of Moses

When we look to the experience of Moses another and fresh moment in divine revelation appears. The children of Abraham now grown numerous are in the land of Egypt as slaves of the Pharaoh. It is the thirteenth century before Christ and the fifth since Abraham. Fearing the power of the Hebrews, the Pharaoh opts for a policy of extermination. This becomes the immediate context for a dramatic intervention on the part of God. This leads to the call of Moses. The story is taken up in chapter three of the *Book of Exodus* where the God of Abraham, of Isaac and Jacob enters into dialogue with Moses. A unique jump in divine revelation occurs during the protracted dialogue of God with Moses. In reply to Moses' question as to the identity of the One calling him, God speaks the striking words, 'I am who I am' (Ex 3:14). This is the Divine Name.

It brings out vividly the sense of being, the wonder of existence, at the heart of the hidden divine Being. The parsimonious language paradoxically manifests and conceals a richness of meaning. The God of Abraham exists truly in contrast to what only appears to exist. He is an infinite ocean of reality in contrast to what is passing away. He is not only the one who remains and lasts, he is also the One who will always *remain with* the children of Israel. After all, he is the God who has heard the cry of his people and who wants to deliver them from their cruel masters (Ex 3:7-10). The future will be as dramatic as the past, in fact even more dramatic, since what is truly living develops in order to continue living. All of his saving interventions will be necessary for humankind to know him. His deeds, in a word, will be the key to his identity. The end of history will be at one with the Being of God.

The event of exodus involves Moses and 'all the children of Israel' in this foundational event. The event of leaving Egypt, of going through the Red Sea, and of going into the Promised Land, has at once historical, religious and paradigmatic layers of meaning. As history, it establishes the Chosen People in the land of Israel fulfilling God's promise to Abraham. On the religious level, it bonds Israel with her God more fully: the covenant at Sinai becomes the effective manifestation of this new level of closeness to God. St Augustine captures the essence of this layer of the exodus in the famous phrase, 'The person who begins to love begins to leave (Egypt)'.[4] Finally, on the paradigmatic level, Yahweh indicates to Israel the pattern for the future and the essential form of Israel's life with her God. God will lead Israel through finite historical situations that will require of her the deepening willingness to be led. Israel's fulfilment, in other words, will require both the readiness and the deed of leaving behind in order to enter into the divine word indicating the new divine space.

This much becomes clear during the drama of the actual exodus and giving of the covenant at Sinai. The extraordinary resistance of the children of Israel, their frequent failure to follow the guidance of their divinely appointed leader, indeed their recurring revolt against the word of Yahweh, all point towards one conclusion. The bonding of Yahweh with Israel is going to be much more difficult than anticipated. In fact, 'the point of intersection where God's sphere and that of the people meet in the covenant is a highly sensitive, explosive spot. Moses stands there as mediator: with the words of God he descends to the people, and with the people's concerns he goes up to God ... [T]he more evident it becomes how poorly the covenant is kept and realised, the more the mediator becomes the expiator as well: God's whipping boy who must vicariously bear the guilt of the people'.[5]

3. The Experience of the Prophets: Hosea

A third matrix of revelatory experience in Israel is that of the prophets. The explosion and 'spiritual outburst' of the prophets articulates simultaneously the pathos-anguish of the betrayed God of the Covenant and the depth of the apostasy of Israel. It also identifies the difficulty of bonding the human and the divine. It will be enough for our present purposes – to indicate and analyse concrete key experiences of the occurrence of revelation in Israel, and only then to define the organising category-concepts thereby being forged – to take the experience of the prophet Hosea. The text in question will be that of chapter eleven (1, 2a, 3, 4a).

> When Israel was a child I loved him
> and I called my son out of Egypt.
> But the more I called to them, the more they turned away
> from me.
> ...
> I took them in my arms;
> yet they have not understood that I was the one looking after
> them.
> I led them with reins of kindness, with leading-strings of
> love.
> ...
> I will not give rein to my fierce anger,
> I will not destroy Ephraim again,
> for I am God, not man.

Prepared by his own experience of an adulterous wife, Hosea participated in the divine pathos of the God of Abraham, Isaac and Jacob, the God who chose Israel in Abraham, liberated Israel in the Exodus and blessed Israel with the Covenant. What should this God now do with Israel, his adulterous bride (2:4-25)? Ought he dismiss her, or punish her according to her sins? No. What should he do with his ungrateful child, Israel? The same? Oh no, for he is God, not man!

There is a step of revelation here that ought to be noticed: the being of God consists in mercy, his might is displayed in the might of his great loving, and this mercy is what happens when the love of Yahweh encounters the perfidy of his Bride. The text of Hosea, in fact, is a flood of tears of this God, a flood that will petrify eventually in the rock of his everlasting fidelity. God *is* faithful love. His nature is characterised by the qualities of loving kindness *(hesed)* and rocklike fidelity *(emeth)*.

4. The Experience Symbolised in the Servant of Yahweh

The final sample of Old Testament revelatory experience will be that of the representative figure of the Servant of Yahweh in Second Isaiah (chapters 40–55). The context is that of the deportation to the slave quarries of Babylon (587–537). Israel now realises that she has become the instrument of her own punishment: her own wrongdoing in fact is this very instrument. In this appalling scenario of self-condemnation in Babylon, the God of Abraham, of Moses and the Prophets will reveal even more of his hidden divine being. Israel may have done great things by way of sinning, but Yahweh will do even greater by way of loving.

The future form of that loving is personified in the person of the Suffering Servant and articulated in the course of the sixteen chapters of Second Isaiah. It is an order of a love that redeems: the project of election and exodus and covenant has collapsed in the face of the inability of Israel to live in the space opened up for covenant existence. However, the God of Israel is not to be outdone. This new revelation is so decisive that everything else moves into the category of 'the former things' to which the 'new things' can be opposed (43:16-9). Yahweh will manifest himself as the redeemer of Israel and of all humankind (Is 41:14; 43:14; 44:6, 24; 48:17; 49:7; 54:5), 'The four Songs of the Servant' (42: 1-9; 49:1-6; 50:4-11; 52:13-53:12) provide a poetic vision of the Servant and his mission.

The fourth song can serve as an articulation of this new phase of the drama of Yahweh's struggle for the heart of Israel and humankind (52:13-53:12). The Servant is a representative sufferer for Israel and for the whole of humankind. In fact, 'God presents the servant as their representative sufferer to the kings and the nations, so that all can accept him and be saved. The God who is first and last has the first and last words in the drama of salvation that reaches from heaven to earth'.[6]

> Yet he was pierced through for our faults,
> crushed for our sins;
> on him lies a punishment that brings us peace,
> and through his wounds we are healed. (53:5)

The concept of representation makes its appearance. The one can stand for the many. He may suffer for the many by 'bearing the faults of many' (53:12a). Israel thus contracts into this Servant who represents Israel and therefore also the whole human family before the God of Abraham. 'The history of Israel as the people under God is consummated in the vision of the unknown genius, for as the representative sufferer Israel has gone beyond itself and become the light of revelation to mankind.'[7] Thus a principle begins to emerge, namely, the one is the benefactor of the many in the designs of God.

The Servant, moreover, is driven by the eternal merciful love of Yahweh.

> And yet ours were the sufferings he bore,
> ours the sorrows he carried. (53:4)

It is not as if there is anything good on our side that attracts or motivates him. On the contrary, 'we had all gone astray like sheep, each taking his own way' (53:6). The Servant, however, is driven by the goodness of mercy. There is something in God, so to speak, that is stronger than God, more original than God! The Servant will be its proof and manifestation. The Servant in fact will come from Yahweh but will come over on to the side of Israel and humankind. The fruits of this love that suffers for the unworthy sinful beloved are unlimited.

> By his sufferings shall my servant justify many,
> ...
> he will divide the spoil with the mighty. (53:11b-12a)

The fruits of the Servant's completed work will be nothing less than the redemption of the world. He will bring about the 'new exodus' and the 'new covenant' that the prophets, Isaiah (10:25-27) and Jeremiah (31:31-3), have foretold. Still, all of this will take place not when Israel or any creature decides, but only when Yahweh decrees it. Thus Israel will have to wait on Yahweh in the humility of hope and with the trust of faith. In that waiting are the faith and the hope and the trust required of a new Israel. When 'the fullness of time' arrives (Gal 4:4), the fullness of revelation will appear (Mk 1:14).

The Emerging Concepts and Figures

Israel's experience is an extraordinary odyssey of change and movement towards the future. Its inspired formulation gives us 'the Scriptures'. A recent document of the Pontifical Biblical Commission states that 'the Jewish reading of the Bible is a possible one, in continuity with the Jewish scriptures of the Second Temple period, a reading analogous to the Christian reading, which developed in parallel fashion'.[8] What such a reading detects is an arsenal of concepts, figures and language that have been forged over a period of almost two millennia in order to symbolise and articulate the profound, if variegated, experiences through which the Lord God has made Israel pass. The opening sentence of the *Letter to the Hebrews* puts it perfectly: 'In the past God spoke to our forefathers through the prophets at many times and in various ways.'

Among these figures, types and concepts there are those of mediator, expiator and priest, law and promise, prophet, sacrifice, and servant, to name but a few. Each, however, has a temporal and developing logic, and therefore suffers from the radical inability to be the last word, for, as we have seen particularly in the instance of the Suffering Servant of Second Isaiah, the future realisation-fulfilment of that prophecy lies entirely with the God of Israel, not with Israel. None of them 'can be brought further in its perfection as image (*figura, typos*)'.[9]

In the call of Abraham, in fact, Israel's religion is oriented towards the future. Time is of the essence, since fulfilment lies in the future, a future that is beyond human control and manipulation, and which approaches us in God's time and according to his wisdom. The future, in a word, will be an advent. Israel's religion cannot be fixed according to its past, as Deuteronomy attempted to do, nor according to its path as the Prophets suggested, nor according to its future, since the events fulfilling both the past and the present remain hidden. 'The inner temporality of Israel's religion makes it impossible to fix one of the time aspects as absolute.'[10]

And there is more. Not only do the figures run into cul-de-sacs, they 'lack a form that can harmonise so many seemingly irreconcilables'.[11] How, for example, can one harmonise the notion of mediator with the notion of the suffering servant? The mediator has to live, the servant has to die. How does one expand the notion of election to incorporate the idea of vicarious suffering? What can join together the faith of Abraham and 'the Law given through Moses' (Jn 1:16)? The figures in the Old Testament 'cannot be linked together into a total picture, even in projection to the future'.[12] Oriented towards a divinely promised future, the very figures and types heuristically naming that future individually run into cul-de-sacs and collectively clash with one another. 'The essential point is that Israel as a whole and existentially is an image and a figure which cannot interpret itself. It is a sphinx's riddle which cannot be solved without Oedipus.'[13]

This horizontal and historical cul-de-sac is compounded further by the vertical cul-de-sac of humankind's representative, Israel's, inability to live in the space and freedom opened up by the covenant. What is impossible to men and women, however, is possible to God: the very profusion of figure and promise makes us hold our breaths as to how the God of Abraham, the God of Moses, the God of the Prophets and the God of the Suffering Servant will bring it all together. Perhaps it will require a kind of new creation that will still be able to subsume all that has been unfolding down the arches of Israel's history.

The First Covenant has to await the event of Jesus Christ, who is the new covenant in Person (see Lk 1:68-79; I Cor 11:25). He alone can put the many figures together. He alone can give unity to the innumerable and clashing types and figures contributed by the revelation made to Israel. From him alone 'the Old Covenant has its unity'.[14]

Revelation: The New Covenant

The revelation to Israel has led to the differentiation of the components of being. In other words, revelation identifies the sectors of reality. These sectors are God, man, society and creation. The Word of Yahweh tells the identity of the person, society and creation. The differentiation, however, has placed them in relationship with each other in a tension of life and love. God is the God of Abraham, Moses and the prophets: he has begun to fill in his *curriculum vitae* as it were by means of the events of the history of Israel. He is the creator of Israel and the creator of the world. The human being is his reflection, in fact, being 'made in his image and likeness' (Gen 1:26-27). The society of Israel is his beloved and chosen people, but with the mission to be the bearer and the instrument of the designs of God's heart for the whole of humankind (Jonah; Jer 1:5). These designs stand forever for they are the designs of his heart (Ps 33:11). Perhaps the psalmist saw this best when he reviews those events litany-like to tell us who God is: 'He led us out of Egypt, for his love is everlasting' (Ps 136). Creation, finally, is his handiwork, his good work, as the priestly author of Genesis says in a refrain, 'God saw that it was good'.

But with the new covenant these differentiated components are recombined and bonded in a manner that amazes, even shocks. This God of Abraham crosses the ontological divide between Creator and creature to become man. And the Word who is God became flesh (Jn 1:1, 14). The people of Israel become the Body of Christ, the Church, while God's good creation is resurrected with Christ and groans with the birth pangs of the new creation (Rom 8:19-25; IICor 5:17; Gal 6:15).

The Pauline corpus employs the word 'fullness' (*pleroma*) to symbolise what has happened with the arrival of the new covenant 'in Christ'. Now the presence of the divine fullness is located within history itself. This fullness is in Christ bodily (Col 2:9). Then it is in the Church as his extended Body (Eph 1:23). Finally, it is in creation, since creation itself finds its fullness in him (Col 1:19). This fullness is by definition always greater. It gives a knowledge that surpasses all knowledge (Eph 3:19). It is always greater than anything we can or will ever be able to say, as the Johannine corpus clearly saw (Jn 21:25). And absolutely no theology will ever be the equal of this divine theology, but will have to recognise its own place and bow in reverence (Jn 20:30-31). As Cardinal Newman clearly saw, 'divine revelation is given to us, not that we should know more, but that we should do better', so that 'the whole duty and work of a Christian is made up of these two parts, faith and obedience; 'looking unto Jesus', the divine object as well as author of our faith, and 'acting according to his will'.[15]

Word-Flesh

The Johannine symbolisation of the event of Christ hits with the power of a sledgehammer. Its impact lies principally in daring to speak of flesh as the new mode of being of the eternal divine Word. The one who was with God, and who *is* God becomes flesh (I Jn 1:1; 14), 'taking on what he was not, not losing what he is' (St Augustine). Flesh is man in his weakness and in his proneness to sin. Above all, it is man in his unavoidable orientation towards death. In stressing the fact that Word became flesh, John stresses the realism of the incarnation: it is in fact an 'enfleshment' of the eternal Son. In the words of T.S. Eliot, 'Here the impossible union of spheres of existence is actual'. Indeed, what could be so distant and disparate as God and our mortal bodily humanity? The Old Testament loved to remind the recipients of the first covenant of this fact: 'I am God, not man' (Hosea 11:9; Nb 23:19).

Secondly, in becoming flesh, the Word speaks and manifests *agape* as the New Testament names it. As flesh, the Word is the very epiphany of this agape. And here one ought to remember the uniqueness of the word 'agape' which in the whole corpus of the Greek Anthology occurs but rarely. The Father shows his Son in a manner appropriate to our human condition. In showing us his Son, the Father shows us his love. 'God so loved the world that he gave us his only Son' (Jn 3:16). God shows by means of a deed, in fact, by means of an event, and this event is the Word appearing in 'the likeness of sinful flesh' (Rom 8:3). In this event of the enfleshment, God reveals the dimensions of his love.

As for ourselves, the event of the giving of the Son by the Father is accessed in the flesh of that Son. It is accessed in the bone taken from our bone, and the flesh taken from our flesh (Jn 6:51f). The words of the *Preface of Christmas* put it splendidly: 'In the wonder of the incarnation your eternal Word has brought to the eyes of our minds a new and radiant vision of his glory. In him we see our God made visible and so are caught up in love of the God we cannot see'. Love motivates the Christ event, and Love appears in this event to the person who perceives it for what it really is (Eph 1:17-8). That is why Paul prays that his contemporaries should know that love (Eph 3:14-19). This Love has loved us first (1Jn 4:19). And the effect of that love is the opening of our hearts to see 'that which has existed since the beginning' but 'that we have heard, and we have seen with our own eyes; that we have watched and touched with our hands' (1Jn 1:1). The revelation of the Son in our humanity, in our very flesh and blood, means that our senses must play an indispensable role in the perception of the Word made Flesh.

Thirdly, the Word made Flesh also radiates into the world and history. In fact, he radiates what the scriptures call 'the glory of God'. Paul brings this out masterfully with a clever use of *midrash* in the Second Letter to the Corinthians. He retells the events surrounding the reception of the Law of the Covenant by Moses on Sinai as this is narrated in Exodus 33 and 34. Moses asks God to see his glory (33:18). God agrees but on condition that Moses look away and into a cleft in the rock, and God covers him with his hand while his glory passes by. Above all, Moses may not look upon the face of God. In spite of these precautions, Moses' face becomes radiant as it reflects the glory which man and woman may not look upon nor survive under the Old Dispensation. The result is that Moses has to wear a veil over his face when he descends from the summit and walks among his fellow Israelites. Even the reflected glory of the God of the Covenant was unbearable for the recipients of that Covenant.

Paul wishes the Corinthians to realise 'the surpassing glory' (2Cor 3:10) of the new covenant made in Christ. In fact, Paul's task is to make known 'the gospel of the glory of Christ' in order 'not to distort the word of God' (2Cor 4:4). This is his ministry. Paul's style is not like that of Moses who 'would put a veil over his face to keep the Israelites from gazing at it while the radiance was fading away' (2Cor 3:13). On the contrary, he wants the glory of that final covenant to shine into the hearts of those who believe in Christ. The impact of that glory, as perceived 'whenever anyone turns to the Lord' (2Cor 3:16), is so great that the Corinthian Christians 'are being transformed into the likeness of the Lord with ever-increasing glory' and are able 'with unveiled faces to reflect the Lord's glory' (2Cor 3:18). That glory is the radiance of the love of God in the Son made man reaching into the hearts of those who believe. It succeeds in giving 'the light of the knowledge of the glory of God in the face of Christ' (2Cor 3:10; 4:4; 3:13; 3:16; 3:18; 4;6).

The utterly unexpected makes its entry. 'What the whole of biblical revelation leads to is the marvellous measure of love: the glorious form of Jesus Christ in the formed formlessness as the obedient one "whom they have pierced" (Zech 12:10; Jn 19:37)'.[16] The centrality of that 'marvellous measure' stands out in the verse of the prologue of John's Gospel. 'We have seen his glory, the glory of the only begotten of the Father, full of grace and truth' (1:14b). In the Son's pitching of his tent among us, there radiate into history the *hesed* (loving kindness) and *emeth* (fidelity) foretold in the Prophets. The Law came through Moses (1:17), the promise of grace and truth through the Prophets, but the very personification of the latter is in the Word made flesh.

Christ is in infinite measure – a measure that is without measure – the loving kindness and the fidelity of God both personified and made flesh of our flesh. As the only Son who is turned towards the Father's heart (Jn 1:18), he is ontologically qualified to be such. The scriptures call this measure 'glory' because the grace and the truth manifest the glory (Jn 1:14b). Glory for its part is the infinite, because divine, and is the counterpart of beauty. According to John, the divine beauty of glory is what sincere believers 'see' (2:11; 11:40). Thus, when Jesus does his first miracle at Cana he gives a 'sign'. The sign lets his glory be seen to the point that 'his disciples believe *into* [sic!] him'.[17] The encounter with the acting Word-made-flesh draws the disciples out of themselves and into the drama that begins to unfold in their midst.

Now it seems that realised Christians all have this in common: they have seen something. It is not a case of 'seeing things' in the ordinary meaning of that phrase. But the 'eyes of their hearts' (Eph 1:18) have been opened to 'see' something, or rather 'Someone'. That 'Someone' made such an impact on them that they got drawn into a deeper life. They discovered a 'life that was the light of men and women' (Jn 1:4). Often that 'life' shone out subsequently in works of service of neighbour and/or of obedience to the truth and the grace given. If the truth were to be told, in fact, one would have to say that the great things have been done by the great lovers. But the great lovers 'saw' divine revelation: as a result, 'they saw his glory', and were moved by the glory-beauty of the love that first loved them (IJn 4:19).

The first Christians could in fact express their faith in a few words: 'We have believed in love (*agape*)'. This is a translation from the ancient Vulgate Latin version. In fact, the complete verse runs as follows: 'And we have known and have believed the love which God has for us' (IJn 4:16a). Both the Latin translation and the Greek original text concur: to be a believer is to believe 'into' the Love that loved us first. A modern author puts it like this employing the metaphor of a bridge connecting distant shores:

> Christianly speaking, faith sees in Jesus Christ the presupposition of faith. He is the substance of faith, the one who makes faith possible. And he stands on both banks of the bridge at one and the same time. He, the Son of God, became human, he took on my humanity, the humanity in fact of us all. And he has taken my humanity, our humanity into his divine mystery, into his relationship with his Father. For evermore man and woman belong to God in Jesus. In him I already stand on the other shore. It is precisely in this fashion that he is himself the bridge, the middle, the mediator between God and man.[18]

In the time of the Church there are innumerable instances in every century of men and women who make this discovery of God as love. Perhaps a good example is that of Charles de Foucauld (1858–1916), an officer of the French army who had been discharged from the army as a result of the amoral life he had been living while in Algeria. As a teenager de Foucauld had abandoned the faith of his childhood. Growing up in Enlightenment France, he heartily subscribed to the view of the day that the Church was ending, that faith was irrational and that Christian living was a 'slave morality'. He subscribed to an agenda that despised faith and dismissed Catholicism.

While on a visit to Paris in 1886, de Foucauld made contact with a cousin through whom he encountered a vibrant parish community with its pastor, the Abbé Huvelin. One Sunday de Foucauld went to the parish Church where he knew his cousin had gone to worship. Arriving late, he stood in the porch. He was struck by a sentence of the homily: 'Jesus Christ took the last place in this world so perfectly that no one will ever be able to take it away from him.' These words impacted de Foucauld with great force. They entered into his mind and invaded his memory and, in some uncanny way, suggested a God that vied with every human being for the last place, and all out of humble goodness. Now this was a picture of a God that was startlingly at odds with the idea de Foucauld had long since repulsed. But it was an idea that turned him around and, if you like, upside-down. He began to see the world with new eyes. The rest is history, as de Foucauld vied with this great love that became obedient unto death, yes death on a cross (Phil 2:8), and even Food and Drink for slaves (Jn 6:55). He spent several years at Nazareth and then sixteen years in the midst of the Taoureg People in Algeria living for the ideal of 'universal brotherhood'.

In Conclusion

It is worthwhile assembling our thoughts together at this point and drawing out some conclusions. First of all, in the words of the Father of Patristic Theology, Irenaeus of Lyons (130–210 a.d.): 'Christ brought total newness by bringing himself who had been foretold.'[19] He is the newness of heaven, he becomes the newness of the earth and of time, catching up creation and time into eternity, and so overcoming the 'ever ageing world' (Augustine).[20] He fulfils the revelation to Israel but does so superabundantly. Accordingly, one sees in him the entry of the utterly unexpected. There is no 'mere melancholy of fulfilment' here (Moltmann), but the entry of 'what no eye has seen, nor ear heard, nor the heart of any man ever imagined, all that God has in store for those who love him' (ICor 2:9). And still, the incarnation of the Word/Son is only the beginning of the drama of the God-Man: we will soon look at his public life and then engage with its dramatic apotheosis in cross and resurrection.

Next, the Word of the Father, the Son who 'is turned towards his heart' (Jn 1:18), illumines our concrete humanity. His light shines over our 'flesh' and gives it eternal value. The Second Vatican Council brings out this insight with vigour in the *Constitution on the Church in the Modern World*: 'The truth is that it is only in the mystery of the Word made flesh that the mystery of man takes on light' (22). Hopkins says it with the poetic power of the poet-theologian,

> I am all at once what Christ is, since he was what I am,
> and
> this Jack, joke, poor potsherd, patch, matchwood,
> immortal diamond,
> is immortal diamond.[21]

The Christ manifests, besides, the love of the Father for us, making it shine out in the darkness which it overcomes (Jn 1:5). Such an event manifesting and communicating such a love shines out as the glory-beauty of the hidden God, the God hidden from all ages. Love, therefore, and Glory-beauty combine to conquer our hearts and to amaze our imaginations. The order of the I-Thou, so attractive to the personalist philosophers of the twentieth century, links up with a divine aesthetic to draw us into life and love. We are addressed by Love and therefore we are! Perhaps the Jewish theologian, Franz Rosenzweig, glimpsed the revealed face of God when he wrote of 'God's eternal being' as 'the freshly discovered, ever young, always first Love that is discovered in every moment'.[22]

Thirdly, the first covenant dramatically portrayed the difficulty of bonding the divine and the human. On the rock of that difficulty the Word of God, carried along from patriarch through prophet to wise man and woman, often shattered to the point where an utterly new initiative from the God of Abraham was necessary. The prophets of Israel participated in that divine *pathos*, highlighting the participation of Yahweh in human suffering and the participation of humankind in divine suffering. They foretold movements either into a future time, as in the case of Isaiah, or else into a space beyond Israel, as in the case of Jeremiah, 'the prophet to the nations' (1:3). In the figure of the Servant of Yahweh there is a heuristic anticipation of the one who will bring about the renewed covenant. Still, not even that figure can suggest the event of the infinite Word 'pitching his tent among us' (Jn 1:14).

Fourthly, this raises the question of the relation of the Old and New Testaments. This issue has traversed the whole history of the Church. In the second century there was the answer of Marcion who wanted to see the Old Testament deleted. The event of the incarnation of the infinite and eternal Word had rendered the words of the Old Testament obsolete! His view was roundly repudiated by the Church. The great 'fragments' indeed were put together into the perfect masterpiece that is Christ and could only have found unity in and through his figure, through what von Balthasar likes to call *Gestalt* or Form. Still, all that had preceded the incarnation retained a permanent value, not only as the essential theological epistemology but also in itself. The event of Christ is hidden in the First Covenant (Lk 24:13-35; ICor 15:3-5). Its discovery, however, is the work of the revealing Son made man in 'the fullness of time' to bring the fullness of revelation.

This question of the Two Testaments is the concern that inspires the thinker who is universally seen, with the hindsight of the centuries, as the founder of Theology, Irenaeus of Lyons (140–210 a.d.). The inspiring insight of his theology he found in a single verse in the Letter to the Ephesians. God had set forth his purpose in Christ 'as a plan for the fullness of time, to unite all things in him [Christ], things in heaven and things on earth' (1:10). The key word is anakephalaiosis or recapitulation. It is the guiding principle of Irenaeus' Against the Heresies. Occurring only here in the New Testament corpus, the word has, like other sole occurrences that go on to a glorious theological development during the time of the Church, inspired a whole world of theology, as the seminal writing of Irenaeus ably demonstrates.

Irenaeus is well positioned to initiate dialogue between the biblical perspective on revelation and the Greek perspective on time which is largely the same as that of all the ancient religions. With the Hebrews there is, as we have seen, the discovery of history. Time is no longer a case of 'the eternal recurrence of sacred origins; they work by a cyclic model. For them there is nothing new under the sun; only that is real which always was and is everlasting. The thought of the Bible breaks through this infernal circle. Here is action and event; here there are real new beginnings which guarantee hope'.[23] History is therefore a purposeful movement towards an ultimate meaning located in the future, an *advent,* when God will do 'a new thing' (Is 43:19). How and when that will happen is another matter. In fact, that is the drama of Israel: the precise form of that ultimate intervention is beyond all guessing.

As we have seen, the figures emerging in Israel are both individually terminating in cul-de-sacs and collectively incapable of combination. Only the God of Abraham, Isaac and Jacob can bring the drama of that history to a head, which will mean quite literally a 'recapping' of it all that is still an absolute newness. This is quite literally the intent of the verse in Ephesians 1:10. Irenaeus expresses his central idea as follows:

> Jesus Christ is one, our Lord, who travelled through the whole order of salvation and recapitulated all things in himself. Man, too, one of God's creatures, belongs to this 'all things'; thus he has also recapitulated all human beings in himself, and to do so the Invisible One became visible, the Inconceivable One became conceivable, the Impassible One became capable of suffering, and the Logos became man. He recapitulated all things in himself.[24]

The basic idea of Irenaeus is that Christianity consists in 'the one economy of salvation, beginning with creation, gradually going up towards Christ in whom God's intention is perfectly realised, and then expanding in him through his Body the Church towards a final consummation'.[25] The intention of God is nothing less than the *divinisation* of man. That intention is the guide and the focus of all God's deeds that make up the history of salvation. Accordingly, it is present 'in the beginning' (Gen 1:1; Mt 19:4; Mk 10:6). It is not an afterthought of God, rather it is his forethought. The truth is that 'the idea of divinised man is the only true idea of man'.[26]

However, God did not create man in this state for the good reason that such creation would not be consistent with man's creaturely condition as someone who begins to exist and so as someone who receives his being from God. As a free being, man ought to experience to the full all the implications of his creaturehood, implications, such as his weakness, his mortality and his need to choose God freely before being confirmed in the possession of eternal life. The logical outcome of the tension between creaturehood and the calling to eventual divinisation is that the human being is a being of growth. Revelation therefore involves a corrective education that brings humankind on a journey involving different stages. God gives himself in the course of this *paideia* in an ever more generous manner, but always according to the receptivity of human beings. Irenaeus puts it like this:

> For the Uncreated is perfect and is God. But it was morally necessary that man should, in the first place, be created, and having been created should grow, and having grown should reach man's estate, and having done so should receive strength, and having got strength should be glorified, and having been glorified should see his master. For it is God who is to be seen. Now the vision of God confers immortality, but immortality makes one near God.[27]

In his overtures to humankind, God follows a method of repetition and addition eventually leading up to Christ in whom the perfect recapitulation of God's self-revelation and man's divinisation occur as the head and the harp of one and the same mystery. With regard to repetition, God's plan was frustrated by Adam's refusal and disobedience. Over and over again God renews his overtures. The more open and welcoming humankind is, through its representative Israel, to the divine Pedagogue, the more rapid will be the incarnational process in history. At last he brought about the Adam-project in the most perfect way in the incarnation of his eternal Son who is God visible among men and women. He is the gift of God fully adapted to the condition of humankind. 'It was incumbent upon the Mediator between God and man, by his relationship to both, to bring both to friendship and concord, and present man to God, while he revealed God to man.'[28] The incarnation, then, is a strategy, inspired by the absolute love of God, to make God become human and to make human beings become God, divinised by participation.

As well as repetition, there is also an addition on God's part. There is a progress in what God does and says. When the 'fullness of time' arrives, God can introduce his Christ. In fact, Christ recapitulates the history of Adam's race. He not only gathers up all that God has done and given and said, but also puts the whole of creation on a new foundation with regard to God. It is to Irenaeus that we owe the first clear formulation of the principle that recapitulation involves the total newness that Christ brought in bringing himself.

Irenaeus is capable of holding God's loving action in tension with our resistance to the divine Pedagogue. He therefore highlights the role of time and of history in the working out of God's abiding design for the human family. He connects God and history in such a manner as to show how the arrival of Christ gathers up the past, fulfils it wondrously in the present, and sets up the time of the Church as the time of the ingathering of humankind *and* creation into the mystery of Christ. This threefold grounds the patristic idea of the threefold Body (*corpus triforme*) of Christ according to which 'the first phase of the incarnation occurred in the old covenant; the second phase occurred in Jesus of Nazareth; and the third phase is currently unfolding in the new covenant'.[29] Or to use a metaphor from Hans Urs von Balthasar, the incarnation should be 'compared with a wave of the sea which, rushing up on the flat beach, runs out, ever thinner and more transparent, and does not return to its source but sinks into the sands and disappears'.[30] The vision and faith-understanding of Irenaeus are both true to life and so truly hope-filled.

The greatest benefit of the Pauline and Irenaean perspective, however, is its capacity to cover the facts of revelation. It explains both the lasting relevance of the Old Covenant, thus re-echoing the sentiments of St Paul in his mini-treatise on the place of Israel in chapters 9 to 11 of the *Letter to the Romans*.[31] It also explains the 'total newness' brought by Christ, which, among other things, combines the uncombinable, bringing about the coincidence of opposites. And it includes the mystery of the Church as the ongoing 'Christening' or divinisation of the components of God's good creation. Thus, to take one example in illustration of the point, Irenaeus suggests the outline of a most original Eucharistic Ecology when he teaches that the 'eucharistised' bodies of the deceased faithful actually continue to eucharistise the earth and creation itself in the period between the first and the second comings of Christ.

Christ therefore is the One who unites the components of reality in an otherwise impossible synthesis. In doing so he is the key to the problem that occupies thinkers both ancient and modern, the problem, namely, of the One and the Many. Christ alone incorporates the many and gathers into the One. He is the totality, the fullness in the particular. This is his wonder for believers, and it is what makes him 'a sign of contradiction' (Lk 2:34) for others. He is 'the inclusive exclusive' for in him alone do we find united the 'fullness' of divinity and the fullness of humanity, without 'confusion or separation', to employ the words of the Council of Chalcedon. In him we find the fullness of creation as the 'New Adam' and the perfect meeting of eternity and time which is now gathered into the granary of eternal life and being.

Of course all of this becomes clearer only in the context of the mystery of the Trinity. The God revealed in the event of Jesus Christ is no monad. Room has to be made in him for Another who is his equal, and for the Spirit who is also his equal! He is a trinity of co-eternal and co-equal Persons. The Father generates the Son out of love and the Son is the eternal response of love to the Father. In their infinite mutual joy, Father and Son spirate the Holy Spirit as their eternal communion of love. This sets up the ultimate source and context for the solution of the problem of the One and the Many. God is one in nature, but multiple in personhood. And since creation bears the stamp of the Creator, it will be logical to expect the same pattern of Unity-in-Trinity in all his works both in creation and in that 're-creation' which we call divine revelation. We will be returning to this subject again in the context of our reflections on the exile and the return of the Trinity in chapter eight.

Notes

1. Abraham Heschel, *God in Search of Man: A Philosophy of Judaism*, New York 1955.

2. It is significant that this blessing is a kind of golden thread running throughout the vicissitudes of the history of Israel and is picked up again in St Paul (Rom 4).

3. See Eric Voegelin, *Order and History*, vol. I, *Israel and Revelation*, edited with an Introduction by Maurice P. Hogan, Columbia and London 2001.

4. St Augustine, *Enarrationes in Psalmos*, 64, 2.

5. Hans Urs von Balthasar, *Convergences*, San Francisco 1983, 86.

6. Eric Voegelin, ibid., 567.

7. Ibid., 569.

8. Pontifical Biblical Commission, *The Jewish People and their Sacred Scriptures in the Christian Bible*, Rome 2002, n.22.

9. Hans Urs von Balthasar, ibid., 85.

10. Ibid., 83.

11. Brendan Leahy, 'Theological Aesthetics' in Bede McGregor and Thomas Norris (eds), *The Beauty of Christ*, Edinburgh 1994, 37.

12. Hans Urs von Balthasar, *Convergences*, 88.

13. Idem, *The Glory of the Lord*, I, Edinburgh 1982, 628.

14. Hans Urs von Balsthasar, *Convergences*, 90.

15. John Henry Newman, *Parochial and Plain Sermons*, I, London 1870, 153–154.

16. Breandan Leahy, ibid., 40.

17. See Henri de Lubac, *La Foi chrétienne*, Paris 1970, 22.

18. Klaus Hemmerle, *Brücken zum Credo*, Freiburg im Breisgau 1984, 23; is not this the true sense of Philippians 2:9-11?

19. St Irenaeus, *Adversus Haereses*, IV, 31, 4.

20. *De catechizandis rudibus*, 22, 39: PL 40, 338 seq.; *De Genesi contra Manichaeos*, I, 23, 35, 42: PL 34, 190 seq.; *De civitate Dei, passim*.

21. Gerard Manley Hopkins, *Poems and Prose*, London 1986, 66.

22. Franz Rosenzweig, *Der Stern der Erlösung*, in *Gesammelte Schriften*, Band 2, Den Haag 1976, 178; see Hosea 6:4 and Rev 2:4.

23. Walter Kasper, *An Introduction to Christian Faith*, London 1980, 179.

24. St Irenaeus, *Adversus Haereses* III, 16, 6.

25. Jan Walgrave, *Unfolding Revelation*, London 1972, 52. St Augustine gives us a hermeneutical principle which was picked up strongly in the Council's Constitution on Divine Revelation, *Dei Verbum*, 16, 'The New Covenant is hidden in the Old while the Old is revealed in the New'.

26. Ibid.

27. Irenaeus, *Against the Heresies*, IV, 38, 3; see also St Augustine, *De civitate Dei*, X, 14 for a summary statement of the same idea.

28. Ibid., III, 18, 7.

29. Kevin Mongrain, *The Systematic Thought of Hans Urs von Balthasar*, New York 2002, 29.

30. Hans Urs von Balthasar, *Origen: Spirit and Fire*, Washington 1978, 18.

31. See Roy M. Schoeman, *Salvation is from the Jews*, San Francisco 2003.

Chapter V

The Unfolding Drama of the Eternal Word

The classical tract of Christology focused very largely on the mystery of the incarnation. It concentrated its attention on the wonder of the eternal Word of God becoming flesh and the radiant vision he thereby brought to the eyes of our minds.[1] As such, it did not go beyond what we saw in the last chapter, remaining tied into the event of the incarnation. It did not address the paschal mystery, itself the nerve centre of the New Testament and its Christology. As for the public ministry of Jesus, it was utterly silent on the subject. Not only that, but it was interested primarily in the history of the elaboration of the language of person and nature in the early centuries and its eventual deployment in the first councils.[2]

A further dissatisfaction with this approach arose from the view that over the centuries the good news of Jesus Christ had been subverted. Greek thought – so ran the contention – had imperceptibly infiltrated the simple powerful message of Jesus of Nazareth who became 'Lord and Christ' (Acts 2:36). Furthermore, the Church of the early centuries had overseen all of this as the Gospel spread into the world of Greece and Rome. The Church, it was claimed, had allowed the Greco-Roman culture the freedom to influence unduly the Gospel of Jesus Christ.

From the beginning of the eighteenth century, the cry went up that the alien categories of Greek philosophy had undermined the Semitic categories of the Gospels. In that way they had infiltrated and subverted the message and the truth of revelation. The language of person and nature had taken over in Christology from the revealed biblical language. This represented the worst possible subversion of the revealed Word of the Gospel. At the beginning of the third century, Tertullian had asked rhetorically, 'What does Athens have in common with Jerusalem? The Academy with the Church?'[3] The abstract categories of the Greek philosophers had invaded the space occupied by the living categories of the revealed Word of God. The philosophers had done what Paul feared they might do in his day when he declared that the Cross of Christ cannot, and never can, be expressed in the language of the philosophers (ICor 1:17).

The 'hellenisation' of the gospel, as it came to be called, became the common complaint, a kind of theological whirlwind. The councils of the fourth and the following centuries were too minute. They made the flesh-and-blood figure of Jesus grow pale with metaphysics. They were also too culture-bound. Besides, they claimed to know and say too much about the revealed mystery of the God of Jesus Christ whose 'home is in inaccessible light' (1Tim 6:16), while at the same time they were quite incapable of speaking to the common humanity of people in such a way as to show how Christ is our 'hope of glory' (Col 1:27). They both smacked of an unverifiable insight into the constitution of Christ, and, at the same time, would say nothing to the average devout believer. It was time for a concerted move against the great councils of the early centuries, particularly that of Chalcedon in 451 a.d. which finally determined the language that was to guide and control the picture of Christ that dominated the minds of believers for the next fifteen hundred years. A divine Person with two natures, the one divine and the other human, was a far cry – so it was claimed – from the picturesque language and vibrant imagery in the discourses of Jesus of Nazareth to the crowds who hung upon his words along the roads of first century Palestine or in cosmopolitan Jerusalem.

In thinkers such as Albert Schweitzer, the issue had become clearer. The Gospel needed to be freed from the encrustation of dogma. 'The Christology of Chalcedon had overlaid the historical figure of Jesus with the concepts of Greek philosophy, and, in so doing, had alienated it from modern historical thought.'[4] This contention, however, does not stand up to scrutiny. Thus, St Augustine consciously alters Greek philosophy by stressing, for example, that 'relation' is predicated of God not as an accident but as essence,[5] while St Thomas stresses that relation is identical with essence in God.[6] Walter Kasper shows that the Fathers use Greek philosophy in order to say something that is quite un-Greek![7]

All of this, however, did not halt the march of mind of historical consciousness. Schweitzer and his colleagues still wished to remove the later layers that had overlain the original painting and to restore the original lustre and colour of the Christ and the Son of God (Mk 1:1).[8] Schweitzer, it has to be said, gathered up a movement that had been around much earlier, in fact, since the end of the eighteenth century. In people such as Hermann Samuel Reimarus, David Friedrich Strauss, Friedrich Schleiermacher, Ernest Renan and Adolf von Harnack there had been growing the desire to read the Gospels as literature and as biography in order to encounter the authentic Jesus of Nazareth. These same authors wanted to give, besides, an account of the truth of the Gospels in an idiom that could convince its 'cultured despisers', to borrow from the title of the famous work of Schleiermacher. In so doing they were convinced they could defend the Gospel figure of Jesus against the attacks coming from burgeoning new disciplines. These disciplines were critical history and literary criticism in the guises of form and redaction criticism. Out of the engagement with the Enlightenment they would be able to present the authentic portrait of Jesus of Nazareth as given in the Gospels and now liberated from the deadening encrustations of dogma.

What was to happen, however, was going to be a surprise. Simplifying somewhat, one can say that this early search for the historical Jesus was to make two striking discoveries. The first was that the Gospels are not 'Lives' in the contemporary sense of close-up factual and psychological descriptions. The second was that eschatology, or the future of God as the future being offered to men and women in and through Jesus of Nazareth and his mission, was the dominating concern of Jesus of Nazareth. 'We are already the children of God but what we are to be in the future has not yet been revealed; all we know is, that when it is revealed we shall be like him because we shall see him as he really is' (1Jn 3:2).

As to the precise nature of the Gospels, there was a consensus that these documents were written with post-Easter eyes. All that the pre-Easter Jesus said and did was seen through the prism of his death and resurrection and glorification to the right hand of the Father (Phil 2:11). In other words, there had been a clear elaboration of the Gospel tradition. This, in fact, was to become Church teaching in the Council's *Constitution on Divine Revelation*.[9] The Council identified three stages in the Gospel Tradition. The first stage consists in what Jesus himself did and taught during his earthly life. The second stage is what the apostles 'handed on ... with that clearer understanding' after the Easter event and in the light of the Holy Spirit at Pentecost. The third stage, the most interesting from our point of view, consisted in the editing of the four gospels. 'The evangelists selected, summarised and clarified in accordance with the situation in which the Church was placed, but preserved the form of proclamation. It is clear, then, that the most fundamental insights of form criticism were officially recognised and accepted by the second Vatican Council.'[10] The work of exegetes such as Ernst Käsemann and others went on to initiate a new quest for the historical Jesus.

The upshot of all of these searches for the historical Jesus was twofold. The first was the progressively dawning insight that the Gospels are to be understood as responses to the figure of Jesus Christ. They are therefore a witness to his greatness, his *Gestalt*, as Hans Urs von Balthasar will name it. It is not the early Christian community that made up Jesus of Nazareth to be the Messiah and the eternal Son of God. Rather, the opposite is the case: it is Jesus who, impacted by his life, and especially by his death and resurrection and the sending of the Holy Spirit so powerfully,[11] 'inspired' the fourfold response of the Gospels to his person, deeds and words. The Gospels, in other words, far from deforming the image of Jesus, are the Spirit-guided expression of the early Christian community's experience of the inbreaking of absolute love into the world in the event of Jesus Christ (Lk 24:13-35; Jn 20:31).[12] They set out to impart a 'knowledge of the love of Christ that is beyond all knowing' (Eph 3:19). This is the basic hermeneutic to be kept in mind in their reading and interpretation.

There was also a second discovery made by the new search for the historical Jesus, namely, the return in a new guise of an ancient heresy. This heresy had already reared its head by the last decades of the first century. It was the heresy of Docetism which consisted in the negation of the authentic humanity taken on and up by the eternal Son of God. It provides a context for reading the text of St John's Gospel and Letters, as we have seen in our last chapter. Docetism will return in the fourth and fifth and seventh centuries as Apollinarianism, Monophysitism and Monothelitism, respectively. Each time, an ecumenical council of the Church will be necessary to eradicate the error. In a sense, the news of the eternal Son of the Father becoming 'flesh of our flesh and bone of our bone' is news that is too good to be true. Docetism in all its versions is a device most cleverly calculated to separate what God in his mercy had joined together in the enfleshment of his beloved Son.

Now the modern separation of the Jesus of history from the Christ of faith clearly smacked of docetism which always resists the very idea of an incarnation of God and prefers to suggest instead a mere 'touch of divinity on the human condition'. The eternal Son had involved himself neither in human nature nor in history. A one-sided emphasis on the risen Christ left out of the reckoning the human nature that he had taken on. But the new quest for the historical Jesus had recovered the importance of the history of Jesus of Nazareth and what he had begun 'to do and to teach' (Acts 1:1). The literary genre of the Gospels was unique in that they proclaimed their message in and through history, and *not in spite of history*. 'It is the theologians' task to look for history in the *kerygma* of the gospels and also to look for the *kerygma* in that history.'[13] The more recent research of scholars such as Richard A. Burridge reinforced the importance of the history of Jesus of Nazareth. Burridge studies a representative sample of ten *Lives* written about heroes of the ancient Greece and Rome. His findings show that the Gospels are 'lives' of Jesus *in that sense*.[14]

Action the Key to the Mystery of Jesus of Nazareth

We have seen in the previous chapter that the God of the First Covenant revealed his identity via the interventions that constitute the history of Israel. Adopting the words of Cardinal Newman, one may say that 'Christianity is a history supernatural and almost scenic: it tells us what God is by telling us what he has done'.[15] It is not surprising, then, if the same principle should obtain in the Second Covenant, which crowns and completes the first superabundantly. This means that the concrete life of Jesus of Nazareth is the key to the mystery of Jesus of Nazareth. In other words, 'Jesus can best be understood by considering his behaviour'.[16] We will learn best who Jesus *is* by looking at what he *does*, claims and teaches. We will look first at his claims and actions. Then we will address that concentrate of his claims and teaching which is the Kingdom of God.

Jesus does not teach as the prophets do. They employ formulae such as, 'The Word of the Lord came to me', or 'Thus says the Lord', or 'A saying of Yahweh'. Jesus, however, never speaks in this fashion. Instead, he makes no distinction between his word and God's (Mk 1:22, 27; 2:10)! His teaching always claims 'greater' authority than that of those who have gone before him. In this 'absolute comparative' there is a living pointer to that tangible yet mysterious source of his freedom and the consciousness of his authority. As St Mark puts it, 'The crowds were amazed at his teaching, because he taught as one who had authority, and not as their teachers of the law' (Mt 7:28-9).

Perhaps this is most visible in the case of John the Baptist in whom the world of the prophets, long since gone dormant, had revived with vigour. 'The Baptist points to one who will come after him. Jesus does not point to another.'[17] In the words of St Augustine, 'John is the voice, but the Lord was the Word in the beginning. John was the voice for a time, Christ the eternal Word in the beginning'.[18]

In the strength of that authority, Jesus went not only beyond the Law of Moses, he also went *above* the Law. The Sermon on the Mount provides striking instances. For example, 'You have learnt how it was said to our ancestors, *You must not kill*. But I say this to you: anyone who is angry with his brother will answer for it before the court' (Mt 5:21-2). There follow in rapid succession in Matthew five similar teachings. Even if the exegetes are not all unanimous as to the authenticity of all of them, there is enough evidence to see that Jesus 'placed his word, not against, but above, the highest authority in Judaism, the word of Moses. And behind the authority of Moses was the authority of God'.[19] This has to mean that Jesus makes the claim to say and to be the last and ultimate Word of the God of Moses.

There is a third aspect of Jesus' teaching that shocks. He challenges each person, or rather the word he speaks (Jn 12:48-49), challenges each person, to decide for or against him. On that decision, however, will depend the person's entry or exclusion from the Kingdom of God. 'Whoever acknowledges me before men, I will also acknowledge him before my Father in heaven. But whoever disowns me before men, I will disown him before my Father in heaven' (Mt 10:32-3). To choose Jesus is to enter the Kingdom of God.

Then there is Jesus' ability to read human hearts. Numerous episodes in the Gospels illustrate this ability. Typical is the incident where Jesus is guest in the house of Simon the Pharisee when a sinful woman enters (Lk 7:36-50). Simon condemns Jesus in his heart for allowing the sinner to touch him. However, Jesus reads the thoughts of Simon. At the Last Supper he knows what is in the heart of Judas, and can forewarn Peter with regard to impending temptation. He is able to know the hearts of those he meets.

Jesus' very presence seems to be of such transparency that he makes others aware of self-deception. That realisation then calls them to radical change of direction or else drives them into total opposition, what the French aptly call *ressentiment*. Perhaps this is the way to understand the antipathy that the gospel of his words and deeds aroused in the hearts of many of his contemporaries, particularly those in high places (Mt 12:14).

When one puts together the elements of his teaching just mentioned, one may accept the claim made by Walter Kasper in his famous study of Jesus of Nazareth, 'In Jesus we see God and his glory. In him we come into contact with God's grace and God's judgement.

He is God's Kingdom, God's word and God's love in person ... And yet ... he is poor and homeless. He is among his disciples like one who serves (Lk 22:27)'.[20] His poverty stands out most vividly in his prayer to the one he calls 'Abba' (Mk 14:36), in his trust in the same Abba (Jn 11:42) and in his obedience to the Holy Spirit (Mt 4:1). Cardinal Newman remarks impressively on the fact that the Holy Spirit was his rule of life. 'He was led into the wilderness by the Spirit; he did great works by the Spirit; he offered himself to death by the Eternal Spirit; he was raised from the dead by the Spirit; he was declared to be the Son of God by the Spirit of holiness on his resurrection.'[21]

As the setting for his shocking claims, this poverty seems in flagrant contradiction of these very claims. How can one reconcile the recurring, 'But I say to you', with the poverty that stands out in his prayer, trust in God and obedience to the Spirit? In the claims spoken with such authority he seems to have authority over others, while in his poverty he appears to be radically powerless. Are not these dimensions simply irreconcilable? The question serves to bring out another attribute which authors such as Hans Urs von Balthasar call 'surrender'. As the one sent into the world as 'the apostle of our faith' (Heb 12:2), Jesus must speak with authority. However, as the 'ambassador' of this God, he receives everything – being, authority, words and grace – from the one sending him. He is therefore 'poor' in the sense that all he has is received. He yields himself utterly to this one who has sent him and under whose mandate he lives (Jn 10:20). The result is that he expresses perfectly the mystery of God's being. Just as St Francis became God's juggler in his day, 'juggling' his way up and down the roads and hillsides of Umbria and Italy to the sound of the unheard divine music he longed others to hear in order to join his merry movement, so too Jesus of Nazareth danced to another tune and marched to another rhythm. To use a metaphor, he loans his humanity to the God who had sent him. In that way God could play on the keyboard of that very humanity the divine music he wanted humanity to hear through Jesus of Nazareth. This explains why certain authors notice a 'triadic rhythm' running through his life and action.[22]

His deeds are even more extraordinary than his words of teaching. We have had occasion already to touch upon these deeds in the course of what we have been saying about his style and the content of his teaching. Now, however, we will look a little in slow motion at the deeds. Jesus was not pious in the ordinary sense. Though we know that he went to both synagogue ('as was his custom', Luke 4:16), and Temple to listen to the Word of the scriptures. He saw the Sabbath as made for man, not man for the Sabbath (Mk 2:27). He was not an ascetic. He shared the banquets of the rich and was accused of being a glutton and a drunkard (Mt 11:19). He associated with the tax-collectors (still looking for good press!), the prostitutes and the adulterers of the day. The result was the charge of even being a blasphemer, the sinner who insults the very name of God! C.H. Dodd remarks that 'the charge suggests an affront to the powerful sentiments of religious reverence and awe, evoking both hatred and fear. The charge of blasphemy expresses not so much a rational judgement as a passionate, almost instinctive, revulsion of feeling against what seems to be a violation of sanctities'.[23]

What is the key to his deeds? Perhaps Mark's Gospel provides the clue. Mark, in fact, may be read as a sequence of collisions with all that hurts and de-dignifies human beings. These hurts to humankind are sickness, sin, the reign of Satan, and spoilt or warped religion. The first seven chapters of Mark are a sequence of encounters with people caught in the death-dealing clutches of these very evils. Mark shows a Jesus of 'great passion, a passionate love'.[24] What drives him is the value of each person in himself or herself, and in the eyes of the One who had sent him. 'Man, not the law, was the norm of authentic piety for Jesus.'[25] Jesus wanted those he met to be whole and free and in contact with the one who had sent him and who had only one thing in his heart, the good of all his children. This 'fire' drove him relentlessly (Lk 12:49). Eventually, perhaps even inevitably, it would call for not less than everything (Mk 10:45).

Jesus Christ, in fact, has made Christians 'universally sensitive about the problem of man', since each person 'is so closely and unbreakably linked with Christ'. Pope John Paul saw each man and woman as 'the primary route the Church must travel in fulfilling her mission: *he is the primary and fundamental way for the Church*, the way traced out by Christ himself'. This is a central message in his first encyclical letter, *Redemptor Hominis*. The Church, for her part, 'finds the principle of this solicitude in Jesus Christ himself, as the Gospel's witness'.[26] A modern exegete, Ernst Käsemann, looking at the public ministry of Jesus, seems to sum up much of the attitude of Jesus as follows, 'Fellow-humanity was the sphere in which his gospel lived, not its foundation or objective'.[27]

The Kingdom of God

The upshot of what we have said so far consists in the realisation that Jesus was consumed by his mission to recompose life and living according to its divine model. That mission he calls the Kingdom of God. It is the hermeneutical key to what he does, says and claims. It is ultimately the key to his mysterious personhood, so that it is valid to say that 'anyone who gets involved with Jesus gets involved with the Kingdom of God'.[28]

What precisely is this kingdom? 'The Kingdom of God is not something limited to a physical space, nor is it bound to a system of truths and commandments.'[29] For the past hundred years the translation 'rule of God' has come to the fore. The Kingdom of God, then, would be where God rules, the space where his presence and life and love are effective in the hearts of people, in their relationships, in society and, above all, in their openness to the God of Jesus Christ. Still, the idea of 'rule' is not the happiest, since many people have quite negative experiences of those who rule them in personal, professional or political life. 'We would like to know first *how* God rules.'[30]

Jürgen Moltmann suggests an approach that is both appealing and penetrating. It is a method which, in the final analysis, is grounded on the insight of the Fathers of the Church, namely, that Jesus is the Kingdom of God in person. Wary of the danger of turning the most wonderful of all experiences, that of encountering the Son of God made man and living among us, into a pale theory, he puts forward the principle that we need to encounter Jesus. Such an encounter requires us first to 'see' Jesus of Nazareth, then to 'judge' or understand him, and finally to 'act' or decide in response to what we see and understand. There is a clear sequence here composed of experience, understanding and deciding. Moltmann explains that 'it is one thing to learn the concept of happiness, and another to be happy. And so it is one thing to reduce the Kingdom of God to a definition, and another to experience it and to feel it, to see it and to taste it. It is not the term that must be allowed to define the experience. Rather, the experience must define the term'.[31] Accordingly, we shall follow a method of 'see – judge – act' in order to encounter the dramatic ministry of Jesus of Nazareth.[32]

A. To See the Kingdom of God: Four Gospel Perspectives

1. The Kingdom of God in Parables

The parables of the Gospels are a unique feature of these unique texts. Parables, in fact, mediate well between the mysterious and the concrete, since they respect mystery while speaking to the whole person. Jesus draws his parables from the worlds of nature and of human beings. Perhaps a really good example of the former is to be read in chapter four of St Mark's Gospel where one finds a sequence of parables drawn from the world of nature: the parables of the sower and the seed, and the parable of the mustard seed. One begins to see that the Kingdom is both a gift and a response.

In Luke chapter 15 we have a set of three parables – the lost son, the lost coin and the lost sheep. Pagoda-like, they reinforce the message that there is more joy in heaven over one sinner who repents than over ninety-nine just and upright people who do not have to repent. In the parable of the lost son, the Father is so overwhelmed with joy that he says, 'This my son was dead, and is alive again; he was lost and is found'(15:24).[33]

2. The Kingdom of God in the Healing of the Sick

Jesus of Nazareth was good news for the sick. It seems as if he was not able to pass by those who were ill. 'That evening at sundown, they brought to him all those who were sick or possessed with demons. And the whole city was gathered together about the door. And he healed many who were sick with various diseases, and cast out many demons' (Mark 1:32f). These miraculous healings were part of the coming of God's kingdom. In the elegant words of Moltmann, 'The kingdom of the living God drives out the germs of death and spreads the seeds of life'.[34]

3. The Kingdom of God in the Companionship of Jesus

What is so striking in the Gospels is the fact that Jesus seeks out the 'sinners and the tax-collectors', setting up table-fellowship with them. The Kingdom comes in the form of mercy of which Jesus is the embodiment. From his person it radiates on those he meets, especially the most abandoned. Mercy, in fact, is what happens when God's goodness meets human misery, and what misery is greater than that of being far away from him who is the source of all life and love? As for those who consider themselves 'just' and so 'better', Jesus had to save them from the temptation to judge others negatively, not noticing the log in their own eyes (Mt 7:3). If undetected and uncorrected, this mindset may prevent their entering into the Kingdom which Jesus is opening up for all.

4. The Kingdom is for the Poor, Children and Women

The logic of solidarity pushes Jesus towards the most defenceless in society. They were principally the poor, women and children. 'The collective term "the poor" embraces the hungry, the unemployed, the enslaved, the people who have lost heart and lost hope, and the suffering.'[35] For all of these Jesus of Nazareth was good news. What he brings to the poor is not primarily the aid of charitable works but the realisation of their true dignity as children of the One he called 'Abba, Father'. In that way they could discover their indestructible worth in the eyes of the Creator. And not only that, but they could find the energy to rise up out of their destitution, material and human, and to bring peace to the violence of the inhumanity and the injustice that enslaved them in the first instance. It is in that way that they rise and take the Kingdom of God by force, and it is in that way that the Kingdom of God belongs to them (Mt 5:3).

As to women, the gospel of Jesus' words and deeds is a very strong statement of their inalienable dignity. 'He does not discriminate against foreign women (he heals the daughter of the Syro-Phoenician woman: Mk 7:24-30). He overcomes the taboo concerning their impurity under the law (he heals the woman diseased with an issue of blood: Mk 5:34), holds them as an example (he lauds the poor widow: Mk 12:41-4), cultivates their friendship (he is a close friend of Martha and Mary, the sisters of Lazarus: Lk 10:38-42; Jn 11)'.[36] Fascinatingly, the longest conversation of Jesus with an individual in the Gospels is the one he had with the Samaritan woman. In her case Jesus even discusses theology (Jn 4)! Jesus transcends the culture of his times and resists the prejudices of his contemporaries. 'The Bible has within its pages a unique history of the greatness, the sovereignty, the wisdom and the courage of women. It is perhaps the most interesting book in connection with the emancipation of women.'[37]

As for children, Jesus nominates them as the norm for all others! 'Let the little children alone, and do not stop them coming to me; for it is to such as these that the kingdom of heaven belongs' (Mt 19:14; see Mk 10:13-6; Lk 18:15-17). Perhaps the great German theologian, Karl Rahner, identifies the reason behind their selection: 'Childhood is openness, is trustful submission to control by another, the courage to allow fresh horizons, ever new and ever wider, to be opened up before one, a readiness to journey into the untried and the untested.'[38] Only these dispositions enable the entry into the Kingdom. The most recent doctor of the Church (and there are only thirty-three such people in the history of the Church!), Thérèse of Lisieux, understood this so well that she opened a new 'way', a spirituality in the Church: in the Book of Proverbs she had read the golden words: 'Let him who is little come to me' (Pr 9:4).

B. Judge the Kingdom: Some Theological Clarifications

In these and other ways, Jesus showed the Kingdom to his contemporaries. It was for them to see and to perceive. They had the experience because they had the experience of Jesus who is the Kingdom in person. However, the Gospels show that many missed the meaning of the experience! Accordingly, if we are not to miss the point of the revelation, we must try to understand the meaning of Jesus' words and deeds as they bear upon the Kingdom. Perhaps the best way to get their meaning is to ask the right questions.

1. Is the Kingdom of God a Present or Future Reality?

The Kingdom of God is experienced in the present in the companionship of Jesus or, alternatively, in the impact of his word and action! Where those lost in evil and in aimlessness are found, where the unjust are changed to care for the weak, where the poor have their dignity recognised, where women and children are treated according to the truth of their status as children of the one Father, there the Kingdom of God begins. The Kingdom is therefore also an object of *hope* since so much of society provides ample evidence of the very opposite state of affairs. The hope of Christians, however, is a hope rooted in both experience and memory. In that way the Kingdom involves the tension between something that exists already but still has to mature into fullness. This explains why Jesus teaches us to pray, 'Our Father … thy Kingdom come!' (Lk 11:2).

2. Does the Kingdom of God belong to this World or the Next?

There are those who have such an exalted idea of the Kingdom as to locate it beyond this world! They appeal to the dialogue between Pilate and Jesus when Jesus says to Pilate, 'My Kingdom is not of this world' (Jn 18:36). However, this is not so much a statement about the place of the kingdom as about its origin.[39] The truth is that the Kingdom is 'in' this world but not 'of' this world. It is not a human achievement but a gift from the Creator of this world from whom every good gift descends (Jn 1:16-17). And it is precisely in the person of Jesus who has come into this world of flesh and blood that it has been situated. However, it encompasses both heaven and earth. That is why Jesus teaches us in the prayer of all prayers that we are to ask that the Kingdom will come 'on earth as it is in heaven'.

3. Is the Kingdom of God Exclusively the Affair of God or are we also Involved?

The eminent philosopher, Eric Voegelin, has shown that the great ideologies of recent centuries all derive from a single aspiration – the desire to bring the Kingdom of God on earth by human means.[40] This would remove the dramatic tension between divine operation and human co-operation, since there would have to be only one principal actor, the great Ideologue-Leader himself, be he a Comte, a Marx, a Freud or a Nietzsche and his Superman. Inevitably God would become superfluous since replaced by a this-worldly leader capable of inaugurating the earthly Kingdom. Since God has not inaugurated the Kingdom, man must do so! Besides, the Christian message of the Kingdom of God, it was claimed, tends to alienate Christians from serious involvement in the project of building the earthly city since its inordinate preoccupation with the City of God engrosses them.

That this can happen *to some Christians* is no doubt possible. In the nineteenth century Cardinal Newman described the danger in these terms: 'When persons are convinced that life is short ... when they feel that the next life is all in all, and that eternity is the only subject that really can claim or fill their thoughts, then they are apt to undervalue this life altogether, and to forget its real importance. They are apt to wish to spend the time of their sojourning here in a positive separation from active and social duties: yet it should be recollected that the employments of this world though not themselves heavenly, are, after all the way to heaven ... but it is difficult to realise this. It is difficult to realise both truths at once, and to connect both truths together; steadily to contemplate the life to come, yet to act in this.'[41] Thinkers like Nietzsche concluded that the 'Christian is a useless, separated, resigned person, extraneous to the progress of the world'.[42]

It is important not to think in either/or terms. The Second Vatican Council addressed the issue in its *Pastoral Constitution on the Church in the Modern World*: 'The Christian message, far from deterring men from the task of building up the world ... binds them, rather, to all this by a still more stringent obligation.'[43] Still it is difficult to realise the interpenetration of heaven and earth for some people. Jesus' own person and teaching show up the true connection. Bringing the total newness of the Kingdom by bringing himself (St Irenaeus), Jesus makes it our responsibility too! One may see this clearly in the instance of the man who was willing to follow him without reservation if only he could first bury his father. Jesus advises him, 'Leave the dead to bury their dead; your duty is to *go and spread* the news of the Kingdom of God' (Lk 9:60).

4. Is the Kingdom of God a Theocracy or is it Union with the Living God?

Far from controlling human beings, the Kingdom is where they find true freedom. The Kingdom in fact is the place where the insatiable human hunger for mystery, love, truth, beauty and freedom is perfectly addressed. St Paul is quite explicit: 'The Kingdom of God is not a matter of eating and drinking, but of justice, peace and joy in the Holy Spirit' (Rom 14:7). The Kingdom in fact is our lasting city (Heb 13:14).

'When God ventures forth to us in his Son made flesh of our flesh then there is the fullest participation of the divine in the human, and there is the correlative possibility of the human to venture into the expansive space of the divine, so that the human participates in the divine.'[44] What a breathtaking adventure! Yet this is the adventure of those who follow Jesus of Nazareth. However, it must begin now or else it will not begin at all! Its full realisation, however, lies in God's future when Jesus will hand over the Kingdom to the Father (ICor 15:24).

C. Act now by making the Unconditional Choice of the Kingdom of God!

In his original preaching, Jesus stresses the absolute urgency of welcoming the Kingdom. 'The Kingdom of God is at hand; repent and believe in the gospel' (Mk 1:15). All procrastination shows that the heart is in bondage to something else, something that is not God. The presence of a reality as great as the Kingdom is both gift and imperative; better, an imperative flowing from a gift. As when treasure hidden in the field or a pearl of great price are found and are instantly preferred to everything else (Mt 13:44-46), so too with the discovery of the Kingdom. As a treasure unparalleled, it has to be chosen at once. The time to enter the Kingdom is now, in fact, this present moment. Whoever postpones the choice is attached to that which is not God, like the rich young man (Mk 10:17-22).

Aware of the transience of time and, in particular, of the manner in which it 'scatters' our very existence and undermines our desire for permanence, we set out to *construct our own future*. We plan our future in order to achieve a measure of control over our vanishing time. This planning is both the driving force of our activity as well as the source of our daily anxiety. There is one thing, however, that that planning leaves completely out of the reckoning: there may be no future, and even if there is, it may not turn out at all as we had planned.

Into this very human situation Jesus now comes laden with love and impelled by the fire of the Kingdom to announce: God comes from the Beyond into the Here. 'The source of the future becomes present for us, God comes from the periphery of time into the centre of time.'[45] He is here and he is now! He is radically *with* us and he is radically *for* us. He desires to have his time with us so that we can have all time with him, and so have his absolute future as our very own future. This explains why Jesus admonishes those who would follow him to set their hearts on the Kingdom of his Father first and on his righteousness and 'all these other things will be given them as well' (Mt 6:33).

The estimate of Elizabeth-Anne Stewart seems to capture what it means to see, judge and act for the Kingdom of which Jesus is literally the personification:

> The new order to which Jesus pointed demands a transformation of consciousness, a completely new way of seeing which, in turn, necessitates new ways of thinking, new ways of being ... To participate in the reign of God, then, means nothing less than undergoing 'an interior revolution' ... How threatening all this is, and yet, as Jesus pointed out, unless we go a complete transformation we will not make any progress, spiritually speaking ... To allow oneself to be transformed is the first step towards renewing the earth.[46]

The Integrating Reality: The Art and the Power of Loving

We have had occasion to note the fire that drove Jesus in the work for the Kingdom (Lk 12:49). Perhaps Luke suggests the concrete expressions of this fire of mission consuming Jesus in his public ministry. At the very opening of his 'account' (1:1-4) the evangelist has Jesus enter the synagogue and read the scroll of Third Isaiah. It is the programme for his mission, transfigured in his person and now to be enfleshed in his ministry of bringing the Kingdom of God. It is not that Jesus is made for the text, but, as with the whole of Old Testament revelation, the text is made for Jesus who will fulfil it superabundantly (Acts 7; Lk 24: 13-35).

What underlines that ministry of and for the Kingdom? The question focuses our minds on what was foremost for Jesus. The encounter with the learned scribe in Mark (12:28-34) who asks which is the greatest of the commandments, makes the point incisively. The same lesson is reinforced by the great parable on the Last Judgement in Matthew 25. Jesus sees his whole existence as obedience to his Father and as service to his fellow-men. These are the very co-ordinates of his ministry, and he lets himself be consumed by them. He wants those who would follow him to be caught up into the same fire to the point where, in the words of St Augustine, 'there will be one Christ loving himself'.[47] We will focus for the time being on his journey towards others. His attitude and action could be summed up in the phrase, 'You are everything, I am nothing'. And this radical disposition is the outflow of his still more central commitment to the cause his Father had given him on coming into the world (Heb 10:1-10).

It is illuminating to look at the style of his life with the men and women he met, at what one might dare to describe as Jesus' 'art of loving'. His public ministry personifies this art of loving. He lives by this art to the extent that he *is* this art (Eph 2:10). This attention to the style of Jesus precludes the danger of letting him disappear in a cloud of generalisation, evaporating him in an over-heated haze of praise. For what stands out in the Gospels, its most winning characteristic so to speak, is what might be called the particularity of attention that Jesus shows to the individual men and women he meets. John Henry Newman puts it splendidly:

> The most winning property of our Saviour's mercy (if it is right so to speak of it), is its dependence on time and place, person and circumstance; in other words, its tender discrimination. It regards and consults for each individual as he comes before it ... it has its particular shade and mode of feeling for each; and on some men it so bestows itself, as if he depended for his own happiness on their well-being.[48]

Certain strands compose the Art of Loving that is the soul of Jesus' ministry and the bedrock of that Kingdom which he embodies. The first strand in Jesus' art of loving is the fact that *he loves all*. Not only the lost sheep of the House of Israel, but also Samaritans (Jn 4), Greeks (Jn 12:20-22) and Romans (Lk 7:1-10) are welcomed by him. He is not there only for the devout and the good. The truth in fact is the opposite: in the case of the call of Levi, he declares that he has come not to call the virtuous only, but the sinners to repentance (Mt 9:13). This is a matter of policy! Jesus did not make distinctions of persons, save in so far as the need of the particular person was greater. In the *agape* he showed he makes no distinctions between the friendly and the unfriendly, the good-looking and the ugly, the great and the little, my own country and the foreign country. All are to be loved. This means in a particular way the enemy: 'If you love those who love you, what right have you to claim any credit? Even the tax collectors do as much, do they not?' (Mt 5:47). And that is the gymnastic that will be required of those who will follow him.

The second strand in his art of loving is that *he loved first*. Jesus did not wait to be loved. On the contrary, he clearly aimed at the primacy of being the first to love (1 Jn 3:19). It was Jesus who noticed Zaccheus and offered to come to his house (Lk 19:10) . It was Jesus who set out to find the sick and the sinful, those under the sway of evil spirits, and those wounded by 'spoilt religion' (Jm 1:27).

The third strand in the art of loving of Jesus is that *he loved with concrete deeds and facts*. To the leper he brought healing (Mk 1:40-45). To the hungry he brought food (Jn 6:1-15). To the blind he gave sight (Jn 9). To the lost and the hopeless, he showed compassion (Lk 15), setting out to teach them and to give them hope so that they could begin again to live and trust in their futures (Lk 7:36-50). To the sinner he brought the most practical of all gifts – the forgiveness of sins and its replacement by relationship with God and others. The spiritual and the corporal works of mercy are inspired over the millennia by this art of Jesus. It is legitimate to read the great charisms of the Camillians, the Vincentians and the Missionaries of Charity as specific embodiments of this strand of the art of loving. This strand in the art of loving is so serious that living it is the key to enter the Kingdom of heaven, while total failure to do so excludes from the Kingdom (Mt 25:30-44).

The fourth strand in Jesus' art of loving consists in his *making himself one with the person loved*. Jesus lived transferred into the other, for the truth is that he loved each person he met *more than he loved himself*. This stands out particularly in the episode of the tears of Jesus at the grave of Lazarus (Jn 11:36f). Later St Paul will exhort the first Christians in Rome with the words, 'Rejoice with those who rejoice, cry with those who cry' (Rom 12:15).[49] In doing so, Paul was but preaching what he had practised: 'I made myself all things to all men in order to save some at any cost' (1Cor 9:22). Perhaps it is in this ability 'to live the other' (Chiara Lubich) that we discover the secret of Jesus' ability to read hearts.

The final strand in the art of loving is what happens when such love becomes mutual. If two or more people live these four strands of loving *among themselves*, their loving becomes reciprocal. This reciprocity works a real wonder of the Gospel, for it brings about a unique presence of Jesus. He both guarantees and explains this presence when he says, 'Where two or three come together in my name, there am I with them' (Mt 18:20). This is a social presence, in a sense a visible presence, at least to the eyes of the soul. It can occur anywhere, in an office, a parliament, in a family, among children, a group of artists, even on the playing field, wherever in fact the strands of the art of loving are operative. Fascinatingly, the Second Vatican Council saw in this mutual love 'the basic law of human perfection and hence of the world's transformation'.[50] In the Johannine corpus there is a veritable treatise on the Law of mutual Love, the New Commandment.

Of course, it will be the passion and the cross that will both manifest and embody this art of loving in a measure that is without measure. On the cross, the crucified Son concentrates, in an incomparable manner, the various strands of the art by which he had lived the Kingdom in the three years of public ministry. Still, it was good to see it there, in action in his public ministry as totally committed to the bringing of the Kingdom of God. To enter the Kingdom, then, requires conversion by which one turns one's back on a previous lifestyle, and begins to live from God and for God and with God. In Jesus this God is present so that the Kingdom of God is here in our midst. To enter the Kingdom, requires us to enter into the very attitude of Jesus and the lifestyle expressing his radical attitude. To live the art of loving is to be placed within the Kingdom of God through, with and in Jesus.

The Kingdom of God: Home for Humankind?

Modern men and women, however, do not easily accept the message of the Kingdom of God. It seems too good to be true, a real Utopia, especially in a world that is claimed to be increasingly controllable by the scientists, the technologists and the entrepreneurs! The question therefore asserts itself: is the gift of the Kingdom of God realistic? Is the way of Jesus of Nazareth true? Does it offer and bring the Kingdom of God into the world? That question preoccupied and exercised the minds of two great thinkers in the modern period, the one Catholic and from the seventeenth century, the other Orthodox and from the nineteenth century. I am referring to Blaise Pascal (1623–1662) and Fyodor Dostoievski (1821–1881). They seem to anticipate and to reply to two principal types of argument made particularly today against the 'good tidings' of the Kingdom of God.

Blaise Pascal has drawn our attention to the grandeur and the misery of human life, what Newman following on St Gregory Nazianzen[51] described as the greatness and the littleness of human life.[52] Man is made a 'little less than God' (Psalm 8:5), yet his 'days are like the grass; the grass withers and the flower fades, with only the Word of the Lord remaining for ever' (Is 40:6-7; Jm 1:10-11). He aims so high and falls so low. He feels called to a higher life and yet is dominated by death in its many forms and its inevitability. Above all, he is threatened by loneliness and isolation which drive home the threat that he is not loved and, even worse, is not even lovable.[53] In this consists the grandeur and the misery of human existence, as the Council commented.[54]

Now it is precisely this dramatic scenario that is addressed by Jesus Christ. His presence and the gospel of the Kingdom of God highlight these clashing dimensions of human existence. Pascal puts it splendidly: 'The knowledge of God without that of man's misery causes pride. The knowledge of man's misery without that of God causes despair. The knowledge of Jesus Christ constitutes the middle cause, because in him we find both God and our misery.'[55] In fact, we find God in our misery, and our misery is taken on by God who comes to heal and save what was lost (Mt 9:9f).

In their encounter with Jesus Christ, men and women are brought face to face with their misery in all its dimensions and expressions. However, Jesus not only deals with the misery of men and women, he offers them a way into a life that surpasses our wildest imaginings: in fact, he is himself that way (Jn 14:6). Jesus saves from despair, and he saves from presumption and pride. In opening up entry into the Kingdom, Jesus saves from despair. In confronting men and women with the truth about life and themselves he pre-empted proneness to pride. In that way Jesus of Nazareth both x-rays the human condition as no else ever could do, and shows how it can be healed and fulfilled still more wonderfully. 'God, you have wondrously created human nature, and even more wondrously restored it!' Or, in the words of Walter Kasper, 'We are therefore bound to ask where else we should and where else we might find such words of life'.[56]

As for Fyodor Dostoievski, he invites us to reflect upon what is perhaps the most subtle and challenging argument against the religion of Jesus Christ, that it is not *practical*. In his epic, *The Brothers Karamazov*, there is the episode of the Legend of the Grand Inquisitor. Jesus is put on trial again. Dostoievski places on the lips of the Grand Inquisitor the most eloquent argument against the Christian religion. Satan himself, masquerading as the Archbishop of Toledo, makes the charge. It consists in the claim that Jesus has indeed given to humankind the most wonderful of all religions, but still a religion that is inappropriate for human beings *as they are*. Not only have they not lived up to it, but they have twisted it and deformed it. Furthermore, they have even deployed it in justification of the most appalling acts of inhumanity. The result is that human beings are worse than ever. They should have been given a more practical religion, a religion where the good would *have to be done* because there would have been no other choice. There should have been no option but to do what was announced and lived and witnessed to by Jesus.

Jesus is charged, therefore, not only with impracticality, but also with the deformation of humankind. 'For fifteen centuries we've been troubled by this freedom, but now it's over and done with for good', thunders the Grand Inquisitor. Aloysha Karamazov, as the brother who believes in God and his Kingdom and puts that belief concretely into action by choosing to live a life of heroic commitment to God and to others as a monk, identifies incisively the root of the Grand Inquisitor's charge: 'Your inquisitor doesn't believe in God – that's all his secret.'[57] And not believing in God, he cannot believe in the final analysis in freedom. The Kingdom of God, in fact, brings the freedom of God to human hearts. It frees them *from* false choices in order to *live by* the Art of Loving personified in Jesus. Living that art directs them into the way of life and on to the path of authentic freedom.

Notes

1. See *Preface I for Christmas*.
2. See Gerald O'Collins, *What are they saying about Jesus?*, New York/Ramsey/Toronto 1977.
3. Tertullian, *De Praescriptione Haereticorum*, VII, 9: *SC* 46, 98.
4. Walter Kasper, *An Introduction to Christian Faith*, London 1980, 38.
5. St Augustine, *De Trinitate*, V, 5, 6.
6. St Thomas, *Summa*, I, q.29, a.4.
7. Walter Kasper, '*Einer aus der Trinität*' in *Kirche und Theologie*, Mainz 1987, 217–227.
8. See especially Bernard Lonergan's review of Leslie Dewart's *The Future of Belief: Theism in a World come of Age*, New York 1966, 'The Dehellenisation of Dogma', in Bernard Lonergan, *A Second Collection*, London 1974, 11–32.
9. *Dei Verbum*, 19; see Herbert Vorgrimler, *Commentary on the Documents of the Second Vatican Council*, vol. III, London and New York 1969, 256–261.
10. Walter Kasper, *An Introduction to Christianity*, 40–41.
11. *Dei Verbum*, 4.
12. See Hans Urs von Balthasar, *The Glory of the Lord, The New Covenant*, vol. VII, Edinburgh 1989; Günter Bornkamm, *Jesus von Nazareth*, Stuttgart 1956, 18.
13. Bornkamm, ibid., 21.
14. Richard A. Burridge, *Four Gospels, One Jesus?*, Grand Rapids 1995.
15. John Henry Newman, *Discussions and Arguments*, London 1872, 296.
16. Kasper, ibid., 44.
17. John O'Donnell, *Hans Urs von Balthasar*, 37.
18. St Augustine, *Sermo 293, 3*: PL 38, 1328.
19. Walter Kasper, *Jesus the Christ*, London 1976, 102.
20. Ibid., 103–104.
21. John Henry Newman, *Parochial and Plain Sermons*, vol. V, London 1869, 139.
22. Hans Urs von Balthasar and Bernard Lonergan come to mind.

23. C.H. Dodd, *The Founder of Christianity*, London 1971, 78.
24. J. Moltmann, *Jesus Christ for Today's World*, London 1994, 31.
25. Walter Kasper, ibid., 45.
26. Pope John Paul II, *Redemptor Hominis*, 14.
27. E. Käsemann, *Der Ruf der Freiheit*, Tübingen 1968, 52.
28. J. Moltmann, ibid, 8.
29. K. Hemmerle, 'Tell me about your God', in *Being One*, 1(1996), 14.
30. J. Moltmann, ibid., 8.
31. Ibid., 9f; Moltmann thereby comes towards the theological methods of both Hans Urs von Balthasar and Bernard Lonergan.
32. Moltmann, ibid., 9f.
33. See Pope John Paul's encyclical, *Dives in misericordia*, 1980, sections 5–6.
34. Moltmann, ibid., 13.
35. Ibid., 17.
36. Theological-Historical Commission for the great Jubilee of the Year 2000, *Jesus Christ, Word of the Father, the Saviour of the World*, 1997, 72–73.
37. Elizabeth Moltmann-Wendel, *The Women around Jesus*, London 1982, 6.
38. K. Rahner, 'Towards a Theology of Childhood', in *Theological Investigations*, vol. 8, London and New York 1971, 48.
39. Moltmann, ibid., 20.
40. Eric Voegelin, *The New Science of Politics*, Chicago & London, 1952, 107–132.
41. John Henry Newman, *Parochial and Plain Sermons*, VIII, 154–155.
42. Pope John Paul I, *Angelus, General Audiences, Urbi et Orbi*, Editrice la Parola 1979, 16.
43. *Gaudium et spes*, 34; see also nn. 39, 7, and the *Message to the World* of the Council Fathers on 20 October 1962.
44. Thomas Norris & Brendan Leahy, *Christianity & Contemporary Expressions*, Dublin 2004, 85.
45. Klaus Hemmerle, *Glauben - wie geht das?*, Freiburg, Basel, Wien 1978, 29: the translation is mine.

46. Elizabeth-Anne Stewart, *Jesus, the Holy Fool,* Franklin, Wisconsin 1999, 90.

47. St Augustine, *Epistula in I Joannnem,* Tractatus XPL 35, 2055.

48. John Henry Newman, *Parochial and Plain Sermons,* I, London 1881, 120.

49. The comment of the Lutheran martyr, Dietrich Bonhöffer, comes vividly to mind, 'Only those Christians who have wept for the Jews should sing Gregorian Chant'.

50. Second Vatican Council, Pastoral Constitution on the Church in the Modern World *Gaudium et spes,* 38.

51. St Gregory Nazianzen, Breviary: Week 32, Monday.

52. See also John Henry Newman, 'The Greatness and Littleness of Human Life' in *Parochial and Plain Sermons,* vol. IV, London 1869, 214–225.

53. See Joseph Ratzinger, *Principles of Catholic Theology,* San Francisco 1987, 52; 75–84.

54. Second Vatican Council, *Gaudium et spes,* 18.

55. Pascal, *Pensèes,* nn. 526, 527.

56. Walter Kasper, ibid., 52.

57. Fyodor Dostoievski, *The Brothers Karamazov,* London 1958, 294; 307.

Chapter VI

Jesus Crucified and Forsaken: The Face of God for the Modern World?

> Evil, helplessness, fear and impermanence are conquered not by ignoring them but by God's entry into them.
>
> (Bishop Donal Murray)

1. Two New Testament Episodes

Talking about God is dangerous. This is the title of the autobiography of the Russian convert, Tatjana Goritschewa, whom we have already met. The great third–century thinker, Origen, agrees.[1] Two sample episodes in the New Testament show why it is dangerous, namely, that even with revelation human beings find it difficult to let God be God the way he wants to be God. The sample episodes are the interrogation scene in the centre of Mark's Gospel (Mk 8:27-33) and the road to Emmaus passage at the conclusion of Luke's Gospel (24:13-35).

Having narrated Jesus' ministry for fully seven chapters, Mark depicts Jesus turning to the Twelve and asking them who people believe him to be. They list the emerging answers to this central question in Mark's narrative. Then Jesus personalises, as it were, the question, 'But who do you say that I am?' Peter answers on the behalf of the others, 'You are the Christ the Son of the Living God'.

Jesus responds immediately by announcing his ultimate mission as a journey to Jerusalem and into his passion. He names himself as Son of Man as if to correct and to fill out the content of his title as Son of God and Messiah.[2] Peter, however, is shocked at the very thought of the Messiah being a suffering Messiah and remonstrates with Jesus, only to be told that his way of thinking is not the way of God but the way of God's adversary, Satan. Peter 'tried to do what Satan had done in the desert, to block the fulfilment of God's plan by persuading Jesus to escape from his suffering'.[3] Peter, in other words, has an ideology of the Messiah into which Jesus and his revelation will have to fit. He personifies man's native slowness to accept God's own self-revelation.

The second episode, occurring in Luke, brings out the same point in an 'exquisite story, found only in this Gospel, that sparkles with Lucan themes'.[4] Two disciples, one of whom is named Cleopas, are travelling from Jerusalem to Emmaus. They are downhearted and dispirited though it is the morning of Easter. They are appalled at the passion and crucifixion of Jesus. In reply to their distress and confusion, Jesus 'starting with Moses and going through all the prophets ... explained to them the passages throughout the scriptures that were about himself' (v. 27). The risen Lord shows that the covenant with Israel had this central astounding dynamic and dramatic thrust 'from one end of the Scriptures to the other'.[5] The Messiah had (dei) to suffer and in that way enter into his glory. In the end, the disciples grasp the point and perceive the glory of the crucified but now risen Lord. For a second time we notice the slowness of human beings in perceiving the true face of God. The comment of Voltaire comes to mind: 'God made man in his image and likeness, and man has paid him back.'[6]

2. The Heavy Baggage of our Pre-conceptions

These two episodes combine to stress the truth that Peter, as well as Cleopas and his companion, have their own idea of the Messiah. Since this idea is in possession, as it were, Jesus' own self-revelation has to struggle to enter their minds and gain reception. Now this is not so because these NT characters are particularly unresponsive or unusually dull but rather because God's self-revelation requires an enormous shift of horizon on our part.[7] And what was true of the New Testament is, mutatis mutandis, true of us. We cannot listen to and perceive God's revelation independently of the heavy baggage of our own presuppositions and pre-understandings. Almost without wanting to, we paint our own portrait of God. *His revelation must fit into our categories.*[8] Only the Holy Spirit, who is both a personal gift to each Christian as well as a communitarian gift to the whole Church as the community of believers, can give us a spirit of wisdom and the ability to perceive what is revealed. Only the Holy Spirit can lead us into the revealed knowledge of God, and enable us to appreciate what hope his call holds for us (see Eph 1:17-18).

This point is well made in *Dei Verbum*, 'The Holy Spirit constantly perfects faith by his gifts, so that revelation may be more and more profoundly understood ... He leads believers to the full truth, and makes the word of Christ dwell in them in all its richness (Col 3:16)' (*DV* 5; 8). Indeed, the very 'fullness of Christ' (Col 2:9) is so disproportionate to our capacity to perceive it and to receive it (Jn 1:16) that the centuries of the Church's time are necessary for that appreciation. This 'fullness', in fact, absolutely requires time for its unfolding, as well as the challenge of each epoch on the Church's journey to stimulate humankind to unpack and to assimilate 'the unfathomable riches of Christ' (Eph 3:8).

The purpose of this article is to propose that the face of God for today is to be sought in his divine Son enfleshed, crucified and forsaken. It will attempt to justify this contention by means of an appeal to a threefold of scripture, patristic tradition and theological reasoning. Finally, it will have to show, by means of a brief analysis of some of the characteristics of contemporary culture in the West, that this is the face of God most appropriate to the men and women of our times.

3. Jesus – the Deed and the Word Revealing God

St Mark brings out this truth in his own inimitable fashion. In fact, he seems so to structure his highly dramatic narrative 'of the Gospel of Jesus Christ, the Son of God' (1:1) that the succession of events is meant to challenge the disciples both to dismantle dramatically *their* notion of the Messiah and to accept increasingly the kind of Messiah being manifested in the ministry of Jesus of Nazareth. Thus after the interrogation scene which we briefly considered at the beginning, Jesus announces three times in rapid succession his passion and death at the hands of the authorities (8:31-3; 9:30-2; 10:32-4): he seems to rush towards the deed of the Cross as a young man might count the days to his wedding. The net impact of these declarations on the disciples was 'that they were in a daze, and ... were apprehensive' (10:32). Worse still for the disciples, this Jesus raises this stunning orientation of his dramatic ministry to the level of programme, 'For the Son of Man himself did not come to be served but to serve, and to give his life as a ransom for many' (10:45).[9]

On the eve of his Passion in the agony of Gethsemene Jesus calls God, 'Abba' (Mk 14:36). He brings his 'sorrow unto death' (Mk 14:34), as well as his imminent passion, to his Father and embraces the will of this Father, his 'Abba', to drink the chalice of his sufferings to the end. In other words, the cross is in the first instance an event between the Father and his Son made flesh. It is not primarily the result of the rejection of his ministry by Israel and humanity.

Still, on the cross He will offer his life 'for the many' to the one he calls 'Abba'. This inevitably means collision with the whole history of refusal on the part of humans to live for God and for others. In this refusal lies the dead heart of sin and its isolating force. On the cross the appalling weight of this refusal will be laid upon the obeying Son.

4. Focus on Jesus' Cry of Forsakenness

A specific moment of that great Deed deserves special attention. It is the moment of his dramatic forsakenness by the one he had called 'Abba' several hours earlier. At the summit of his loving of the Father and of us, Jesus experiences the summit of his suffering when he cries out 'with a great voice' (Mk 15:34; Mt 27:46). And so both Mark and Matthew highlight this experience of the Redeemer, giving in Aramaic and Hebrew, respectively, the words uttered by Jesus – 'Eloi, Eloi, / Eli, Eli, lama sabachtani' (Mk 15:34; Mt 27:46). This cry, interestingly, was not considered in any depth during recent centuries, having been seen as the first line of Psalm 22. In the early centuries, however, this was not the case. The early Fathers were interested in this logion of Jesus, though not without certain anxieties lest they should slip into any form of Patripassianism or Arianism. This century has seen a flourishing interest which is not embarrassed or defensive but rather intriguing and fascinating.

The cry ought to be read in the context of Mark's Gospel and its tradition on which Matthew draws.[10] A keyword in the cry is the word *sabachtani*. What does it mean? To arrive at the answer one is obliged to go to the Hebrew of Psalm 22 from which the word is taken. The Hebrew word suggests 'leaving a person alone in a grievous situation without intervening'.[11] And since this cry is not given in either Luke or John, its content and meaning should be determined *without* recourse to the other Gospels. Furthermore, the cry of abandonment is the *only* word spoken by Jesus on the Cross in both Matthew and Mark. It ought therefore to be interpreted as, yes, the opening verse of Psalm 22 *but redeployed here* to express both the summit experience of the Saviour in his death and the genuine meaning of that death for all humankind.

Surprising insights result. First of all, the God to whom Jesus cries his 'Why?' is the God whom Jesus has called 'Abba' ('Dad'; 'Father') only some hours previously. There is infinitely more involved than in Psalm 22 where the innocent suffering of the Just One makes him cry out to YHWH, the God of the Covenant. In that sense, 'this psalm exists for Jesus, not Jesus for the psalm' (Balthasar, Moltmann). Secondly, the content of the cry is the abandonment felt in Jesus' human soul because the Father does not intervene to take him out of the situation of abandonment in which he finds himself. He no longer enjoys the beatifying light and presence of his Father. This absence constitutes the core and the summit of his suffering. Finally, the cry happens in the context of Jesus' fidelity to his Father and to the mission he has received from him to give his life as a ransom for many (Mk 10:45) and to drink the chalice of suffering to the dregs (Mk 14:36). The 'many' are not any longer beyond God but have been reached in their distance and difference from the Creator and redeeming God.[12]

Here the extraordinary words of a recent *International Theological*

Commission document on Christology come to mind: 'No matter how great be the sinner's estrangement from God, it is not as deep as the sense of distance that the Son experiences *vis-à-vis* the Father in the kenotic emptying of himself (Phil 2:7), and in the anguish of "abandonment" (Mt 27:46)'.[13] Or in the poetic words of Romano Guardini, 'In his forsakenness the infinitely beloved and crucified Son of the eternal Father reaches the absolute depths from which the omnipotence of love raises up the new creation'.[14]

This immense suffering, consisting as it does in his forsakenness by his Father, is still the expression of the Son's love both for the Father and for those who crucify and reject him. In all authentic love, the lover exalts the beloved, and so enlarges the beloved, as it were. Through this forsakenness, which results precisely from the Son's love for the Father's redemptive will in our regard (Mk 14:35-6), he says to his Father, 'You are everything, I am nothing', and, more wonderful still, he says to sinners, 'You are everything, I am nothing'! In that way he loses everything except that which binds him to the Father and to humankind, namely, his love. By doing so he places that very love precisely where it seems to be most absent, namely, in the sin-dominated history of humankind and in the appalling impact of that history of sin which results in fallen humankind's godforsakenness, their abandonment by God.

5. An Early Hymn: Philippians 2: 6-11

Paul, the earliest writer of the New Testament, in his *Letter to the Philippians* quotes an existing hymn, recognisably such from its rhythmical structure and parabola-like movement.[15] Its ancient character adds to its significance for our present theme, namely, the particular face of God one reads in the crucifixion of Christ. In the RSV text the first three verses (2:6-8) read as follows:

> Though he was in the form of God, he did not count equality with God a thing to be grasped, but emptied himself, taking the form of a servant, being born in the

likeness of men. And being found in human form he humbled himself and became obedient unto death, even death on a cross.

The next three verses (2:9-11) are symmetrical to these three verses and describe an ascending movement of Jesus Christ consisting in his exaltation from the nadir of death on a cross to the zenith of being Lord (*Kyrios*) who is the glory of the Father (11). The significance of the explicit nomination of God as God the Father will be important for the interpretation of the text, particularly the first three verses which are our principal concern.

The protagonist of the action of these verses is 'he who was in the form of God' (6). It has to follow that the subject who thus empties himself by taking the form of a servant is not the already incarnate Christ but he who abides beyond this world, being in the form of God.[16] This subject actively empties himself by taking on the form of a slave in the Incarnation. This first *kenosis*, however, leads as a matter of course to a second *kenosis*, that of death. Paul adds the telling qualification, 'death on a cross'.

The connotation of cross in the Old Testament and in the Hellenistic world of Paul's time was both stark and terrible. The Romans reserved this form of execution for traitors, public criminals, rebels and those guilty of sedition against the State.[17] In Israel, the significance of death by crucifixion was even more appalling since it connoted expulsion from the Covenant and its incalculable benefits and, as a result, the notion of perdition. 'Cursed be anyone who hangs on a tree', was the recognised teaching of the Old Testament (Dt 21:23; see Acts 5:30;10:39; IPet 2:24).

This meaning is validated by Paul explaining in *Galatians* the purpose of Jesus' crucifixion as a reaching after those hitherto considered beyond any hope of redemption, that is, the Gentiles (3:13-4). By his crucifixion Jesus was cursed with the accursed in order to redeem the accursed and include them in the blessings of Abraham's posterity. This is the soteriological function of the incarnation and the Cross.

What is of first importance, however, is not soteriology but theology, or rather the theology that is glimpsed *through* this soteriology, the new image of God that emerges from taking seriously the self-emptying of Christ for the world.[18] Cardinal Newman grasps well the wonder of the fact in this passage, 'The chief mystery of our holy faith is the humiliation of the Son of God to temptation and suffering...In truth, it is a more overwhelming mystery than that which is involved in the doctrine of the Trinity. I say, more overwhelming, not greater, for we cannot measure the more and the less in subjects utterly incomprehensible and divine; but with more in it to perplex and subdue our minds'.[19]

6. Coming to Terms with the Novelty: The Early Church

To summarise the drift of the argument to date: both the theology of Mark's gospel, in particular the deep theological riches of the *Eloi, Eloi, lama sabachtani,* as well as the theology of Paul as condensed in the *kenosis* of the Letter to the Philippians, show that the Son of God revealed his Father and completed his work in terms of the forsakenness of the cross and the *kenosis* of crucifixion. In this resides the wonder of the faith. What did the Church of the Fathers do to articulate this blinding mystery in the early centuries?

For the great heresiarchs of the fourth and fifth centuries, 'the overwhelming mystery of this self-emptying of the Son did not arise. In the case of the Arians, the Son did not enjoy equality of essence with the Father'. As for the Gnostics, the Word took on only an apparent body, while Nestorius had the notion of a human Christ and a divine Christ which makes any consideration of *kenosis* fall entirely on the human side. But for the Fathers who championed the orthodox faith the mystery was not only affirmed but even confronted with their reverent yet daring efforts to understand. Their great concern was to steer a middle course.

> On the one hand, God's changelessness must not be defended in such a manner that in the pre-mundane Logos

nothing real took place. On the other hand, this real event could not be allowed to degenerate into theopaschism.[20]

What would a middle course look like? What line did Athanasius follow against Arius after Nicaea, Cyril against Nestorius at the time of the Council of Ephesus, and Leo against Eutyches less than twenty years later? 'The divine design to let the Logos become man meant for the Word a genuine humiliation and lowering, the more so when the historic condition in which sinful humanity found itself was taken into consideration.'[21] Thus Leo speaks of the incarnation as 'inclinatio majestatis' and so as 'humilitas'. Cyril speaks of the Logos accepting 'an emptying out of fullness' and 'a lowering of what was exalted'. As for Athanasius, he describes the basic movement of Jesus' existence as descent. Citing the Philippians text he goes on:

> What could be clearer or more probative than these words? He did not pass from a more wretched state to a better one, but, being God, took the form of a slave and, by the event of assuming, was not lifted up but cast down.[22]

The post-Nicene Fathers were alive to the real possibility that their efforts might indeed damage the truth of the unchangeability of God and so of the abiding glory of Son of God, even in the days of his flesh. In doing so they would be in conflict with Paul's teaching in First and Second Corinthians where the crucified Christ is 'the power of God and the wisdom of God', and 'the Lord of glory' who shines into the hearts of believers 'with the light of the knowledge of the glory of God' (ICor I:24;2:8). They would also be at variance with the central emphasis in St John for whom the glory of Christ shines out on the cross because 'it is there that he goes to the (divine) extreme in his loving, and in the revelation on that love'.[23]

How, then, could one steer that true course between the Scylla of a divine unchangeableness, for which the incarnation is only an addition, and the Charybdis of a divine mutability of such a kind that from the time of the Incarnation the divine self-consciousness of the

Son is 'alienated' into a Nestorian-like human awareness? That is the question which the Philippians text sternly poses, that the Fathers grappled with, that the German and Anglican kenoticists of the nineteenth century struggled to clarify, not without serious exaggeration, but which leads inevitably to 'an altogether decisive turn-about in the way of seeing God'.[24] Perhaps one should now look for the real key to this breakthrough.

The key to the breakthrough is to be located in the mystery of the Blessed Trinity or, more precisely, in the Persons in their processions, relations and missions. The God of Jesus Christ is not a monad, but a communion of Persons. This God is not an 'I' but a 'We', the We of Father, Son and Holy Spirit. 'God does not exemplify loneliness', claims Henri de Lubac, 'but ec-stasy, a complete going-out-from self'. This means that 'the mystery of the Trinity has opened to us a totally new perspective: the ground of being is *Communio*'.[25] This communion is lived in the mutual ecstatic outgoing of each Person to the Others, in what the Fathers saw as the *perichoresis* of the Persons in one another. The Trinitarian *perichoresis* constitutes the very life and being of God and makes it triune. Here one finds the eternal exteriorisation of God, his tripersonal self-gift. It is this eternal exteriorisation of God that is the condition of possibility of the temporal exteriorisation of God in the Incarnation. The Trinity is therefore the key to the *kenosis* of the Eternal Son in his incarnation and death in which he reveals 'the glory of God the Father' (Phil 2:11).[26]

What is the upshot of all this for our new picture of God, for the seeking and for the discovering of his authentic Face (see Ps 26:8; Ps 104)? Von Balthasar seems to answer convincingly:

> If one takes seriously what has just been said, then the event of the Incarnation of the second divine Person does not leave the inter-relationship of these Persons unaffected. Human thought and human language break down in the presence of this mystery: namely, that the eternal relations of Father and Son are focused, during the 'time' of Christ's

earthly wanderings, and in a sense which must be taken with full seriousness, in the relations between the man Jesus and his heavenly Father, and that the Holy Spirit lives as their go-between who, in as much as he proceeds from the Son, must also be affected by the Son's humanity.[27]

'The Lame Slain Before the Foundations of the World' (Rev 13:8)

This raises inevitably the question of the immutability of God. More specifically, a way must be found between two exaggerated, and therefore false, understandings of the divine immutability. This is 'the way of the Lamb' (Rev 5:6-14), who has been 'slain before the foundation of the world' (Rev 13:8). This slaying cannot be understood in a Gnostic sense, as a heavenly sacrifice that is offered independently of the sacrifice of Golgotha. It must indicate rather the eternal aspect of the historic and bloody offering of the cross. As we have just seen, the condition of possibility of this 'slaying', this *kenosis*, is the 'selflessness' of the Persons. This exit-from-self of each of the divine Persons for the Others is already a *kenosis*. It is the eternal and therefore enduring *kenosis* of the love constituting the Blessed Trinity.

Of course this *kenosis* must be thought of analogically. This means that however great the similarity is between the *kenosis* of the Incarnation and Cross, and that of the processions of the Persons in the most holy Trinity, the dissimilarity is still greater.[28] In that way it should be possible to avoid the excesses of the kenoticists and, instead, address the root of the mystery of the Son's *kenosis* in the light of the divine generosity of the Persons in their relations of procession and mission. 'God, then, has no need to change when he makes a reality of the wonders of his charity, wonders which include the Incarnation and, more particularly, the Passion of Christ ... All the contingent "abasements" of God in the economy of salvation are forever included and outstripped in the eternal event of love.'[29]

7. The Aspirations and Problems of Today

The governing theological perspective of the Second Vatican Council, it seems, highlighted two dimensions of the mystery of faith. The first was the mystery of Christ,[30] while the second was the necessity of addressing the central issues and questions of the age, what the Gospels call 'the signs of the times', in order to continue the dialogue of salvation with the men and women of our times.[31] Every authentic theology x-rays the human condition. This is the undeniable lesson of the history of theology.[32]

The practical import of this principle is that, having painted, however inadequately, the Face of God according to what the riches of revelation mediate in scripture, the patristic tradition and in the best of contemporary theology, we must now show the striking relevance of such a christo-theology to both the aspirations and the problems of the men and women of our times.

Aspirations

Our era emphasises two concepts more than others. First, it emphasises freedom. The Council pointed out that 'many of our contemporaries seem to fear that a closer bond between human activity and religion will work against the independence of men, societies, or of the sciences'.[33] The fact of a Supreme Being whose laws govern human activity, whose Word demands 'the obedience of faith' (Rom 16:26), and whose providence decides the destiny of individuals and of nations, seems to restrict human initiative and the yearning for autonomy inordinately and unacceptably.

This emphasis is sometimes so strongly made that there results the denial, or at least the marginalisation, of the idea of God. If there be a God and He is everything, how can I be anything? And in the name of this freedom, such a mentality plans society and designs culture in such a way as to marginalise God. We well know how this inspires frequently a rejection of God and of religious faith, or at least a practical agnosticism leading people to live as if God did not exist.

The second aspiration is that of the aspiration to human solidarity or community. Many movements in our time, as well as many of the world's recent ideologies, emphasise this central aspiration. Our age seems to be moving towards unity on a world scale in spite of the many obvious contradictions. The signs of the times point in that direction. The technological revolution has made the globe one great village. The great trading and economic conglomerations of nations have tended to make the world into one enormous market.

The search for unity among the Churches is a sign of a more reconciled humanity. The beginning of the dialogues with the Great Religions, as well as with the men and women of other persuasions, underlines the same aspiration. One could say that a certain unitary consciousness now pervades the human family. This aspiration to community, however, often makes little or no room for the religious dimension. Sometimes, in fact, the achievements of science, technology and commerce are proffered as a replacement for the universal bonding value of religion and faith.

How relevant is the God revealed by Jesus Crucified and Forsaken to the search for freedom and community? Is he not the God of Communion, as we have just seen? And is he not the God of freedom since his whole Being consists in the event of Trinitarian love? He is a God who both emphasises freedom and brings communion. As Trinity, he is the transcendent source of variety, plurality and possibility, for the One God is a plurality of Persons. The very distinction between the divine Persons – a distinction that is manifest in Jesus' dialogue with his Father ('Abba') in Gethsemane, in his forsakenness by him on Golgotha, and in his resurrection from the tomb by the Father's glory (1 Pet 1:3; 1 Cor 15:15) – highlights the space opened up by this Trinitarian God for human freedom and its expression. To use an image, the 'nots' distinguishing the Persons (the Father is *not* the Son, the Son is *not* the Father, and the Holy Spirit is *not* the Son nor the Father) reveal a gap, as it were, through which the whole human family can enter into God, the Holy Trinity, as the famous Rublev icon masterfully depicts.[34]

The God whom Jesus reveals and communicates to the world, is a God whose very life is infinite unity in communion. The Persons of the Trinity are one, not only through the one divine nature that each One possesses in full, but also through the infinite mutual love through which they indwell each other, and which the classical Greek theology of the divine *perichòresis* underlines. Here vistas are opened up for a human community built on mutual love which surpasses our wildest imaginings: 'The Lord Jesus when praying to the Father that they may all be one ... even as we are one' (Jn 17:21-22), has opened up new horizons closed to human reason by implying that there is a certain parallel between the union existing among the divine Persons and the union of the sons of God in truth and love. It follows, then, that if man is the only creature on earth that God has wanted for its own sake, man can fully discover his true self only in a *sincere giving of himself*.[35]

Tragically, it is true that the mystery of the Holy Trinity has not been much adverted to for its astonishing relevance to the human aspiration to communion and solidarity. Both Karl Rahner and Hans Urs von Balthasar speak of a certain 'Islamisation' of Christianity. The practical effect of this loss of substance is quite serious: in fact, if the doctrine of the Trinity were dropped in the morning from the Church's profession of faith, the spiritual life of many believers would not be substantially affected! The triune God seems to be as far away from our life patterns as He is from our thought categories.

What makes Christianity unique is the God of Christianity. This God is the most perfect unity in trinity, and *vice versa*. The contrast between this revelation of God and the perception of God in Judaism, Plotinus and Islam stands out. Every otherness in these latter is a simple falling away from perfection. In Christianity, however, there *is* the fact of the *Other* at the heart of reality: the Son is other than the Father and the Holy Spirit is other than the Father and the Son. Here we find the transcendent Ground for the centrality of the neighbour in Christian revelation which teaches the way to the neighbour at the same time as it opens up the way to the Father.[36] The Other is always 'the brother for whom Christ died' (1Cor 8:11) entering forsakenness by the Father so that every neighbour's forsakenness could be accompanied and overcome. Here one finds the revealed antidote to every form of individualism.

Problems

As well as aspirations, however, there are also great problems confronting the human family, a couple of which we shall briefly mention. There is the phenomenon of atheism in its various guises, a phenomenon that was considered in some depth in the *Pastoral Constitution on the Church in the Modern World* (GS 19–21). Atheism of whatever kind either forgets or deliberately abandons God. But in the reality of Jesus Crucified and Forsaken we have the fact of a God abandoned by God for the sake of those who are without God. And in that great moment of Calvary, Jesus though always being the only begotten Son no longer *senses* the presence of the loving Father. Is not this Jesus Forsaken, the God for the atheists? He is so full of love for the Father of all that He can be fully with those who have no love at all for the Father. What is even more wondrous is that he can lose everything for love, except love!

Then there is the problem of the great divisions that mark the panorama of modern culture. There is the division between generations, divisions between the rich North and poor teeming South. There are the divisions within the Christian family itself, and now, in the wake of the Enlightenment, the division between faith and culture, perhaps the most startling phenomenon of the contemporary world. Once again Jesus Forsaken who stretches out his limbs on the wood of the Cross in order to gather together the scattered children of God (Jn 11:52) and to draw all unto himself is the God for divided and fragmented humanity. His ideal, indeed, the very 'purpose' of his forsakenness, consists in the overcoming of the many tragic divisions: 'May they all be one. Father, may they all be one *as* You and I are one' (Jn 17:21).

This 'as' is one of those 'as' expressions that make the Gospels so attractive,[37] since it suggests a community of human beings that not only mirrors the communion of the Three but actually participates in this communion and in that way embodies it on earth. This participation-embodiment is nothing less than the Church, which for the Fathers as well as for the Second Vatican Council is 'a people made one from the unity of the Father, Son and Holy Spirit' (LG 4). To be worthy of their calling (Eph 4:1), Christians are now invited to put on 'the mind of Christ' (Col 2:5). In so living they are attuned to the inner life of God. 'They become heirs to the New Covenant, singers of a new song, and a new people' (St Augustine), or, in the words of St Ignatius of Antioch written to the Christians of Ephesus: 'By your love you are united as the strings are united to the lyre. The result is a harmony which sings Jesus Christ.'[38]

Thirdly, there are the phenomena of science and technology. Technology has already produced a type of human being who can be well-described as *homo technicus vacuus*. The key characteristic of this technological civilisation is a turning outwards and away from the interior, from the inside of reality, as it were. It leads inexorably towards a culture devoid of human and spiritual content, and unresponsive to the Divine. Jesus Forsaken, who loves 'to the end' (Jn 13:1) and in that way locates the divine where it seems most absent, turns the pain of his crucifixion and abandonment into a way of 'putting love where there is no love' (St John of the Cross). In that way He both humanises and divinises. He is the perfect antidote to the spiritual and human emptiness threatening contemporary culture. He challenges believers to give a soul to our society and thus a context necessary for the proper placing and use of science and technology.

8. Jesus Crucified and Forsaken: The Pedagogue for the Third Millennium

Jesus crucified, then, reveals the face of God as Trinitarian communion in love, and brings this same communion into humankind. However, he also teaches us the art of living both communion and suffering in all its forms. And while we have already seen this Art in operation as it were as we considered the mission of Jesus to bring about the Kingdom of God, it is both necessary and practical to see the operation of the same dynamic at the higher level of the Cross where Jesus finishes and consummates his mission received from the Father (Jn 19:30).

First of all, he enables us to be architects of unity wherever we live. Jesus does not cease to love on the wood of the Cross. On the contrary, he loves to the point of giving his life for those who had no love for him and who did not know his Father. Since in his crucifixion and abandonment he still continues to love, reaching those furthest away from his Father, and bringing them into communion with this Father, he points the way for us to follow. Like him, we must know how to build this communion. But such a communion is impossible without Christians 'walking in love *as* Christ loved us and gave himself up for us' (Eph 5:2 RSV), enduring suffering even to the extreme of Godforsakenness.

It is in this context that we can perhaps best understand that commandment which Jesus describes as 'his' and 'new' (Jn 13:34-35; 15:12), 'Love one another *as* I have loved you'. Having achieved through his *kenosis* of Incarnation and death an extrapolation on earth of the life of the Blessed Trinity, he gives to us the commandment to live by the law of love at the heart of the Blessed Trinity. Like an emigrant going to a foreign country and there having to adapt to new customs, culture and language, while bringing the culture and language of his own homeland, so too the Son of the Father adapts perfectly to our human condition experiencing even its abandonment, but brings with him as the culture of the new creation he is founding the basic law of heaven, namely, mutual love among equal persons. By keeping this commandment we will bring about the unity for which he prayed (Jn 17:21ff), suffered, rose, and sent the Holy Spirit (Acts 2:42). The fruits of this unity will be a fresh credibility for the Gospel in society (see Jn 17:21-23).

Secondly, he teaches us how to live every suffering and turn it into a springboard towards communion. In fact, he enables us to see every suffering as a reflection of his own. In each suffering, whether it is personal or social, we are invited to perceive a face, the Face of Jesus Forsaken and Crucified, since he has entered into each and every suffering, and has paid the price for the bringing of divine love where it was previously absent. It remains for us to live in tune with what He has already done and so to complete in our own bodies what is lacking in Christ's sufferings for the sake of his body, which is the Church (Col 1:24).[39] Of course the achievement of such *attunement* is the task of the Christian life (see Phil 3: 10; ICor 1:17-25).

It has always been a cornerstone of Christianity that Jesus crucified and forsaken is the way to live communion with God. Thus St Bonaventure in the thirteenth century wrote: '*Nemo ad Deum entrat recte nisi per crucifixum*'. The encounter of God and humankind requires a reciprocal *kenosis*, that of God's Son becoming flesh and a sacrifice for us and our reciprocal responding in order to be that nothing (*nada*) that is the pre-condition for union with God. This fact is brought out frequently in the specific experiences of the founders of the religious Orders, such as, to mention one poignant example, St Paul of the Cross and the Passionists.[40]

Jesus crucified and forsaken, however, is also the way for us to reach union with each neighbour, particularly in their difference and distance from us, as well as in the difficulties they sometimes pose for us. Why is this the case? Jesus Crucified loved even those who were so different and difficult for him that they actually killed him. 'Christ also suffered for you, leaving you an example that you should follow in his steps ... When he was reviled he did not revile in return; when he suffered he did not threaten' (IPet 2:21, 23 RSV). He is what we might call the authentic style of neighbourly love. If up until now the neighbour was often seen as an obstacle for us on the holy journey to God (Ps 84:5) and sometimes even as a temptation, Jesus crucified teaches us the centrality of the neighbour and the way to love him. He is the key to what might be called a 'technique of unity' which is alluded to in the pages of the New Testament, and which calls us to serve Jesus present in each brother and sister, and to make ourselves one with him or her in everything but sin. Is not this the practical message shouted out in the Cross of the Word made flesh, foolishness indeed in the eyes of the worldly-wise and a stumbling-block to those who do not believe, but to those who do believe, the power and the wisdom of God (ICor 1:23-5)?

There is still more. If this is the inner logic of love as shown in the Incarnation and as culminating in the forsakenness of Calvary, if this is the very life of the Blessed Trinity, it is *also* the imperative for Christians to follow in order to walk worthy of their calling (see Eph 4:1f). It is the technique that the Apostle of the Gentiles employs. He made himself a Jew to the Jews, a Gentile to the Gentiles 'so as to save some by all means' (see ICor 9:19-23). Jesus crucified and forsaken is the model for whoever would make himself one with every brother or sister as Jesus crucified did. The fact is that one cannot enter the spirit of another person without being poor in spirit. And the eternal model of such poverty of spirit is the one who, not only taught the corresponding beatitude (Mt 5:3), but who moved by love for the lost (Mt 9:12-3), lost everything for love except love!

Notes

1. Hans Urs von Balthasar, *Origen. Spirit and Fire. A Thematic Anthology of His Writings,* Washington D.C., 1984, 'The Mystery of God', 317–319.
2. Roch A. Kereszty, *Jesus Christ. Fundamentals of Christology,* New York 1991, 97: 'Jesus reprimands Peter because Peter wanted to prevent Jesus from suffering in Jerusalem.'
3. Ibid; see G. O'Collins S.J., *Christology. A Biblical, Historical, and Systematic Study of Jesus,* Oxford 1995, 62–66.
4. Robert J. Karris, O.F.M., *The Gospel according to Luke,* in *The New Jerome Biblical Commentary,* London 1993, 720.
5. Ibid.
6. Voltaire, *Notebooks,* ed. Theodore Besterman, Toronto 1952, I, 231.
7. Bernard Lonergan, *Method in Theology,* London 1971, 235–237.
8. Of course it is true that 'if God reveals himself to humankind, if God speaks to humankind a divine Word, all that must happen in a human word' (K. Hemmerle, *Thesen zu einer trinitarischen Ontologie,* Einsiedeln, 1976; 1992, 14 – translation my own). It is an entirely different matter, however, to resist the very accomplishment of that revelation as it actually happens. Such a resistance (see Acts 7:51-53) both belittles the divine design *and* the very capacity of the human to carry and express the divine self-communication!
9. In that way Mark explicitly identifies Jesus as the personification and fulfilment of the Suffering Servant prophecies in Second Isaiah: see E. Voegelin, *Order and History,* volume I, *Israel and Revelation,* edited with an Introduction by Maurice P. Hogan, Columbia and London 2001.
10. Gerard Rossé, *Il grido di Gesù in croce,* Roma 1984, 23–36
11. Mark and Matthew both translate the Aramaic/Hebrew with the Greek *enkataleipo* which means, 'Why do you leave me in this sorrowful situation?' It must follow from the philogical point of view that Jesus in that moment felt the Father abandoning him in

the sense that the Father did not take any steps to intervene in order to take him out of the plight of abandonment.

12. Ibid., 107–112.

13. 'Select Questions on Christology', in *International Theological Commission*, 1979, S. IV, 8.

14. See *Der Herr*, Herder 1985, 475.

15. See Brendan Byrne, S.J., The Letter to the Philippians, in *The New Jerome Biblical Commentary*, London 1993, 794 for a commentary on the text.

16. H.U. von Balthasar, *Mysterium Paschale*, Edinburgh 1990, 23–24.

17. Thus Cicero, *In Verrem*, V, 66, 170; see M. Hengel, *Crucifixion in the Ancient World and the Folly of the Message of the Cross*, Philadelphia 1977; and *The Atonement: a Study of the Origins of the Doctrine of the New Testament*, London 1981.

18. H.U. von Balthasar, op. cit., 24.

19. J.H. Newman, *Parochial and Plain Sermons*, III, London 1868, 156.

20. H.U. von Balthasar, op. cit., 251.

21. Ibid., 25

22. Athanasius, *Adversus Arianos* I, 40-41: PG 26, 93; for the texts of Leo and Cyril see von Balthasar, ibid., 21f.

23. H.U. von Balthasar, op. cit., 29.

24. Ibid., 28

25. H. de Lubac, *La Foi chrétienne*, Paris,1970, 14

26. Von Balthasar, op. cit., 30.

27. Ibid.

28. DS 806.

29. H.U. von Balthasar, op. cit., ix.

30. See, for example, *Lumen gentium*, 1; *Dei Verbum*, 1; very powerfully *Optatam totius*, 14.

31. See *Nostra aetate*, 1–2, and especially *Gaudium et spes*, 4, 8, 9; 22: 'The truth is that only in the mystery of the incarnate Word does the mystery of man take on light.'

32. That is why every epoch-making theology is the fruit of the encounter between revelation and the Great Tradition, on the one

hand, and the cultural ideal of the society in which the Gospel of Christ is being sown, on the other.

33. *Gaudium et spes, 36.*
34. Thomas Norris, 'The Intellectual Formation of the Priest', in B. McGregor O.P. and T. Norris, *The Formation Journey of the Priest*, (Dublin, 1994), 162–174.
35. GS 24; italics mine.
36. K. Hemmerle, *Glauben, wie geht das?* Freiburg Basel Wien 1978, 16–20.
37. See C. Lubich, *Servants of All*, London 1979, 33.
38. *Letter to the Ephesians*, 4.
39. See C. Lubich, *l'Unità e Gesù Abbandonato* , Roma 1984, 49–100.
40. S. Breton *La Mystique de la Passion. S. Paul de la Croix*, Paris 1962.

Chapter VII

Articulating the Experience

> There is no chronicling in the New Covenant. Everything is
> summed up in a single, final Word from God (Heb 1:2). All
> the same, this Word unfolds dramatically in Jesus'
> development, work, suffering and resurrection. It is the acme
> and the timeless conclusion of dealings between God and
> man.[1]

Christianity is eminently an historical religion. It is founded and
grounded in great historical events, and in a sequence of persons who
are at once its actors and its protagonists. However, it is no museum
religion, for its power is in the present and its final act is the very
omega and goal of human history.[2] The Gospels, as we have seen
when considering the unfolding drama of the incarnate Son, do
provide access to the historical Jesus. They do so, however, in a fashion
that is peculiar to themselves as inspired documents where the Word
of God lives and expresses itself in the words of human authors. The
corollary of that interpenetration is that the evangelists proclaim their
message, not in spite of history, but in and through history. It is the
theologian's task to find history in the *kerygma* and to find the same
kerygma in that history.[3]

One may read one of the earliest formulations of 'the word of
faith' (Rom 10:8) in Paul's *First Letter to the Corinthians*. The text reads
as follows:

> For what I received I passed on to you as of first importance:
> that Christ died for our sins according to the Scriptures,
> that he was buried,

> that he was raised on the third day according to the Scriptures, and that he appeared to Peter, and then to the Twelve. (15:3-5)

The text pre-dates Paul. It was in fact the teaching of the early Christian community built upon the foundation of the apostles and the prophets (Eph 2:20). As such the teaching had great authority. Paul had 'received' it in order to 'deliver' it in turn to the Corinthians as the bedrock of their faith, 'the Gospel that saves' (15:1-2). Like an athlete running in a relay race, Paul saw himself as receiving the most sacred trust imaginable in order to hand it on to others. To lose or to change that Gospel is to lose the chance of salvation. Paul is responsible for the *kerygma*, just as the Corinthians are responsible for their response to 'the word preached to them' (1Cor 15:2).

The *kerygma* contains four components. They include the death of Christ, his burial, his resurrection and the appearances. The four facts or 'words' constituting the *kerygma* can be divided into two sets of two. The first set describes the descent of the eternal Son, while the second set describes the ascent of the Son. The truth of that descent-ascent literally puts flesh and blood on the Gospel and the Word of Faith of the early Church.

'Kephas' and the 'Twelve' (see Mk 3:13) are the recipients of these appearances. This component of the *kerygma* has great importance. The primitive Christian community listed the recipients of the appearances in its very own 'creed', and these eyewitnesses are the Apostles. The point is that the faith of Christians is dependent upon the witness of the Apostles who saw the risen Christ. The 'word of the Apostles' enjoys a special role, since 'faith comes by hearing' (Rom 10:17). Thus the responsibility of the Apostles for the transmission of the Gospel is underlined, as well as the source of their competence to do so.

What is also striking is the fact that the phrase 'according to the Scriptures' occurs twice. What is its significance? The scriptures of the first covenant contain the *kerygma* in some fashion. The oft-quoted words of St Augustine come to mind, 'The New Testament is hidden in the Old and the Old is made manifest in the New'.[4] The early apostolic Church lived with the consciousness of Israel being 'recapitulated' in Christ, not merely fulfilled. This was the core contention of our fourth chapter.

This pre-Pauline *kerygma* suggests, even leads towards, the Johannine *kerygma* that 'God is love' (IJn 4:8, 16). The key verses in 8–10 deserve to be cited in full:

> God is love.
> God's love for us was revealed
> when God sent into the world his only Son
> so that we could have life through him;
> this is the love I mean:
> not our love for God,
> but God's love for us when he sent his Son
> to be the sacrifice that takes our sins away.

A masterpiece of Johannine brevity, the text carries a content of great richness. The very first phrase gives the sublime description of God. Its brevity, however, does not hint at any banality. The brevity in fact makes it the fountainhead of insight. The three words are the distilled essence of what has been going forward throughout the whole of history, as the very next component vividly demonstrates. The author is reflecting back over the events of our redemption in the revelation of the Father through the Son in the Holy Spirit. This very revelation occurs so that we could have life in that Son, a fact highlighted in the double use of the phrase, 'for us'.

The next component stresses the utter divine originality and goodness of such a gift. To that end it contrasts the love of the Father and the Son with 'our love'. It does so with an arresting vigour. The great Johannine theme, so beloved of St Augustine, comes to mind, 'God loved us first' (4:19). Perhaps von Balthasar gets close to the dramatic message of the Apostle:

In this love of God which humans meet in Christ, they experience not only what true love is but also at the same time, and uncontradictably, that they, sinners and egoists that they are, have no true love. They experience both aspects in one: the creature's limited love, and its guilty frigidity ... It is face to face with Christ crucified that the abysmal egoism of what we are accustomed to call love becomes clear: when the question is put to us in ultimate seriousness, we say no where Christ in his love said yes, and in our lack of love we say yes without a qualm to his bearing our sins: all is right for us, if he is willing to do it![5]

By a clever technique of contrast:

John sets the Father's love and 'our love for God' in opposition in order to highlight the selfless and boundless freedom of the divine initiative: nothing in us attracted or motivated the divine love to act in such an unheard of and astounding fashion for us. Rather, there is in God something greater than God, so to speak, something not measurable by any human criterion whatsoever ... It is this 'more' that is the motor force in the whole plan of God.[6]

Combining the two texts, that of Paul and that of John, we arrive at:

the primitive Christian core of dogma: God is love; the immanent Trinity is revealed in the economic and precisely as God's 'orthopraxis' in the giving of the Son to divine abandonment and hell, which is the greatest possible conception of God; he is (with Hegel) identity of identity (God is all; he is eternal life) and of non-identity (God is dead, in so far as he identified himself with godlessness). He is so full of life (so very much love) that he can afford to be dead.[7]

The incomparable originality of this revelation of God needs to be stressed. It means that, in Jesus, God made himself present in the world not only by creation and conservation of his creation, but substantially and personally. He is not only present in the world but he interprets himself (Jn 1:18) to us and for us *in the very language of the world's sorrow and suffering*. He employs that which is his very opposite – pain and failure, yes even death and lostness – to say who he is! Unlike all other systems of religion, he descends into that which is his very opposite and contradicts his very being. All other religions consist, understandably, in the movement out of this world in the search for the blessed life. He condescends to live in this world in order in due course to die for it. Divine revelation shows that 'Christian love is God's final word about himself and about the world ... The world wants to live and rise again without dying; but Christ's love wishes to die, in order that through death, it may rise again beyond death in God's form'.[8] An American author puts it in these terms, 'The mystery of the incarnation and the Eucharist would destroy us if we took them, I don't say seriously but to the fullness of their significance'.[9]

This brings before us a staggering 'theology' of God, precisely as that knowledge of the love of Christ which surpasses all knowing. (Eph 3:19) This is a truly 'theological theology',[10] God speaking himself to us, and not God as spoken by us. God 'says himself' to us rather than 'we say' God to God! The Father has, as it were, painted his self-portrait for us in giving us his Son. That same Son, however, becomes the sacrifice that bears away the sins of the world. God can no longer be thought of as only the first principle or cause. Neither can he be thought of as detached from his creation and his creatures. He is not a distant horizon nor an absent Lord nor a superior principle reminiscent of Aristotle's 'Unmoved Mover'. Rather, as Charles Pèguy noticed, he has made himself the prisoner of his hope that all will be saved (Jn 17:1; 1 Tim 2:4). He is therefore the passionate God whose Son's passionately lived life inevitably leads to the most dramatic passion. In fact, he gives his life as a ransom for man (Mk 10:45). 'No religion or world view has dared to think and proclaim something of this kind about God, human beings, and the world; therefore

Christianity remains without analogy, and it rests not on an "idea" but on a fact – Jesus Christ – which, in the unity of claim, cross and resurrection, remains an unsplittable atom'.[11]

The Key Relationship: Differentiating and Articulating the Experience

The content of divine revelation overwhelms. 'The divine Ocean forced into the tiny wellspring of a human Heart! The mighty oak-tree of divinity planted in the small, fragile pot of an earthly Heart! God, sublime on the throne of his majesty, and the Servant – toiling with sweat and kneeling with the dust of adoration – no longer to be distinguished from one another! ... All the treasures of God's wisdom and knowledge stored in the narrow chamber of human poverty! ... The rock of a divine certainty floating on the tides of an earthly hope!'[12] The rhetoric in the passage attempts to wake us up to wonder that spring of all philosophy, science and discovery. It wants us to realise at least a little the unfathomable riches of Christ' (Eph 3:8), for, as Cardinal Newman saw, 'realisation is the very life of religion'.[13]

Still, that articulation is difficult. It may, however, be viewed from the perspective of a unique relationship that shines through the whole of the New Testament. The relationship in question is that of Jesus to God, to the one he called 'Abba'. This relationship is dealt with progressively throughout the whole of the New Testament. It is in fact among its core concerns. Its treatment, in fact, largely differentiates the Synoptic gospels, the Pauline writings, and the Johannine corpus. Joachim Jeremias shows that Jesus in the Gospels always addresses God as 'Abba' with the one exception of his cry of forsakenness on the Cross (Mk 15:34; Mt 27:46). When one remembers that devout Jews had such a respect for the divine Name that they did not use it outside of the Liturgy, one begins to realise the unique nature of Jesus' rapport with the God of the patriarchs and the prophets.

Since this relationship of Jesus to God is a dominant concern of the whole New Testament, one ought to consider the components of the relationship. It is possible to do this by careful consideration of the poles of that relationship, namely, 'God' and 'Jesus'. This consideration will show that there is a progressively nuanced refinement in the use of the terms determining the relationship, and that this very refining serves to clarify the very nature of the relationship involved.

Following the research of Jeremias,[14] Bernard Lonergan outlines the refinement in the use of the term 'God' as between the synoptics, Paul and John.[15] Synoptic usage advances to 'God the Father' in Paul and then to either 'the Father' (seventy-five times in John) or 'my Father' (twenty-eight times in John). There is a remarkable parallel refinement in the use of 'Jesus' across the same threefold. In the synoptics, Jesus is generally called by an Old Testament title such as 'Son of Man', 'Son of God', 'Messiah' or something similar. However, in Paul he is called 'Son of the Father' or 'his Son', while in John he is called 'the Son' which occurs fourteen times in John's Gospel, while only once in Mark and Luke and twice in Matthew (11:27).

In order to underline the significance of this refinement across the three great sectors of the New Testament, it is appropriate to lay it out in table form.

	Synoptics	Paul	John
(A)	'God'	'God the Father'	'Father' ('the', 'my')
(B)	'Son of Man' or 'Son of God'	'Son of the Father' or 'His Son'	'the Son'

When one reflects on the refinement of the terms 'God' and 'Son of Man/God', one will become aware at once of a very precise refinement in the grasp of the relationship between Jesus and God. In Paul, God is 'defined' relationally as 'God the Father', while Jesus is also defined relationally as 'Son of the Father' or 'His Son'. One notices a principle of correlation clearly emerging. This correlation-principle is even clearer in John. There 'God' is 'the Father' or 'my Father', while Jesus is 'the Son'. In the Johannine corpus, 'God' and 'Jesus' are related as Father and Son, better, as '(the/my) Father' who is God, and 'the Son' who is the same God. 'I and the Father are one' (Jn 10:30) brings out the kind of reality confronting the disciples and the Jewish people. A similar refinement can be observed in the use of the term 'Spirit' across the same threefold.

Our realisation of the mystery of God as a Trinity of Persons has been deepened. The God of Jesus Christ *is* the event of the Father, the Son and the Holy Spirit. God is the Father, and this same God is the Son, and this same God is also the Spirit. One has to make room in God for a 'Second' who is the one, eternal God, and one has to make room in God for a 'Third' who is the same eternal God. The words of the great *theologus* of the Greek Fathers come to mind, 'As soon as I start to ponder Unity, I am overwhelmed by the splendour of the Trinity. And as soon as I start to ponder the Trinity, I am completely taken by Unity'.[16] Our God, in other words, is ordinarily too small. Not only, but he runs the perpetual hazard of continuous reduction to the dimensions of the God of the philosophers. That is why Karl Rahner could write in the 1960s that if the dogma of the Blessed Trinity were to be dropped from the Church's confession of faith, such a drastic step would have little or no bearing upon the prayer life of Christians![17] In the meantime, however, there has been a great recovery of the Trinity to the point where an Italian theologian could recently write that 'Trinitarian theology is the grammar of the whole of theology'.[18]

Now what is extraordinary about this is that it was manifested through the mystery of the Cross of Jesus and the godforsakenness that he endured thereon. For it is there that we glimpse the Father's love for us when he gave away his Son for us (1Jn 4:10; Rom 8:32). Here one is not face-to-face with a Trinity who floats above history and humanity, as it were, but a Trinity who is the very heartbeat of history and is perceived in the rhythm of creation, redemption and the life of the world to come. The crucified, but now glorified, Christ as 'one of the Trinity' has in fact 'expresses humanly the divine ways of the Trinity'.[19]

There is a further implication of this great event of the death and the resurrection that deserves attention. The event achieves a mysterious yet intelligible breakthrough in the image of God. This breakthrough moves both upwards and downwards. The Johannine 'God is love' does not primarily mean that God loves his creation and has re-created it in the Blood and resurrection of his beloved Son and in the sending of the Holy Spirit. Rather, it means that God is *in himself* the very Event of Love, and that being such he is Trinity! He does not *need* Israel or creation or to offer eternal eschatological salvation to humankind in order to be love. 'Rather, God is Love in himself, namely absolute, that is, triune love, which does not need man in order to possess an object of love'.[20]

To suggest, then, that God needs creation or humanity to be love would immediately lead to a situation where the creature would have power over the Creator. This option has in fact been followed out in the West. The name of Hegel comes to mind at once. God became himself only in the encounter with his creation, and became Trinity in the clash with the mystery of evil on the Cross. The Cross does not reveal the Trinity: the Cross makes the Trinity!

The event of Christ achieves, then, an extraordinary enlargement in our perception of God upwards. This enlargement moves downwards also. So much is given to us to the end that an appalling destiny can be avoided, the destiny of a lost eternity. For 'God loved the world so much that he gave his only Son, that whoever believes in him may not die, but may have eternal life' (Jn 3:16). Here one sees the opposite abyss to that of the Trinity, namely, that of eternal death.[21] To be outside of God and his Son and their Holy Spirit is to be outside of the life that is true, good and beautiful.

A Network of Relationships

The New Testament, then, provides the experiences of the event of Christ on the part of the first Christian communities. As we have seen, this became the *realisation-experience* of who God is as Trinity, and who God is for us as our eternal future. We saw how difficult and demanding the articulation of those experiences was for the inspired authors of the New Testament. And we saw how in John that articulation reached its culmination and summit. Just as a lofty peak in a circle of mountains enables the climber to reach a certain view and perspective of the whole range, so too does the theology of John provide the highest viewpoint for viewing the other New Testament authors. His articulation of 'the life which was with the Father' but which has now appeared (1Jn 1:2) becomes a source of endless wonder and stimulating insight. John concentrates the mind on the divinely new (13:34; 15:12), and engages the imagination with the vision of a life exceeding our wildest imaginings – the life of God as the very life and future of humankind (Jn 1:4). His is an overturning of habitual ways of thinking and, even more importantly, of living. We will look at three relationships which he spells out in the Gospel, and then study three dimensions in the dynamism of the third relationship. This will open up an amazing set of relationships that both define our new existence (ICor 5:21; Gal 6:15) and invite us to live the new existence with joy and vigour.

I. The Father and Jesus

The first fundamental theme of the Gospel is the relationship obtaining between Jesus and the Father. The Gospel begins with the declaration that the Son's identity consists in being towards the heart of the Father (1:18). This is because the Son is with God and is God (1:1). Jesus desires only one thing, to please his Father (5:30 and 8:29). His food in fact is to do the will of the one who sent him (4:34). Jesus relates all he does and says to the Father in as much as its authority depends upon his being one with the Father and in being sent by him, 'The Father who has sent me has himself testified concerning me'

(5:37). What Jesus teaches is from the Father, 'I can speak just what the Father has taught me' (8:28). 'Jesus is never "Jesus on his own", but is "Jesus and the Father". He has his identity only in as much as the Father is in him.'[22]

The relationship of Jesus and the Father is the key to his identity, as well as to his deeds and words and very presence. It is captured in chapter ten when Jesus utters the mysterious words, 'I and the Father are one thing [hen]' (10:30). Each is an infinite 'You' for the Other.[23] This stands out with particular prominence in the discourse on the Good Shepherd in chapter ten. There Jesus names himself as the Good Shepherd. In doing so he is taking on the function of Yahweh who alone may rightly say, 'I am the shepherd of my people'. How can Jesus act and claim in this fashion? The reason is that on the basis of the most intimate relationship of Jesus with the Father, Jesus is the same reality as the Father and the Father has given him all that the Father is.

John shows the enormity of what Jesus claims by means of the reaction of Jesus' contemporaries. They see in Jesus' claims a blasphemy and pick up stones in order to stone him (10:31-8). The charge of blasphemy is laden indeed with an explosive association but here it points unmistakably to the claim and impact of Jesus' person and ministry. Those who hear and see the 'works' of Jesus are shocked by his claim. This shock in fact runs through the chapters of the Gospel, arriving in chapter fourteen at the summary of the claim in Jesus' saying, 'He who has seen me has seen the Father' (14:9). In Jesus there is not only the Son of the Father, but also the Son who reveals the Father to men and women.

II. Jesus and we are one Thing

The insistence on the relationship of Jesus and the Father has a very precise purpose. It is intended to lead to a second relationship, that of Jesus with us. Jesus wishes to live in us and to bring us everything he has brought from the Father in heaven. There is a single verse in chapter six where this relationship is strikingly stated:

> I live because of the Father,
> (and) the living Father sent me,
> so the one who feeds on me
> will live because of me. (6:57)

Line one repeats the first relationship of the Father and Jesus. This relationship is grounded in the eternal origin of the Son from 'the Father'. Here we are in the realm of the Trinity. Now this Father sends the Son into the world. This is the incarnation. The incarnation, however, becomes sacrament when Jesus makes himself into Eucharist 'for the life of the world' (6:50). The effect of the Eucharist is that the eternal life of the Father given to the Son in the 'heart' of the blessed Trinity arrives in human hearts. The result will be that human hearts will arrive in the bosom of the Father, being placed there *by* the Eucharistic Heart and *beside* the Eucharistic Heart. In that way, the eternal Son makes human creatures to be sons and daughters of his infinite Father in and with himself. The words of St Augustine jump to mind, 'Give me someone who loves and he will understand … But if I speak to someone cold and without ardour, he will not know what I say'.[24]

A classical 'short formula' in 14:20 is able to 'concentrate' the mutual indwelling of the Father and the Son, and of the Son and ourselves. It reads as follows, 'On that day you will realise that I am in my Father, and you are in me, and I am in you'. Jesus has extended as it were to human creatures his own relationship with the Father. Creatures of flesh and blood, creatures here today and gone to-morrow, blooming only to perish like the flowers of the fields if left to themselves, are lifted into the eternal and life-giving relationship with the Father of life and love. There are, in fact, many other passages in John where the mission of Jesus in relation to us is stated as precisely this 'glorious relocation' of lost humankind. By means of the Word of Jesus, the Eucharist of Jesus, or the love and the gift of Jesus we are in Jesus, and he is in us. Being grafted in that fashion on to the divine Vine, Jesus, we too will be living branches and we will bear much fruit (15:5-8). Christians are 'internally connected, as branches from a tree, not as parts of a heap. They are members of the Body of Christ. That divine and adorable form, which the Apostles saw and handled, after ascending into heaven became a principle of life, a secret origin of existence to all who believe, through the gracious ministration of the Holy Ghost'.[25]

III. Believers are a New We

The third substantial relationship one notices in St John is that of the rapport of believers *with one another*. John spells this out in an incomparable manner. Christians are one because they participate in the communion of Jesus and the Father. There is a new communion in the history of humankind and of the world. 'That all of them may be one (*hen*), just as (*kathos*)[26] you are in me and I am in you. May they also be in us so that the world may believe that you have sent me' (17:21). Christians are not like solitary satellites orbiting around Jesus. Rather, *the very relationship of Jesus with the Father now becomes their relationship*. For their part, they embody and express and realise this relationship in space and time with enormous implications for the unfolding of human history. What vistas are opened up here! They are the very vistas that the Second Vatican Council held up for the People of God from out of the heart of divine revelation.[27] If the world is to believe, if we as believers are to be credible, that 'horizontal' relationship must shine. It, and it alone, is the key to our life and our witness before the men and the women of our times, indeed of all times!

This life of the Trinity, as brought down to earth by the Son made flesh by the overshadowing of the Holy Spirit, is not for the few. It is for all. Jesus prays for this precise purpose on the evening before he will climb the Cross to die for it. However, if the world is to believe in such a life on earth as it is in heaven, it can only be by the witness of the disciples who *live among themselves* the relationship that obtains between Jesus and the disciples. What is the case in virtue of the incarnation and the paschal mystery must be the case between the disciples. The hallmark, then, of the life of the disciples, as revealed and communicated and articulated in the Fourth Gospel, consists in reciprocity, the reciprocity of the mutual indwelling of each one in the others. The words of Klaus Hemmerle say it splendidly.

> Our being one in reciprocity is the decisive point where the Trinity becomes visible for the world ... Only if we are ready to live the Trinity among ourselves will the Trinity be manifested again. In this sense the connection of the three levels of unity of the Gospel of John is an essential connection: the unity of Jesus with the Father becomes the unity between Jesus and us, and in this we become one thing in reciprocity. These levels constitute the supporting structure of the Gospel of John.[28]

What is so striking here is what one might call the principle of Trinitarian reciprocity. Christians are not called to mutual relationship that is based only upon a certain commonality of faith: since all believe in the same Lord Jesus, they are united through this common profession of faith. Nor is their relationship to one another merely the result of external association through membership of the Church. Their relationship and virtue must go deeper than those of the scribes and the Pharisees. Rather it is due to the fact of Baptism and initiation (Eph 4:5). Perhaps Paul says it vividly, 'You have clothed yourself in Christ, and there are no more distinctions between Jew and Greek, slave and free, male and female, but all of you are one in Christ' (Gal 3:28), and again, 'When people are in Christ they are a new creation' (2Cor 5:17; Gal 6:15).

Where Christ is, however, there is the Father and, of course, the Holy Spirit. And where Christ is, there are also his members – the one Christ who is both Head and Members. In other words, Christ connects us upwards as it were, since it is in him that we have access to the Father in the power of the Holy Spirit (Eph 2:10). But he also connects us horizontally in his Body, the Church, having re-located us in the heavenly places, as the Letter to the Ephesians memorably puts it (Eph 2:6). However, St John articulates for us, *in a particularly explicit manner*, the sets of relationships that actually constitute that 'total Christ' (St Augustine). And he does this in order that we might be able to live the life that he has come to give us in abundance (Jn 10:10; Eph 4:1). His articulation of the originating experience, that results from the inbreaking of absolute love into the world, combines insight and life. His purpose, in other words, is both explanatory and practical. It is full of vision and it shows how to put that vision into practice. We learn not primarily in order to know more but to live better the one life that we have. That life, in fact, can be lived according to a revealed rhythm. The remainder of this chapter will attempt to draw out this rhythm.

John now focuses on the dynamic of that third horizontal relationship. He identifies in fact three aspects of the dynamic. They can be named by means of three key words or phrases. The first is a 'reciprocal one-being-in-the-other' of the divine Persons. John speaks constantly of this: you in me, I in you; I in the Father, the Father in me; ye in me, I in ye; the one in the other, the other in each one. In order to express this reciprocal indwelling – for that is what it is – the Fathers of the Church invented the expression *perichoresis*. The word originally indicates a dance: the one dances around the other, the other dances around him so that all move in and with each other in harmony. In fact, this is how that love flows and moves which Jesus brings to us out of the bosom of the Trinity. The other person is the axis of my life, I am the axis of his life. God is the axis of my life, I am the axis of his life, for he wanted it to be so. This is a 'dance' from which there is no dispensing. For as long as we fail to live the 'dance of this love' by living mutually in and for each other in the Church, we will not show the life that Jesus brought down to earth 'for the life of the world' (Jn 6:51).

A second key phrase consists in 'the communion of goods'. Jesus states it as follows, 'All I have is yours, and all you have is mine' (17:10). It is possible to be friendly and courteous with each other. But do not the pagans do as much (Mt 5:47)? Christians are called to go much further! If God the Father of our Lord Jesus Christ has given all he has for us, if he has not spared even his own beloved Son but given him up for us all (Rom 8:32), we can be sure that we are called to give all and receive all. If our lives are going to be a reflection of the life of God which is the life of the Trinity, where the one divine nature is 'owned' by each of the three Persons, the same rhythm of life must characterise our life together. Being 'one person' means something concrete, not something spiritual only. And if we are not willing to share our material goods, the question has to arise as to how much we cherish the spiritual or realise its proper sense and purpose. How can we have real communion in what is higher if we are unwilling to be in communion in what is lower? 'Our life and my life, our goods and my goods are not opposites that mutually exclude one another, but are realities that contain each other with the one making an imprint on the other.'[29]

The third keyword that distinguishes the special 'we relationship' of believers is 'glory' or 'to glorify'. Out of the reciprocity of the concretely lived mutual love of Christians shines glory which is the splendour or beauty of such love. The eternal perichoretic love of the Persons brought down to earth by 'One of the Trinity' and given to believers as the very form of their real life which is hidden with Christ in God (Col 3:3), shines forth as glory-beauty. In living by reciprocal love, and in putting that reciprocity into concrete expression by a communion of both material and spiritual goods, believers show forth the style and the rhythm of the life of God the Holy Trinity. What appears then is the beauty of such a lifestyle, a beauty that is both human and divine, just as Jesus was the fullness of both divinity and humanity.

Where am I? You? S/He? We?

The category of place is of little importance in Aristotle's metaphysics. It contributes little to our understanding of reality. However, this is not the case with the revelation symbolised in the inspired literature of the New Testament. If in Aristotle, place is one of the lesser accidents, in the revealed religion of Christianity, place has special importance. The eternal Son who became bone of our bone and flesh of our flesh descended below all others, 'assuming the condition of a slave' (Phil 2:7). However, he did so in order to 'place' the whole human family between himself and his Father: 'now the life you have is hidden with Christ in God' (Col 3:3). And since the communion of the Father and the Son constitutes the Holy Spirit,[30] Christians are *within* the life of the blessed Trinity. In that place they are vulnerable to the Spirit of Love who is the communion of the Father and the Son.[31] We have seen how on the basis of these pillars of salvation history, John 'defined' God as Trinitarian love. We are 'placed' within that very love, so that Christian existence consists in 'waking up to the love that sleeps inside us' (Origen). God, in fact, has revealed himself to the human family, not as a mighty and solitary Being who commands and conserves creation, but rather as the Reality of Communion who loves 'to the end' (Jn 13:1; 19:29). We know the divine Persons in virtue of their 'economy' in our regard, and so we discover ourselves to be human persons placed in their divinising company. 'O Christians, recognise your dignity', was the repeated reminder and exhortation of the Fathers.

This placing enables us to 'define' the key words of Christian existence in a surprisingly new fashion. Since 'God loves *me* immensely', 'I' am responsible to that very love. '*He/she*' is also loved immensely. Then '*you*' are as important as I am, indeed in 'you' I encounter the same Lord. '*You*' are, in point of fact, 'the brother for whom Christ died' (1Cor 8:11). '*We*' have a unique task, that of 'loving one another' 'as he loved us' (Jn 13:34; 15:12; 1Jn 4:19). To live in the awareness of the new identities of all the persons who constitute the web of my human existence is to live in a Trinitarian fashion. And this means not only a new understanding *of* God but even more importantly perhaps a new life *in* God the blessed Trinity. In other words, we arrive at a new way of thinking the faith *and* of living the faith. Theology and spirituality are thus brought into fruitful contact: they begin to rhyme and so to inspire each other mutually.

1. The 'I': where am I?

The most elementary Creed is that God is Trinity and that this Trinity has loved me. The truth in fact is that it was through the concrete loving by the Trinity that I discovered that God is love, namely, that 'the mystery of the Trinity has opened to us a totally new perspective: the ground of being is *communio*'.[32] It has to follow that 'at the very heart of Being there is communion, the ecstasy from self'.[33] If I can believe in this love and then entrust myself to it, then I live the reality of Jesus, the firstborn of many brothers. I begin to live as a son or a daughter *with* the only-begotten Son and *in* the only-begotten Son. I am, in fact, addressed by the Father who loves me in his only begotten Son and therefore as his only-begotten Son (Jn 17:24). I have been called and chosen, and so I can live as the Son with the Father. Jesus heard himself being addressed at his baptism in the Jordan and on Mount Tabor with the words, 'This is my beloved Son' (Mt 3:17; 17:5). I can say 'yes' with him to the same Father who has only one thing in his heart, namely, the good of all his children, his Eternal child as well as his adopted. And Jesus continued to say 'yes' to that Father, even in Gethsemene, 'Abba! Father! If it is possible, let this chalice pass. Yet, not my will but yours be done' (Mk 14:36). Not only, but on the Cross Jesus spoke the most radical 'yes' with his death and abandonment. In that way, he placed his eternal 'yes' to the Father in time and space.

My 'I' may be a very troubled one. 'I' may not understand even my own life which I may perceive as confused and pain-filled and as scattered in a thousand misadventures that add up to little or nothing. I may feel that I have not followed the better inspirations in life. I may even believe that my existence has been inconsequential. However, if I can accept the address of the Word to me, if I can welcome the welcome he has brought from the Father, then I begin to live as a son/daughter.

What an amazing God! No longer a God who sits on the summit of reality, issues commands, and distributes favours! Here is a God who calls me to be and to live (Ez 16:6). I am no longer 'condemned to do what I like'. On the contrary, a landscape opens up in front of me where the child becomes son/daughter, an extension-expression of the eternal Son. In the words of G.M. Hopkins,

> ... Christ plays in ten thousand places
> Lovely in limbs, and lovely in eyes not his
> To the Father through the features of men's faces.34

This is a God who is other than the God of explanation, or even a God so great that none greater may be thought! He is in fact a God who is so full of love and therefore of life that he can bring the sinner to life, and the living to be a 'beloved son/daughter' (1Thess 1:14). In the words of Klaus Hemmerle:

> This is a God who embraces me completely. My saying, 'I believe in love', and 'Here I am! I am ready! He loves me!' are enclosed and traced out, rendered possible and rooted in the living relationship between Father and Son. He makes such an eternal mystery shine out in his human nature, in his praying to the Father and in his struggling with the Father.[35]

Now we know full well that baptism plunges us into this divine milieu of the blessed Trinity.[36] Through baptism, in fact, I am placed within the milieu of the Father, the Son and the Holy Spirit. I become, through the merciful love of the Father of mercies (Eph 2:4), a son/daughter of the Father, a brother/sister of Christ, and a temple of their Holy Spirit of communion. Unheard of relationships opening up even more wonderful vistas! However, there is an enormous difference between 'the being of substance' and 'the being of consciousness'. To realise, as Newman insisted again and again, is to turn notion into reality and so find the life of authentic religion.[37]

2. The 'You': Where are 'You'?

'You' are with me in the very same Son. As the Son made man has said 'yes' to me, so has he also said 'yes' to 'you'. And he has said that 'yes' to you 'to the end' (Jn 13:1), for 'you' are 'the brother for whom Christ died' (1Cor 8:11). 'You' are his very presence, his place, to the point that what I do to 'You' he takes as done to himself: 'I was sick, and you visited me' (Mt 25: 32). This explains why the Gospel does not allow me to exclude anyone from that 'yes' which the Father says to the Son and, through the Son made flesh, to me and to you. I begin to understand what it means to love the neighbour as oneself (Mt 22:39).[38] I begin to realise the meaning of the Golden Rule that fulfils the Law and the Prophets and that, as a 'Seed of the Word', travels across all the religions. In each and every 'you' I encounter the Son. 'You' are, as the Fathers of the Church love to repeat, 'the eighth sacrament of Christ'.[39] Every man and woman shows your face.

Perhaps this fact explains why the risen Lord Jesus was never recognised by anyone to whom he appeared after his resurrection until he prompted them, as it were, with a deed or a word: his face is now the face of every man and woman. 'You' are another 'I', not only in the unity of the one human nature, but now in the One Christ. 'You' and 'I' are members of each other. Mahatma Gandhi saw the implication of this with striking clarity, 'I cannot harm you without harming myself'.[40]

3. 'We': where are 'We'?

This, then, is the vista opened up by John's articulation of the Trinitarian life given to humankind. I may not, I am not 'allowed', to pursue an individual way to the Father. A great space has opened up. I and you and s/he are together in that space. The Holy Spirit, in fact, in our hearts makes us cry out as one, 'Abba! Father!' (Gal 4:6; Rom 8:15). A new communion exists, a 'we' that is not the addition of individuals, but the birth of a unity. The many have become 'one thing' (Jn 17:21). Better, the many have become one new Person, just as Gal 3:28 insists because the Father answers the prayer of his Son, 'that all of them may be one, Father, just as you and I are one' (Jn 17:21). The very 'place' of that communion is indicated in the next breath, 'May they also be *in us*'. There is a new communion on earth. This communion does much more than merely resemble the Communion of the Eternal Three: it actually is a participation in the Eternal Communion. This, after all, is the sense of that recurring New Testament preposition, 'as' (*kathos*).[41]

Dialoguing with the Culture of Descartes

At the beginning of the modern period there is what Karl Rahner and others like to call 'the turn to the subject'.[42] This turn intended to enrich the subject by a deeper and more 'critical' appropriation of 'the sources of the self'.[43] History, however, shows that that turning took place in the context of a deepening worry about the ultimate basis of certainty. Where certainty becomes the only great issue, there is already an anxiety about the meaning of being and the experience of life. Eric Voegelin and others show that the great Religious Wars of the Reformation Era had effectively tended to diminish seriously confidence in Revelation as the locus par excellence of such certainty.[44]

What Descartes sought was the certain foundation of all reality. He went, not to the revealed experience of the love of God flooding our hearts through the Holy Spirit who has been given to us (Rom 5:5), but to the immediate experience of the Self as thinking, indeed self-consciously thinking. There he found his axiom, *Cogito ergo sum*. He was so happy with his discovery that he wanted to make a pilgrimage to Loreto to thank the Holy Virgin. As a corollary of his insight, a 'methodic doubt' could be raised about everything else. A solitary 'I' was now going to reconstruct the world of God, man, society and history all by itself! This is the inspiring spark, the abiding presupposition, of modern culture in the West.

As we have just seen, my 'I' had been given to me in the revelation 'given once and for all to the saints' (Jude 3). That gift had also been made to all the others as the 'You's', the 's/he's' and the 'we's' within the divine-human network of relationships constituting the human family as made in the image and the likeness of God (Gen 1:27), and re-made by divine revelation in the image and the likeness of the God of Jesus Christ. The Tradition had handed on this matrix of life and love, not as the preserve of the elite, but as a legacy for all and so as truly 'catholic'. But now there is a break in that Tradition. This is something that we already considered in the very first chapter. Here we should perhaps look, however briefly, at the landscape and climate in our culture that is overshadowed by the figure and concerns of Descartes.

In illustration of the point it is enough to look at a passage in Immanuel Kant where in the *Critique of Pure Reason* he writes:

> The *Cogito* ought to be able to accompany all my concepts, because otherwise a reality could be conceived by me which could in no way be thought, which means then that the concept was either impossible, or, at least for me, could not exist ... I call it apperception in order to distinguish it from empirical apperception, or also original apperception, since it is precisely that self-consciousness which, in as much as it produces the concept 'I think' – which should be able to accompany all the other concepts and be one and the same in every consciousness – cannot be accompanied anymore by any other concept.[45]

This is a clear programme, and a critique of all others.

However, one would like to propose an alternative starting point, such as, for example, one that might wish to set out from the experience of the love of another, such as a mother or a spouse, or even of God who might want to address a loving Word to each of us. Can we give ourselves existence and being (Acts 17:28)? Is not the first word of every child 'Mama', and not 'I'? And what is one to say about the phenomenon of language? Surely language is a pre-existing datum and as such a gift for each I? Is it not designed to generate communion, and not merely communication, among persons?[46] Interpersonality and dialogue are surely a better grammar of human existence than the solitary I.

The major outcome of the enterprise of modernity has been the emergence of the individual subject, a solitary monad, and the presumed source of meaning and order on his own. The world in the West is increasingly peopled by lonely monadic individuals for whom others and personal relationships are only *secondary in importance*, if they feature at all. The crisis of modern culture, in the judgement of the Austrian philosopher, Ferdinand Ebner, consists in the isolation of the I. One encounters increasingly 'the loneliness of the I' (*Icheinsamkeit*). 'The I is cut off from others and dreams of breaking out of its isolation but does not know how.'[47] The result is 'the wounded ego', to employ the striking phrase of Paul Ricoeur.

Of course the turning to the subject at the beginning of the modern period brought with it as well a fresh attention to the world that surrounds us. If Aristotelian science was interested in the universal, the necessary and the certain, the science that developed with Newton was more concerned with the particular, the contingent and the probable. In fact, that could open up a way to comply with the mandate of the Creator in Genesis (1:28). In any case, the rest is history. The benefits flowing from the resulting modern science and technology for the betterment of humankind are a daily experience and a reason to thank the Creator.

There was a price, however: the world could now be studied independently of God, its Maker. This could lead to a 'bracketing' of God, even to his eclipse.

Blaise Pascal foresaw this with characteristic clairvoyance. In one of those great insights of his, the *Pensées*, he makes the statement, 'The silence of those infinite spaces frightens me'.[48] If one considers that the first and foundational word is the word emerging from one's own I, then there opens up inexorably the spectre of silence. Since one begins from the self, dialogue with another I is not essential. In the words of Klaus Hemmerle, 'The human being becomes an entity who receives no answer because he is no longer a being who answers anyone. At the conclusion of modern development there is a collective or individual loneliness, isolation'.[49] He does not even expect a primary word addressing his I. In the end there will be only monologue, and since that begins and ends with himself, there has to follow 'the silence of those infinite spaces'. That silence is unbearable, since it drives home the devastating message, 'You are alone in the universe ultimately'.[50]

Such a threatened I simply has to expand. The I must rediscover the You and the S/He in order to enter the communion of the We. This human milieu is then addressed and x-rayed by revelation. The result is the knowledge of a love that is beyond all knowing (Eph 3:19). We human persons find ourselves located in a Trinitarian milieu. There is a 'new whereabouts'. The Father of Our Lord Jesus Christ has truly raised us up with his Son and given us a place with him in heaven (Eph 2:6). That has been the concern of this chapter: to unfold the content of divine revelation in the categories of relationship among Persons, both divine and human. Being is relation, and revealed Being is Trinitarian relationship, so that society is to become communion. [51]

Finally, since the revelation has to enter the existing culture, there is a need for dialogue with that culture. The heirs of Descartes have been the instruments of many blessings for humanity, at least in the West, but they have weakened both the human and divine blessings of Persons. Indirectly, though, they might now make us all more aware of what the elementary declaration of divine revelation is saying, much as illness both reminds us of health and increases our yearning for its return. 'Father, I want those you have given me to be with me *where I am*, and to see my glory, the glory you have given me because you loved me before the creation of the world' (Jn 17:24).

Notes

1. Hans Urs von Balthasar, *Theo-drama. IV:The Action*, San Francisco 1994, 60.
2. See Thomas Norris, 'On the personal appropriation of the meaning of Revelation' in I.T.Q., 46(1979), 40–50.
3. Günter Bornkamm, *Jesus von Nazareth*, Stuttgart 1956, 18.
4. St Augustine, 'Novum in vetere latet, vetus in novo patet', *Questiones in Heptateuchum 2, 73*: PL 34, 623.
5. Hans Urs von Balthasar, *Love alone the way of Revelation*, Einsiedeln 1969, 40, 43.
6. Thomas Norris, 'The Theological Formation of Candidates for the Priesthood', in *I.T.Q.*, 64 (1999), 389–402.
7. Hans Urs von Balthasar, 'Wer is Jesus von Nazareth - für mich?' in H. Spämann (ed,), *Wer ist Jesus von Nazareth – für mich? 100 zeitgenössische Zeugnisse*, Munich 1973, 17 as translated in Medard Kehl and Werner Löser (eds), *The von Balthasar Reader*, Edinburgh 1982, 113.
8. *Idem, Love Alone*, 112.
9. Herbert A. Kenny, 'Herbert A. Kenny and Patricia Buckley Bozell: A Correspondence' in *Communio*, vol. XXX, 3(2003), 510.
10. See Walter Kasper, *The God of Jesus Christ*, London 1984, 316.
11. Hans Urs von Balthasar, *Wer ist Jesus von Nazareth für mich?*, ibid., 17.
12. *Idem, Heart of the World*, San Francisco 1996, 46.
13. John Henry Newman, *Oxford University Sermons*, London 1890, *passim*.
14. J. Jeremias, *The Prayers of Jesus*, London 1967.
15. Bernard Lonergan, *De Deo Trino*, I, Rome 1964, 124f; *De Verbo Incarnato*, Rome 1964, 48–50.
16. St Gregory Nazianzen, *In sanctum Baptisma*, 40, 41: PG 36:417.
17. See Karl Rahner, *The Trinity*, New York 1970, 11–12.
18. N. Ciola, *Teologia trinitaria, storia, metodo, prospettive*, Bologna 1996, 198.
19. *Catechism of the Catholic Church*, n.470.

20. Hans Urs von Balthasar, *Convergences*, SanFrancisco 1983, 91–92.

21. Hell, or eternal perdition, is therefore a Christological revelation. The paschal Christ of course 'descends into hell', as the Apostles' Creed teaches. In doing so, he ratifies the gift of human freedom to the end and 'pays' for the abuse of that gift to the point of becoming dead with the dead out of love. Hell is the most dramatic *aporie* of Trinitarian love and human freedom; see Hans Urs von Balthasar, *Dare we Hope that all will be Saved?*, San Francisco 1988.

22. Klaus Hemmerle, *Partire dall'unità*, Roma 1998, 36.

23. See Michael Mullins, *The Gospel of John. A Commentary*, Dublin 2003, *passim*; John Redford, *Bad, Mad or God*, London 2004.

24. St Augustine, *Homily 26,46 on John*: PL 35, 1608.

25. John Henry Newman, *Parochial and Plain Sermons*, vol. IV, London 1869, 170.

26. C. Spicq, *Agape dans le Nouveau testament*, 173, n.1, points out the strong theological import of the word *kathos:* 'In his "departing words" (13:17) *"kathos"* has a strong theological meaning: imitation and similarity, extension and similarity: *as* the Father loves Jesus, so Jesus loves the believers (cf. Jn 15:9; 17:23) and the believers must love each other with the same love (cf. Jn 15:12) ... *as* the Father and the Son are one, the disciples must be one (cf. Jn 17:21)'.

27. See The Pastoral Constitution on the Church *Gaudium et spes*, 24.

28. Klaus Hemmerle, *Partire dall'unità,* Roma 1998, 38-9: the translation is mine. The famous words of St Augustine come to mind, *'Imo vero si vides caritatem, vides trinitatem'*, *De Trinitate*, VIII, 8, 12: quoted in Pope Benedict XVI's first encyclical *Deus caritas est*, n.19.

29. Klaus Hemmerle, *Partire dall'unità*, 40.

30. Joseph Ratzinger, 'Der heilige Geist als *Communio*' in *Weggeminschaft des Glaubens*, Augsburg 2002, 34–52.

31. For example, Leo I, *Sermo I in Nativitatem Domini*, 1–3, PL 54, 190–193.

32. Henri de Lubac, *La Foi chrétienne*, 14 as quoted in Joseph Ratzinger, *Principles of Catholic Theology*, San Francisco 1987, 22–23.

33. *Idem*, 13.

34. Gerard Manley Hopkins, ibid., 51.

35. Klaus Hemmerle, ibid., 33–34.

36. See Liam Bergin, *O Propheticum Lavacrum: Baptism as Symbolic Act of Eschatological Salvation*, Rome 1999.

37. See John Henry Newman, 'Unreal Words', in *Parochial and Plain Sermons*, vol. V, London 1869, 29–45

38. J. McNerney, *Footbridge to the Neighbour*, Edinburgh 2003, *passim*.

39. See Olivier Clément, *The Roots of Christian Mysticism*, London Dublin Edinburgh 1993.

40. Wilhelm Muehs, *Parole del cuore*, Milano 1996, 82.

41. See M. Cerini, *God who is Love*, New York 1992, 44; 81–82.

42. Karl Rahner, *Theological Investigations*, vol. IV, London 1966, 324.

43. Charles Taylor, *The Sources of the Self*, Cambridge MA 1989.

44. Eric Voegelin, 'Equivalences of Experience and Symbolisation in History', in *Published Essays, 1966-1985*, Baton Rouge 1990, 117–118.

45. I. Kant, *Kritik der reinen Vernunft*, in *Werke*, vol. 3, Frankfurt 1968, 136.

46. See St Augustine, *Sermo 293,3*: PL 38, 1238 where the '*verbum in corde*' becomes the '*verbum prolatum*' to reach the *cor* of the other, and *vice versa*.

47. See John O'Donnell, *Hans Urs von Balthasar*, London 1992, 141.

48. Pascal, *Pensées*, Fragm. 206, ed. Brunschvicg.

49. K. Hemmerle, *Wie Glauben im Leben geht*, München 1995, 228–229.

50. See the comment of C.S. Lewis in the film, *Shadowlands*, 'You need to know you are not on your own', and the repeated motif of abandonment and the absurd in Samuel Beckett's work.

Chapter VIII

The Exile and the Return of the Trinity

We stand at the centre of this prodigious drama, we are at the very heart of the Most Holy Trinity. What does it mean? To be inside God himself, inside his incomprehensible hurricane? It seems unbelievable to you, doesn't it, since the only God you can imagine is a logician, an organising intelligence. But this is not the first definition of God. No, God is first of all charity. He is Absolute Love. Absolute Love! Just try, by the movement of our miserable hearts, to measure such an unheard of power! We live comfortably and unaware in the midst of this great whirlwind, and if, unimaginably, the unwavering course of its spirals were displaced to the slightest degree, entire worlds would be uprooted. For love, nothing is mediocre; everything is great.[1]

God can be thought about more truly than he can be talked about, and he is more truly than he can be thought about.[2]

St Paul stresses that 'if one man has died for all, then all men should be dead with him' (2Cor 5:14), while the Johannine tradition puts it like this, 'We have believed in the love which God has for us' (I Jn 4:16). From this love there radiated the splendour of God in Christ. Beauty, in fact, is the splendour emanating from the concrete form of love. To take but one example of a work answering to this specification, there appeared in 1938 Henri de Lubac's *Catholicism: The Social Aspects of Dogma*, whose very title intriguingly connected Catholicism, socialism and dogma in an era dominated in the political arena by socialism and fascism: de Lubac shows how 'Christianity is obsessed with the vision of a united world', and therefore 'refuses to pass through this world with a rose in its hand'.[3]

The Fathers from Justin (+165 a.d.) onwards were convinced that the splendour and attractiveness of the content of the faith are the best evidence for the truth of the faith. Augustine puts it memorably, 'If the poet can say, 'Everyone is drawn by his delight', not by necessity but by delight, not by compulsion but by sheer pleasure, then how much more must we say that a man is drawn by Christ, when he delights in truth, in blessedness, in holiness and in eternal life, all of which mean Christ?'[4] Beauty was the unerring pointer to truth and the good. 'Something that has existed since the beginning, something that we have heard, and have seen with our eyes; that we have watched and touched with our hands: the Word, who is life – this is our subject ..., We are writing this to you to make our own joy complete (IJn 1:1, 4). The Second Vatican Council adopted this text as its leitmotiv in its ground-breaking constitution on divine revelation.[5] As we have seen, it was the conviction of that great stirring of minds and hearts that if the world could hear the message of divine revelation, it would believe, by believing it would hope, and by hoping it would love.[6]

Theologians such as Hans Urs von Balthasar are so persuaded of this order of reality and of its primordial role in our accessing reality in knowledge that they invert the traditional order of the transcendentals of being as they have been traditionally deployed in the theological enterprise. Whereas ordinarily theology began with the truth, then advanced to the good, it rarely reached the beautiful. Still, beauty remains 'the tangible manifestation of the idea' (Hegel). More pertinent still is the fact that God let his glory-beauty radiate on the face of his beloved incarnate Son and from there into the hearts of believers (Jn 2:11; 2Cor 4:6).

In the modern period, dogmatics were not steeped in the glory-love-beauty that we have been describing in section two of this study. In fact, during the centuries since the Reformation, the category of the beautiful largely disappeared from theology. Both Catholic and Protestant theology aimed at a statement proving the superior truthfulness of their respective versions, as well as the evil of the untruths in the accounts of the others. However, modern men and women are challenged by the good and so are reluctant to choose it. As for the true, they are threatened by its seeming 'severity' (an Irish proverb speaks of the truth as '*searbh*' or bitter). But they are vulnerable to the beautiful. Without the beautiful, in fact, the good loses its attractiveness and the true its cogency. It is in this context that the American Orthodox theologian, David Bentley Hart writes, '[B]eauty is a category indispensable to Christian thought; all that theology says of the triune life of God, the gratuity of creation, the incarnation of the Word, the salvation of the world makes room for – indeed depends upon – a thought, and a narrative, of the beautiful'.[7]

This explains why it is often the artists, whether the poets, the sculptors, the painters or the musicians, who best captured during that long era since the sixteenth century the glory of the God of Jesus Christ, the glory shining on the face of his Son, Jesus (2Cor 4:6). It is enough to think of The Messiah of Frederick Handel, the poetry of Patrick Kavanagh, the painting of a Grunewald or a Jacques Rouault, or the cinematography of André Tarkovsky. The philosophical transcendental of beauty finds its revealed equivalent in glory. From Plato to Simone Weil there is the conviction that beauty is the most 'influential' of the transcendentals, those colours of Being that introduce us to reality and enable reality to impact us. As for Plato, beauty is a ray which, from the face of God, as from a beautiful sun, is handed down and shared with created nature; having thus rendered nature beautiful and gracious with its colours, it returns to the same fount from where it came.[8] For Weil, in true art 'there is almost a kind of incarnation of God in the world, the sign of which is beauty. This beauty is the experiential proof that the incarnation is possible'.[9]

The intuitions of these two thinkers, so separate in time and so different in context, make their insights truly independent of each other. However, they converge on the revealed form of Christianity. He who was in the form of God 'empties' himself to be in the form of man (Phil 2:6-7). What 'made' him do so was love. Christ in fact came not only to teach the truth and to bring about the good. Of course, his mission included these also, and necessarily. But above all, he came to radiate in the world the splendour of the love that wished to die 'from what was ours' (Augustine) so that we might live 'from what is his' to his Father forever, participating in 'what no eye has ever seen, nor ear ever heard, nor the heart of man ever imagined', namely, 'all God has in store for those who love him' (I Cor 2:9-10).[10] He is not a messenger from God, but the Son who allows us to see his glory as of the only begotten Son who is nearest the Father's heart and is full of grace and truth (Jn 1:14; 18).[11]

It is little surprise, then, that St Augustine should call the eternal Son 'the art of the Father',[12] and echoing the Letter to the Ephesians should call Christians 'God's work of art' (2:10). In his *Letter to Artists* (1999), Pope John Paul II writes that 'the Son of God in becoming man has introduced into human history all the evangelical wealth of the true and the good, and with this he has also unveiled a new dimension of beauty, of which the Gospel message is filled to the brim'.[13] The truth is that in '[M]aking its appeal first to the eye and heart, as the only way it may "command" assent, the Church cannot separate truth from rhetoric, or from beauty'.[14] Theologians such as Henri de Lubac have noticed that in the Fourth Gospel the signs done by Jesus make his glory shine out: the impact on those who saw them is put typically in these words, 'They believed into Jesus' (2:11).[15] The author of the Gospel deliberately adopts a formula which is, syntactically speaking, a 'barbarism' – the rules of syntax had to be stretched in order to facilitate the inbreaking glory.

A new perspective comes into view, the perspective of beauty-glory. This perspective has three characteristics that seem both to challenge and, at the same time, complement the more 'cosmological' and 'anthropological' elaborations of revelation. It contains a certain resistance to an exclusive turning to the subject. The turning to the subject at the beginning of the modern period has indeed inspired the search for a critical perspective and presentation. This is not only a valid perspective, it is also a necessary one, especially since it shows that the question of God is the most human of all questions, a conviction encompassing thinkers as diverse as Dostoievsky and Karl Rahner. Still, it is not adequate on its own: having shown that an authentic anthropology is incipient Christology, as this anthropological method undoubtedly does, it would then be necessary to unfold and to paint the resultant divine milieu that opens to us in the love of the Trinity where Christians with unveiled faces may advance from one degree of glory to the next (2Cor 3:18). Otherwise there exists the real danger that the cosmos and the human will be made the 'measure' of the divine whereas their true calling is to be its real 'sacrament'. For Christ is not only the answer to the human search for meaning: he is more truly the answer that questions all other answers.

No individual 'I' can dominate the 'Thou' without violating the dignity of the 'Thou' and the truth and freedom of both. David Tracy puts this in the same personalist categories:

> The real face of our period, as Emmanuel Levinas saw with such clarity, is the face of the other: the face that commands, 'Do not kill me'. The face insists: do not reduce me or anyone else to your narrative ... God's shattering otherness, the neighbour's irreducible otherness, the othering reality of revelation (not the consoling modern notion of 'religion'): all these expressions of genuine otherness demand the serious attention of all thoughtful persons.[16]

Is not the heartache of modern men and women in the claim to be self-made, and therefore to be able to dispense with the only one who is truly self-made, namely, the God of Jesus Christ? Next, there is the fact that it is God the holy Trinity who comes towards us relentlessly, since, as the *Constitution on Divine Revelation* stresses, 'in his goodness and wisdom God chose to reveal himself and to make known to us the hidden purpose of his will (cf. Eph 1:9) by which through Christ, the Word made flesh, man has access to the Father in the Holy Spirit and comes to share in the divine nature (cf. Eph 2:18; 2Pet 1:4)'.[17] St Irenaeus, as we have seen, saw in the missions of the Son and the Holy

Spirit the outstretched arms of the Father calling and enfolding his children.[18] This was in fact the [last] chapter's concern, for there we looked at the extraordinary 'whereabouts' of Christians and the resulting 'Trinitarian relations' in which we participate and which constitute the core of the Christian life. 'God has sent the Spirit of his Son into our hearts by which we cry, "Abba! Father!"' (Rom 8:15; Gal 4:6).

The third characteristic of this perspective underlines what constitutes the credibility of the faith. As the title of one of von Balthasar's books puts it, only love is credible, the love that is the glory-beauty of God the Holy Trinity. What we have shown is that such love is Trinitarian, crucified and glorified because the Father loved humankind so much that he did not spare his own Son but gave him up for us all, not allowing his Holy One to see corruption but glorifying him in resurrection by the Holy Spirit, and then lifting humankind in him and with him to his own right hand (Rom 8:32; Acts 2: 31; Phil 2:9-11; ICor 15:54-57). The revelation recorded in the New Testament and by the living Tradition of the Fathers contains 'the unfathomable riches of Christ' (Eph 3:8). Those riches unite impossible spheres of existence.

That makes Christ the 'Catholic' par excellence in that he is the One who includes and unites the many. Vertically Christ unites humankind to his Father, horizontally he unites himself to every man and woman, as Pope John Paul II stresses.[19] He is 'the second Adam' as also the eternal Son. He is the one 'through whom all things are made' (Jn 1:3) and re-made so that 'all things hold together in him' (Col 1:15). In fact, 'there is one Lord, Jesus Christ, through whom all things come and through whom we exist' (ICor 8:6). In the language of Chalcedon, he is 'consubstantial with the Father according to divinity, consubstantial with us according to humanity', even if the latter was not recognised in the tradition as it ought. As such he is the mediator of unity in all directions! To present such a revelation is to suggest necessarily a dynamic theology of the Trinity, for the Trinity is the only possible hypothesis capable of covering both the experience of the first Christians and the revealed data of the New Testament.

The Loss of Revealed Substance: The Exile of the Trinity

This 'fullness' of revelation was unequivocally defined in the teaching of the early Councils and wonderfully thought through in the great work of St Augustine, On the Trinity. Augustine spent over twenty years between 399 and 421 in the composition of this tantalising text.[20] However, in spite of the conciliar teaching and the theological legacy of the Doctor of Charity, the reality of the Trinity as the core mystery of the faith did not enter, in some of its essential dimensions, into the daily consciousness of believers. For example, the mystery got locked into what Walter Kasper calls an *'Ichgeschlossenheit'* which connected the mystery so tightly to the individual's journey to the Father that it lost all significance for human co-existence or society.[21]

Thus Immanuel Kant in the eighteenth century could write that the doctrine of the Trinity has no practical relevance to living.[22] By the middle of the last century Karl Rahner lamented that, if the doctrine of the Blessed Trinity were dropped from the Church's confession of faith, the faith of the majority of believers and – what is worse still – their spirituality would be unaffected.[23] Other authors, such as Catherine LaCugna, speak of a 'defeat' of the doctrine of the Trinity in the fact that it became irrelevant to daily living.[24]

Von Balthasar even spoke of a certain 'Islamisation' of Christianity where the specific core of faith in Trinity and in the Paschal Mystery would have largely melted down. This fact obliges us to look at the work of Augustine: historically his *De Trinitate* was destined to influence the Church's thinking for many long centuries, while theologically it set a standard of excellence that continues to inspire the whole tradition, though not without certain criticisms.[25] We will have to look briefly at the history of the understanding of God the holy Trinity in subsequent ages. We will do so in broad strokes and with a view to showing how the great recovery of lost truths in the last seventy years has led to a new inspiration for Christian living, specifically the emergence for the first time of a spirituality of communion in which believers go to God, not only beside one another, but above all with and through the brother or sister for whom Christ died (I Cor 8:11).[26] What was utterly unlikely only a half century ago is now a real fact and an attractive challenge – a truly Trinitarian and communitarian lifestyle.[27] The prayer that expresses the dying wish of the Saviour is becoming flesh, 'May they all be one, Father, as you and I are one' (Jn 17:21). If these synthesis words of the Gospel become flesh in daily living, might not the Church thereby enter upon the Springtime foretold by popes and longed for by many? One thing, however, is certain: no sooner do Christians overlook a vital component of divine revelation than society begins to complain and to proffer its own substitute.[28]

1. Horizon Analysis: Discerning Augustine's Perspectives

The context of Augustine's profound and prolonged reflection was a post-conciliar one. The Councils of Nicea (325) and Constantinople (381) had defined the consubstantiality (homoousia) of the Son and of the Holy Spirit with the Father, respectively. This was the 'rule of faith' he adhered to strictly after his conversion. If the Father, the Son and the Holy Spirit were each one and the same eternal God, and a believer wanted to avoid the facile solution of modalism, then one had to give an account not only of how the God of Jesus Christ was both one and triune, but also endear the mystery to believers as the mystery of God's love for us par excellence.[29] This was the objective of Augustine who realised full well the enormity of the challenge involved, 'There is no subject in which error is more dangerous, inquiry more arduous, and discovery more fruitful'.[30]

The *De Trinitate* is a work of charismatic quality, not only in the sense of personal brilliance and theological insight, but above all in the sense that Augustine himself was the recipient of a great charism. Chosen by God, captured by Christ and endowed by the Holy Spirit, Augustine wrote a *Rule* which has been the basis of innumerable religious orders in subsequent centuries. That makes him a founder of religious life in the Church, as Francis, Dominic, Teresa and Ignatius were to be in the next millennium. The significance of this fact for his theology of the Blessed Trinity is vital. For his charism was a gift for the whole Church given through him. Agostino Trapè stresses how 'in his theological penetration, which was exceptionally profound and sure, his mystical experience exercised a decisive influence'.[31] For Augustine was typical of all the Fathers for whom thinking about the Faith could never be separated from living by the same Faith, a fact that keeps their theology evergreen and inspirational: it seems to contain a life which much theology of the second millennium tends to lack.[32]

The truth is that charisms 'provide insights into the centre of revelation, insights that enrich the Church in ways that are as unexpected as they are lasting. They are always charisms in which understanding, love and imitation are inseparable ... The Holy Spirit does not reveal any particular aspect without making the totality also stand out'.[33] This principle will enable us later on to compare Augustine's insight into the mystery with that of others in the second millennium who were also the recipients of charisms destined for the whole Church.

Augustine's spiritual experience, so poignantly described in the *Confessions*,[34] always accompanies and guides his intellectual probings of the mystery. Contemporary commentators stress this as the hermeneutical key to all his theology, which is to be a tasting knowledge of the things of God. In his view of things, life and understanding nourish each other mutually. God the holy Trinity, in fact, beckons us into a spiritual and intellectual itinerary with him in Their 'space', the Church. That itinerary both corresponds to the wonder of the revealed mystery and speaks to the abyss of human existence, the *infinitum internum* at the core of each person.

The works of Plato, as well as the Neoplatonists like Plotinus, had 'turned him towards' the unchanging Truth whose Light pointed him towards the Love that lasts forever. That Truth resides within, *'in interiore hominis'*, so that one should journey inwards in order to discover God, 'Do not wander far and wide but return into yourself. Deep within man there dwells the truth'.[35] This is his way of interiority which leads him to seek wisdom 'with an incredible desire of the heart'.[36] Little wonder, then, that he will make the discovery of the triune reality of the soul reflecting the triune reality of the eternal God, 'O eternal Truth, and true Love, and loving Eternity!'[37] Vladimir Solovyov has noticed here an insight that has not been appreciated in the tradition of the West. 'Already in the *Confessions*, Augustine has noticed how being (*esse*), knowing (*scire*) and willing (*velle*) each contain the other two in their distinctive character, and consequently, each inwardly already contains the whole fullness of the triune spirit.'[38]

Upon his conversion in 386, Augustine made the profound experience of life in the *Catholica*. In a particular way, he was struck by the reality of *caritas* and of the Church as the Body of Christ vivified by this same charity. Famously, he described the Church as the *Christus Totus*, composed as she is of Christ as Head and of us as his members or Body. This led him to the conviction that the core of the Christian life lay in the commandment of love since the God of the Old Covenant completed the revelation of his being (Ex 3:13-4) with the revelation that this very Being is love as *agape*.[39]

It is important to remember that this is the foundation on which the *fides catholica* of his Baptism will be built culturally and philosophically. 'When Augustine comes to faith, he feels himself driven to harmonise the philosophical and experiential datum at which he had arrived (God, the Truth, the ineffable Light that illuminates with its grace the souls of those seeking wisdom) with the doctrine of faith that said to him: God, the God whom you have found and whom Christ reveals in full to you, guiding you in the process towards him, is Trinity – Father, Son, Holy Spirit. The theological search of the great doctor is profoundly marked by this personal struggle.'[40] In that way, Augustine provides a theology that is truly the fruit of an interaction between divine revelation and the cultural ideal of his time, just as all epoch-making theologies will do during the subsequent history of the Church.

The mystery of the unity and the trinity of God are to be read economically in the event of Christ. Now that event was a design of unity: Christ, in fact, is the mediator of unity for humankind and creation, a unity which is the design of the Father and the work of the Holy Spirit (Eph 1:10). He describes in Book IV how that design is fulfilled in the three phases of creation, redemption and participation in the life of God the Holy Trinity. Here Augustine opens up the meaning of the One, the Many and the Other. Here is how he sums up the unifying mediation of the Son made flesh:

> He did not say, 'I and they are one thing', even if as 'head' of the Church and 'the Church' being 'his body' he could say, 'I and they are, not one thing, but one person', because then 'the Head and the Body are one Christ'. But showing his divine consubstantiality with the Father, ... being consubstantial in the same nature, he wished his own to be 'one thing' but in him ... And this is the sense of the expression, 'May they all be one thing as we are one thing', just as the Father and the Son are 'one thing' not only by means of the equality of substance, but also by means of the will, so those who have the Son as the Mediator between themselves and God must be 'one thing' not only because they are of the same nature but also by means of the commonality of one and the same love. Later the Lord will indicate that he is the 'Mediator' thanks to whom we are reconciled with God by means of these words, 'I in them and You in me, so that they might be consumed in unity'.[41]

In the *Confessions* there is the famous incident of the ecstasy which he and Monica lived in that garden in Ostia: though only a 'momentary intuition', they tasted the rapture of being one in God the Holy Trinity. It is no exaggeration to say that Monica and Augustine had a glimpse of the life of the Trinity and so had lived a moment of Trinitarian unity. There is a corresponding theological method in the great doctor. He stresses that both in the one who reads as well as in the one who writes there must be a living faith and love for the truth. 'In this way let us set out along Charity Street together, making for him of whom it is said, "Seek his face always"' (Ps 105:4).[42] Here we can hear the voice of the pastor exhorting his flock in Hippo, 'Show me a lover and he will understand what I am saying. Show me ... someone wandering in this wilderness, thirsting and longing for the fountains of his eternal home, show me such a one and he will know what I mean'.[43] Both his prayer and his Trinitarian theology follow the way of charity in its vertical and horizontal dimensions, and graft that on to the cultural ideal of Neoplatonism in which he detected the vestiges of the life at the heart of Being, the life of being, knowing and loving.

The Sequence of the Books: A Key to their Content

In the first seven Books he wishes to outline the content of the mystery as taught by the Church and as witnessed in Scripture. He will follow here the sequence of expounding the mystery of faith (*regula fidei*), understanding it (*intelligentia fidei*) and experiencing it (*experientia fidei*). In Book V, however, he makes a stupendous discovery, namely, that each of the divine Persons is a relation. He noticed this in his exposition of the Scriptural witness: the very names of the Persons in the Scriptures are relational. And even if the name of the Holy Spirit is not as obviously such as the names 'Father' and 'Son', still the Scriptures call him 'the gift of God' (Acts 8:20; Jn 4:10) and 'charity', and this again strongly points in the direction of relation.[44] He writes, 'Sometimes one speaks of God according to relation (*secundum relativum*); thus the Father expresses a relation to the Son and the Son to the Father, and this relation is not an accident, since the one is always the Father, the other always the Son'.[45] The implications of this insight are quite extraordinary. While Aristotle in his doctrine of substance and accidents, relegates the category of relation to an insignificant place among the nine accidents of reality,[46] Augustine discerns in New Testament revelation that the Father, the Son and the Holy Spirit may be understood as relations, and that this opens up a most original approach to the understanding of the mystery of the unity and the trinity of God while respecting its transcendent ineffability.

God is not only being in-himself, or by-himself, 'substance' to use the language of Greek philosophy. He is above all relation. Relation is no longer the weakest of the accidents, but rather expresses something essential – the very life of God the Holy Trinity. Augustine explains further in these terms, 'Even if being Father and being Son are not the same thing, still the substance is not different, since these appellations do not belong to the order of substance but to that of relation, relation which is not an accident because it is not changeable'.[47] This allows Augustine to harmonise the two 'inspirations' that guide him, namely, that of philosophy and of the Mosaic revelation, as well as the revelation contained in the New Testament. 'The two data are connected in such a way that the unity of the divine esse (which is concerned with the order of consubstantiality) is not broken by the otherness of Father, Son and Holy Spirit, which indicates the relation of the one to the other.'[48]

Here Augustine transforms the traditional and classical metaphysics which he inherited. Now God is not only the Absolute Substance as the Absolute One, but also the One Being who expresses himself in the reciprocal relations of a distinct Three, the Father, the Son and the Holy Spirit, each of whom is the one true God. This represents a revolution in our understanding of reality or being. Cardinal Ratzinger expresses it in these terms in his now famous Introduction to Christianity, 'In this simple affirmation (each divine Person is a relation) there is evident a genuine revolution in the form of the world: the absolute supremacy of a thinking focused on substance is displaced in as much as relation is discovered to be an original and equal modality of the real ... and a new thinking about being emerges in reaction. It must be also said that in all probability the challenge arising for philosophical thought from these circumstances is in fact far from having been addressed'.[49] The implications of this breakthrough will be identified at key moments in the subsequent chapters of this work.

Between Books IX and XV Augustine sets out his understanding of

Trinity. He chooses not to employ his newly discovered category of relation. Instead, he turns to the Genesis revelation that the human being is made 'in the image and the likeness of God' (1:26). In this truth he was sure that he had 'found an object of study more familiar to us'.[50] He was sure that he had found a 'vestige' of the Trinity in the fact that each person is, knows and loves.[51] It was the way of interiority but in its individual mode. His profound exposition in these books has impacted mystics, inspired theologians and influenced philosophers. But what is to be said of the other analogy, the analogy of love? The decision not to explore this avenue of inquiry in the main corpus of his research has had an epochal impact on the history of theology in its various fields.

Great mystic and insatiable searcher that he is, Augustine sets out in spite of all in Book VIII of his opus to look for an 'experience' of the Trinity. Already convinced from both philosophy and divine revelation that there has to be some similarity between the ineffable mysterious God and the creature, – revelation tells us there is – he seeks again a foothold in experience to assist in this fresh 'assault' on the mystery. Love is clearly the highest peak in human experience, the summit of human action and being. It has to follow that 'in the issue of the Trinity and the knowledge of God we should principally investigate what constitutes true love, because the only love worthy of the name is true love'.[52] In any case, the *First Letter of John* clearly stresses that 'God is love and that whoever lives in love lives in God' (4:8, 16). Since this is the case, 'why go running towards the highest heavens, or in the depths of the earth in search of him who is with us, if we wish to be with him?'[53] This search for an experience leads him to what is possibly the second great insight of the *De Trinitate*, namely, that the life of mutual love is the most perfect analogue for the great mystery, even if it can be used only by those who live by this love with sincerity and in truth.

His words speak for themselves. 'If you see charity, you see the trinity. I will push myself, if I can, to make you understand that you see it, but let the Trinity help us.'[54] In the following passage he seems to summarise his experience and insight:

> Love belongs to someone who loves and who with love loves something. So there are three: the lover, and that which is loved, and love. What is love, if not a life that unites, or that desires that two realities unite, and that is the lover and that which is loved? And it is like that in loves that are more base and carnal. But in order to reach a source that is more pure and crystalline, the flesh having been subjugated, let us lift ourselves up to the soul. What does the soul love in the friend if not the soul? Therefore also here there are three things: the one who loves, that which is loved, and love. It remains therefore for us to raise ourselves still higher and to begin to do so.[55]

Augustine discovers that he has found the place where he can seek.

However, he decides to stop there rather than push on to its full discovery and appropriate exposition.[56] As he finally concludes the marathon work, he writes not without a hint of nostalgic regret:

> If we try to recall where it was in these books that a trinity first began to appear to our understanding, it will occur to us that it was in the eighth book ... But when we came to charity, which is called God in holy scripture, the glimmerings of a trinity began to appear, namely lover and what is loved and love. However, that inexpressible light beat back our gaze ... So here we are, after exercising our understanding as much as was necessary in these lower things, wishing and not being able to raise ourselves to a sight of that supreme trinity which is God.[57]

This extraordinary page, reminiscent of the conclusion of John's Gospel where the evangelist admits that his work has had to leave out most of what could be written (Jn 21:25), is an ardent desire for a further grace of the Holy Spirit and a new theological *kairos*. In effect, Augustine concedes that he should have developed the interpersonal analogy for our more fruitful understanding of the highest mystery of faith, but decided not to do so! Like Moses contemplating the Promised Land from the heights of Mount Nebo but not being able to enter!

If it is true that the Eternal Ocean has broken upon us in divine revelation, then it is to be expected that it will take time for the appropriate exploration, articulation and 'unpacking' of that divine depth. A fortiori is this the case with the most central mystery of divine revelation, the Holy Trinity. This point was powerfully made in the last Council when it teaches that 'the tradition which comes from the apostles develops in the Church with the help of the Holy Spirit. For there is a growth in the understanding of the realities and the words which have been handed down … For as the centuries succeed one another, the Church constantly moves forward toward the fullness of divine truth until the words of God reach their complete fulfilment in her'.[58] John Henry Newman famously formulated in 1845 in the *Essay on the Development on Christian Doctrine* this dynamic understanding of the assimilation of divine revelation. Development is now recognised as one of the constitutive first principles of Catholicism.[59] It is not at all accidental that the Council should have named the Holy Spirit as the guide of this development. We have seen that he inspired Augustine with a charism both in his life as a founder of monastic communities, an original communicator of the Word of God, and in his career as a luminous meteorite for the work of theology and theologians. As he did then, so he will continue to do while the Church advances on her pilgrim way.

In spite of the reserve inserted into the tradition against the search for understanding in the case of the Trinity by a genius such as Dionysius the Areopagite, the Middle Ages still sought out fresh understanding. Man has an insatiable desire to know and to understand. This meant that Augustine came to the fore strongly again, or rather his desire to 'seek what is to be sought and to seek what is found, since what is to be sought is hidden, and what is found is immense'.[60] However, as in the case of the *Doctor Caritatis*, so this time charisms were to play a special role. Specifically, the great spiritual charisms given to Dominic and Francis inspired further searches into the mystery. It was as if the fresh glimpses gained by Francis and Dominic signalled unprecedented avenues of access for theologians or else suggested unexpected dimensions of the revealed mystery.

2. Thomas Aquinas (1224/5–1274)

Inspired by the charism of St Dominic consisting in the principle of *contemplata aliis tradere*, Aquinas picked up the issue of the 'understanding of faith' where Augustine had left it. He tried to penetrate into the mystery of the Trinity by seeking a new understanding. Theology, in fact, was the *'intellectus fidei'*.[61] He described, with exceptional mastery, the life of God as revealed and communicated to humankind in the Persons of the Trinity. His analysis of the eternal origin of the divine Persons may be equalled, but it will never be surpassed. The treatise may be read in the *Summa Theologica*.[62]

In his search for understanding, Thomas remains in the realm of what has been called the 'psychological analogy'. It was the realm opted for by Augustine, albeit with much heart-searching since, as we saw, he felt more attracted to the 'interpersonal' analogy of mutual love where one could 'see' the Trinity, as it were. Thomas brings to his elaboration of the 'psychological analogy' the most acute analysis. In particular, he turns to the interior in order to discover and hone the tools of analogy. These he finds in the soul's threefold faculty or capacity of memory, intellect and will.[63]

Thomas shows how the Father generates the Word in whom he sees himself and all creatures. He then shows how the Father and the Word together 'spirate' the Holy Spirit by loving one another and all creatures. Thus the Son proceeds from the Father by way of 'generation', and the Holy Spirit proceeds from both by way of 'spiration'. In that way Thomas connects in an intelligible pattern the cardinal notions of person, procession and relation. In God the holy Trinity, then, there is one nature or substance, two processions, three Persons and four relations. The four relations are those of the Father to the Son (paternity), the Son to the Father (filiation), the Father and the Son to the Holy Spirit (active spiration), and the Holy Spirit to the Father and the Son (passive spiration). He also connects the missions of the Son and of the Holy Spirit to their respective processions within the Trinity. Thomas' theology of the Trinity is therefore an exceptional contemplation.

The role of relation, therefore, is pivotal. In fact, Thomas arrives at the insight that 'the divine Persons are subsistent relations'.[64] The Father, the Son and the Holy Spirit exist as reciprocal relations that are subsistent, since being-in-itself and relation coincide in God. Now this insight, which is already present in Augustine as we have just seen, has enormous implications for our theology, philosophy and particularly for our daily living. I live fully when I relate and see myself as a gift for the other(s). Aquinas, in fact, writes that 'the person is love: *amor est nomen personae*'.[65] As Walter Kasper writes, 'the ultimate and highest reality is not substance but relation ... The meaning of being is self-communicating love'.[66]

Thomas does not attempt an experience of faith in relation to the Trinity. His Trinitarian theology is the fruit of his reason illuminated by faith and nourished by the Eucharist of whose wonders he is a passionate singer. It is true that Thomas had entered the gateway, but more in the mode of thought than in that of experience. His existence in fact stayed very largely outside. Many have commented on his silence over the last months of his life on foot of that extraordinary experience while saying Mass.[67]

3. St Francis of Assisi (1182–1226) and St Bonaventure (1221–1274)

Bonaventure is the theologian of St Francis in that the extraordinary charism given by God to Francis found its mouthpiece in the seventh general of the Franciscan Order, just as Thomas Aquinas did for St Dominic. Bonaventure saw in the experience of Francis 'an anticipated representation of a new state of revelation'.[68] Like the other great charisms in the history of the Church, this one too had given a glimpse of an aspect of divine revelation. What constituted that 'state' in the case of 'the little poor man' of Assisi?[69] In a particular way, Francis discovered the Crucified Christ to be the way into the bosom of the Father and so into the inner life of the Blessed Trinity. This represents an authentic novelty in the understanding of God the Holy Trinity.

Perhaps the crowning event in the spiritual itinerary of Francis was the gift of the stigmata of the Crucified in September 1224, two years before he died. According to Bonaventure's *Legenda Maior*, Jesus had shown Francis that what most pleased the Lord was Francis' predilection for meditation on the Passion. This had stimulated a fresh ardour in Francis to be conformed in body and soul to the Crucified. It was in that condition that Jesus Crucified appeared to Francis, imprinting upon him the wounds of the Passion. 'The true love of Christ had transformed the lover (Francis) into the image of the Beloved.'[70]

The stigmata are the visible sign that Francis is now so much one with Jesus that he has entered with the risen Jesus into the bosom of the Father (Jn 1:18). Remaining in the flesh, he sees his brothers and sisters, the poor and the lost, the whole of creation itself, all of which he already deeply loved, with totally new eyes of the body and of the heart. This is the context of the *Canticle of the Sun*. In the Christ who had gathered together all of reality (Eph 1:10), things in heaven and things on earth, uniting them in an impossible union of spheres of existence, and in that Christ crucified, Francis had entered into the bosom of the Holy Trinity. The theological, spiritual and cultural implications of this experience gave rise to the Franciscan Order in its many branches, and impacted the whole Church powerfully. The spiritual impact, to take just one of the three aspects, has been such as to inspire both the art of Giotto and the literature of Dante Alighieri (1265–1321).[71]

Bonaventure writes the famous short work, *The Itinerary of the Mind to God*, probably in 1259, in order to describe the stages of the journey to perfect union with God the holy Trinity. With the witness of Francis before his mind, he writes in the Prologue that 'no one penetrates properly into God if not by means of the Crucified ... John in his Apocalypse says, "Blessed are those who wash their robes in the Blood of the Lamb, for they shall have access to the tree of eternal life and shall enter by the gates into the Holy City" (Ap 22:14), as if he were saying that contemplation is not enough to enter into the heavenly Jerusalem, but that it is necessary to pass by means of the Blood of the Lamb who is indeed the entrance'.[72]

4. The Crucified and the Trinity in the 'Interior Castle': Carmelite Mysticism

It is permissible to read the drama and the 'charismatic' experience of Francis as a sign that, in the assimilation of divine revelation, the Crucified Christ becomes a key to our understanding of the Blessed Trinity. The New Testament already stresses the fact that the event of the crucifixion is a Trinitarian event. It is enough to remember that in Luke's account the dying Jesus turns towards God with the words, 'Father, into your hands I commend my spirit' (Lk 23:46). This follows another saying, that to the 'good thief', 'Today, you shall be with me in Paradise' (Lk 23:43). The fact is that the event of the Crucified Christ brings lost humanity, as symbolised in the thief, into the bosom of the Father. That becomes humanity's 'place', as it were. What has happened with Francis, what has been symbolised by Bonaventure, the 'theologian of Francis', is the truth that the Cross is a key to both experiencing and understanding the mystery of the Trinity. Spirituality and theology therefore 'rhyme' in the event of Christ crucified, while the Pauline stress that 'Christ crucified is the power and the wisdom of God' (ICor 1:24) has attained further and fascinating currency.

This becomes a key to reading the pneumatic history of the West in the subsequent centuries. In illustration of this contention, it would be sufficient to mention some strands of that history. For example, in the philosophical strand, one could study the thought of Meister Eckhart or of a Heidegger. In the theological strand, one might mention the contribution of Luther and of three theologians of the last century representing respectively the Orthodox, Protestant and Catholic traditions, namely, Bulgakov, Barth and von Balthasar. Here we will follow the mystical strand as personified in the Carmelite theologian-mystics of the sixteenth century, Teresa of Avila and John of the Cross. It is significant that the Church has named these two as Doctors, a title which indicates that their doctrinal and theological insight is of a unique quality, a quality capable of opening up fresh vistas on what is hitherto concealed or immense, as Augustine did in the fifth century and Aquinas did in the thirteenth.

Both doctors stress that the way that leads to God is the way of self-annihilation, the way of the *nada*. This annihilation is to be lived in the strictest unity with the Crucified Son, since it is he who emptied himself out in the *kenosis*, even to the nothingness and the folly (ICor 1:23) of the cross (Phil 2:8). This allows the very life of the Blessed Trinity to enter the soul. For Teresa, the soul is created to become the 'interior castle' where the Blessed Three may take up their dwelling.

It seems best to begin with the saint of Avila. She stands out as the very personification of the Johannine phrase, 'If anyone loves me, he will keep my words and my Father will love him and we shall come to him and take up our dwelling in him' (14:23). As with Thérèse of Lisieux who seems to 'incarnate' the Scriptural word, 'Unless you change and become like little children you will never enter the kingdom of heaven' (Mt 18:3). Teresa of Avila is the very verification of the Johannine promise. She comments on her 'experience' in these words:

> As soon as one has entered this mansion, the soul discovers as by an intellectual vision the Three Persons of the Blessed Trinity, as in a representation of the truth, in the middle of a fire resembling a shining cloud that comes to its spirit. The three Persons are seen distinctly, and the soul, assisted by a wonderful understanding, with which it is favoured, knows with certainty that each and the three are one only substance, one only power, one only wisdom, one only God; in such a way that what we know by faith the soul knows

almost by sight, although not with the eyes of the body nor the eyes of the soul, it not being an imaginary vision.[73]

As for her colleague and mentor, John of the Cross, he describes the soul's actual participation in the life of the very Three into whose company the soul is ushered by the reality of the Crucified:

> The soul which is united to and transformed into God spirates in God to God the very spiration that God, being in her, spirates in himself to her, which is what I believe to have understood St Paul saying when he wrote, 'Since you are the children of God, God has sent the Spirit of his Son into your hearts who cries out, Abba, Father (Gal 4:6), which is what happens to the perfect in the manner just described.[74]

This brings back the insight of St Augustine who, as we saw, developed the analogy of the operations of the human soul to provide some understanding of the life of the Trinity in itself. There is something very new in John, however: while the operations of the human soul mirror the life of the Blessed Three for Augustine, for John the Blessed Three are contemplated as living and inhabiting the soul of the baptised, eucharistised and sincerely living Christian. Besides, John and Teresa confirm, on the 'experiential' level, both the 'rule of faith' of the Church and the Augustinian and Thomistic 'understanding of faith'.

5. The Adventure of Christian Thinking: The Making of an Omission

We live in an era which is concerned to overcome the exile of the Trinity, that eclipse of the true form of God in the minds of sincere believers. The task, however, is not an easy one, and it requires more than a theological solution. Can one be more precise as to the task involved? To respond to that question, it is perhaps necessary to step back and to reflect on the adventure of Christian revelation in the world it found. As we have seen when considering revelation in relation to the quest at the heart of philosophy in our third chapter, the search for the Absolute, the Beginning, is the constant in all the great cultures, whether mythical, philosophical or religious. Christian revelation also announced the Absolute, and the absolute Beginning (Jn 1:1; I Jn 1:1; Acts 17:20f; Rom 1:18f). That Absolute had a 'face', the Face of the Father of our Lord Jesus Christ. However, revelation was a shock to the point that its first hearers must have marvelled at its bearers (see Acts 17; Jn 9). This Absolute One is Trinity: he is a communion of distinct and co-equal 'subjects', the Father, the Son and the Holy Spirit. The Absolute of Judaism and of Islam, however, is a perfect monad: there is no 'differentiation' in his Being. But with the God of Jesus Christ it is otherwise: the Father is the one eternal God but he is not the Son, the Son is the one eternal God but he is not the Father, and the Holy Spirit is the one eternal God but he is neither the Father nor the Son. To employ an image, these 'nots' are the 'gaps' through which we can enter into the very life and the love of God the holy Trinity, as the famous Rublev icon of the Trinity of Persons so memorably depicts.

This Trinitarian Absolute reaches me: it is not I who go out in search of this Absolute in the first instance. Rather it is this God who comes in search of me, extending towards me and the whole of humankind his 'two arms' in the Persons of the Son and the Holy Spirit. Just as He comes towards me, so he also comes towards the others: the others are precious to Him just as I am. He takes the initiative (IJn 4:19) to seek us out, the Son descending from the Father and descending as far as the cross, the Holy Spirit waking us up to our new belonging (Eph 4:2) as the beloveds of the Father (2Thess 2:13). The events of Easter and of Pentecost 'open out' and communicate to us a God who is both communion in himself and who communicates that very life of communion to us in the Economy, 'gathering together the scattered children of God' (Jn 12: 51f). In a word, the God of Jesus Christ is both ontologically and economically communion. And so it is no surprise that the greatest 'law' that he gives to humanity is the law by which the Holy Trinity live and the Church spreads in the world the sweet odour of the risen Lord, the law, namely, of mutual love.

Now this fact deserves some attention. In all other religions, the other people are my competitors, as it were, on the way towards the Absolute. Since the Absolute is one, other beings represent multiplicity, a falling away from the perfection of the One. All such multiplicity takes from the perfection of the One. The many are the rivals of each other on the journey towards the One. Thus I must renounce the many if I am to arrive at the One. These religions solve the abiding problem of the 'one and the many' simply by eliding the many in the journey to the Absolute who has to be an undifferentiated One. This is essentially the way of Philosophy and of the Great Asian Religions. Thus the great ancient thinkers withdrew from the company of others and from the cosmos in order to be free to journey towards the One-Absolute.

This was the culture that the Apostles entered after Pentecost. Christianity had to make its entry into Greco-Roman world. It, too, announced the Absolute. However, it had to face great difficulty. For example, it had to explain that the One, the Absolute, is Threefold. The episode of Paul at the Areopagus of Athens makes the point vividly. Tertullian (160–240) coins the initial language for that mighty inculturation into Greco-Roman culture as *substantia, persona* and *essentia*. In this One (divine Substance) there are Three (*Personae*): thus the insuperable clash between the One and the Many is solved 'divinely', even if the process still had a long way to go.

Variety and otherness and plurality are no longer a threat on the journey or a falling away from unity, fullness and perfection. On the contrary, the others are in truth a blessing, since both singly and all together we have but one Father in heaven, we are brothers and sisters of the one Son on earth (Heb 2:14f), and are the living temple of the Holy Spirit who rouses us up to realise the greatness of our Father in heaven (Gal 4:6). The many are a source of fullness, enrichment and variety. They are not me, but that 'not' is the expression, the rejoicing and the feast of Being, of the One who is and who is a Trinity of infinite Persons. The first two Ecumenical Councils, in fact, bear testimony to the effort required to establish this 'outline of reality'.

However, all the great thinkers have articulated the Trinity by finding its traces within the individual person, not interpersonally. Beginning with Augustine, they have located those traces in the individual's faculties of memory, intellect and will. The great mystics and 'charismatics' have followed the same path. The framework within which the Christian life happens is and remains the framework of the quest for God within the individual. It is very definitely not a quest for the God who bonds brothers and sisters in unity, giving the gift of his presence in their midst (Mt 18:20). In fact, there was a flight from the brother as there was from the world in order to pre-empt distraction or even temptation. Silence was preferred to the word, and solitude to assembly. *The Imitation of Christ*, to take a famous example, quotes Tacitus to the effect that to go out among others is to suffer automatic damage both humanly and spiritually! We definitely do not go to God together! We definitely are not a family on the holy journey that leads to our true homeland (Heb 13:14)! St Augustine's *City of God* is an exaggeration as to the lifestyle of the city of believers, a Utopia as to its practical and daily living! There has never been a 'spirituality of communion' in the history of the Church.

Now at the same time as the most 'social' of all the mysteries was being 'individualised' and 'privatised', a further development was afoot. This consisted in the affirmation of the value of the human being as human being. The anthropology was individualist, however, not Trinitarian. It owed more to Boethius' idea of the person than to that of Augustine. There was the affirmation of the autonomy of creation as such. Each person should fulfil him/herself, not only in the quest for the Absolute, but also in his or her self-expression at the level of secular reality. To fulfil myself, it is not sufficient, in other words, to plunge deep within myself to find there the Absolute that is Trinity. To fulfil myself I also need to go outside myself to others and to created reality. But the others and created reality are not perceived as connected to the Trinity, and less still as within the mystery of the revealed Trinity. Rather, the Trinity is a mystical reality, while other people and creation are a second and further project. There is a profound parting of the ways.

Spiritual life is organised around the Trinity understood in the individualistic mode, but the life of culture is organised around what is secular. Culture is increasingly placed in opposition to the spiritual experience of the mystic and of believers.

It is enough to look at the history of theology or of spirituality to perceive this parting of the ways. There one notices that the Trinity is relegated to the realm of 'the spirituality of the individual', while the secular and human spheres take on a life of their own outside the great space opened up by the revelation of the Trinity in Christ. With time these two orientations separate and go their own ways in spite of the efforts of the great 'spirituals' such as Ignatius or Teresa or John of the Cross. Theology anchored to life should have kept them together as it had largely done in the first millennium.

From approximately the end of the fourteenth century, however, the theologian travels in one direction, the 'spiritual' in another direction. Referring to that history, Hans Urs von Balthasar is well within the mark when he writes:

> The impoverishment brought about by the divorce between the two spheres is all too plain; it has sapped the vital force of the Church of today and the credibility of her preaching of eternal truth ... (T)hose who have to preach to the modern pagans ... long to discover the living organism of the Church's doctrine, rather than a strange anatomical dissection: on the one hand, the bones without the flesh, 'traditional theology'; on the other, the flesh without the bones, that very pious literature that serves up a compound of asceticism, mysticism, spirituality and rhetoric, a porridge that, in the end, becomes indigestible through lack of substance.[75]

John Henry Newman identified, in quite another context,[76] what happens when a component part of reality is omitted. He named three results. They are the ignorance of the omitted component, the resulting distortion and deformation of the whole, and the usurpation on the part of something else of the area vacated by the omitted component. By deploying this phenomenology of Newman, we may perceive better the bitter fruits of the inadequate appropriation of the revealed Trinity in the life of the People of God and in the course of the history of the Church of God.

Since the Blessed Trinity is not appropriated in its essential implications for the life of Christians with God and with one another, since the essential dimensions of relation and communion disappear from the popular horizon, the great mystery fades from the living awareness of believers. People soon become ignorant of the omitted component. This is what theologians and Church historians call 'the exile of the Trinity'.

The Jerusalem community, according to the witness of the Acts of the Apostles, lived by four principles, 'These remained faithful to the teaching of the apostles, to the koinonia, to the breaking of bread, and to the prayers' (2:42). The second pillar of that Pentecost community was communion in both its vertical and horizontal dimensions. This community made them 'one mind and one heart' (4:32). As for St Paul, he loved to remind his communities that they are members of each other, so that 'if one part is hurt, all parts are hurt with it. If one part is given special honour, all parts enjoy it' (1Cor 12:26). As for St John, he proclaimed to his communities the extreme love of God for them (Jn 13:1; 19:31-37), and then concluded, 'If that is how God has loved us, we too should love one another' (IJn 4:11). From the revelation of God as Trinitarian Love there flows the imperative of mutual love! This is the only way by which the 'world' will see the God of Jesus Christ (Jn 13:35)! This is the sure way to manifest the religion of Christ to the whole of humankind.

Secondly, there is a certain deformation of the whole. St Thomas had identified completeness and proportion and radiance as essential components of the beautiful.[77] Since the Trinity as the central mystery in the total Mystery of Faith has been greatly reduced, with major dimensions being lost and forgotten, there follows inevitably an imbalanced version of the Faith. The account of the hope that Christians are called upon to give to their unbelieving brothers and sisters (IPet 3:15) suffers a major deficit. What may be marginal is made central, and vice versa. The unifying light of fullness no longer shines over the contents of faith. The analogy of faith becomes irrelevant, and, grotesquely, a part may begin to stand for the whole. Just as the human body loses its beauty when member(s) are amputated or misshapen, so too the Body of Christ (ICor 12) does not shine as it ought in the world (Phil 2:13) nor radiate the light for humankind (Mt 5:14-16).

Finally, the place of the Trinity as the integrating and illuminating core of the whole will be occupied. The human spirit with its insatiable thirst for order and sequence will still look for the core. Something else, invariably further down the 'hierarchy of truths',[78] will therefore usurp the very place and functions of the Trinity in 'the faith given once for all to the saints' (Jude 3). Accordingly, the 'catholicity of the real' will be dented and diminished. Thus the phenomenon of the pursuit of the 'first principle' of revelation emerges.[79]

We have seen how the reflection of the Church, drawing as it does from the sources of divine revelation over the past two millennia, guided by the Holy Spirit and under the intellectual handling of seminal thinkers, has inspired a remarkable 'understanding' of the central mystery of divine revelation. Invariably, a particular charism engendered a fresh 'experience' of the mystery, a kind of 'tasting knowledge'. A number of features of that understanding have stood out. It would be helpful to name them at this juncture in our inquiry. By doing so it would perhaps be easier to realise more thoroughly the indispensable elements of the 'understanding of faith' hitherto achieved, as well as anticipate some new horizons in the search for further understanding.

First, the category of 'relation' emerged. St Augustine was our benefactor here. He saw that the very life of love among human beings was relational, in fact, 'tri-relational'. In the light of the Johannine texts extolling mutual love and stressing that 'anyone who lives in love lives in God' (IJn 4:16), he set out to enable us to 'see the Trinity'. Then there was the category of 'person' thanks to Augustine and to the Cappadocian Fathers of the fourth century, Basil the Great, Gregory Nazianzen and Gregory of Nyssa. A divine Person is a relation, a subsistent relation. Then there was Thomas Aquinas. He employed these breakthroughs in an original synthesis which, however, remained strictly within the 'psychological analogy'.

The remarkable charism of Francis of Assisi led to the discovery that no one 'may properly enter the mystery of the Trinity except via the Crucified Christ'. If the bosom of the Father is the locus for the theological project, then the love for the Crucified who unites humankind to the Father, each person to every other person, and all humankind to creation, is the 'method' par excellence for the doing of theology. He stressed universal humankind, and famously sang a hymn for a creation caught up into the risen Christ, an ecology become canticle. St Bonaventure gave this experience its theological form, even highlighting how all the human sciences and works – the *artes* – could be united in Christ, 'the Art of the Father'.[80] As Thomas drew out the theology contained in the 'experience of faith' of St Dominic, so Bonaventure drew out the experience of Francis into a theology.

The great doctors of the Carmelite movement in sixteenth century Spain, Teresa and John, drew on all these acquisitions. However, they evolved a further 'experience of faith', namely, that of the actual indwelling of the Blessed Trinity in the soul and the resultant Christian life. This experience in turn yielded a new theology. Their insight, focused and sharpened by the acquisitions of the ages, led to a simple reading of Scripture that was, at one and the same time, a further charism in the Church. Thus Teresa personally appropriated the text of John 14:23, 'If anyone loves me, he will keep my words, and my Father and I shall come to him and make our dwelling in him', to the point that she seems to be their very 'personification'. John of the Cross assimilated the accumulated insights of the tradition to attain a similar 'appropriation' of Galatians 4:6: 'God has sent the Spirit of his Son into our hearts by which we cry, "Abba! Father".' Together they highlighted for the whole Church a new way of accessing and of living out the life of the Holy Trinity. Still, it was a life within an 'interior castle'. Why not an 'exterior castle' as well? Does not the same Trinity exist in the souls of one's fellow-Christians? Should not this be recognised so that Christ could dwell among those united in his name (Mt 18:20)?

The 'understanding' of the Trinity, then, remained within an 'individual mould'. It concerned our access to the Father, through the Son and in the Holy Spirit (Eph 2:18). The net result has been that even the 'articulated access' and divinely structured way to the Father through the mediating Son, in the sanctifying Holy Spirit, has 'flattened out'. For all practical purposes, the names of the Persons are but names for God. A practical nominalism thus reigns at the core of the Faith. That nominalism washes out the content of faith, flattens the dynamism of the liturgy, and walls off the holy space opened up by the Redeemer of humankind for his brothers and sisters. Perhaps most injurious of all for the Gospel that is obsessed by the unity of the human family (Henri de Lubac), it excludes the other, 'the brother for whom Christ died' (ICor 8:11). It makes the most communitarian of all faiths an individual duty. Liturgically and publicly we are Trinitarian, privately we are monotheistic. Could it be that Catholic faith has nothing essential to do with society or with the great dilemmas of modern men and women?

How can Christians now conceive that they are actually located by the sacraments of initiation, as celebrated in the divine liturgy, in the space opened up in the Spirit between the abandoned Son and the Father of Mercies? How can they know that they are members of each other? Although Augustine himself had seen quite clearly that mutual love and the experience thereof provided the locus for both and experience and understanding of the ineffable mystery, he did not go in there, as we have seen. Besides, although the categories of relation and of person are well forged in the tradition, it was the individualist notion of the human person that gained the ascendancy, not the relational. Famously, Boethius defined in the sixth century the human person as 'an individual substance of rational nature'.[81] His definition became practically dominant. It effectively reduced person to substance, and banished the notion that the living out of relation as

authentic love is essential to becoming a person. It is now only a short step to understanding the Divine Three as Three Individuals. The charge of 'tritheism' is around the corner.

But there was a still greater lacuna: the very text of divine revelation was overlooked, particularly the witness of the Fourth Gospel. Christ had prayed, on the night before he suffered, that 'all may be one'. He specified that unity in clear personal and relational categories, 'As you, Father, are in me, and I am in you'. The Trinity is the *Lebensraum* of Christians, while the Mystery shapes and forms the communion of believers to the extent that, as the Council reminds us, 'They are a people made one from the unity of the Father, the Son and the Holy Spirit'.[82] The Redeemer, further, indicated the necessary prerequisite for that 'trinity-stamped' unity: it consists in the law of mutual love. Reciprocity or mutuality is of the very essence of our life and place with the God and Father of our Lord Jesus Christ!

He specifies the measure of this mutual love: 'Love one another *as* I have loved you.' It is a measure that is without measure. And he names the fruits, the extraordinary fruits, of that life when he adds, 'By this love you have for one another, all will know that you are my disciples' (Jn 13:35). It will be the secret to the credibility of the Church. We will be able to say 'God' only if we are communion! And lest anyone might think that all this is anything less than the deepest desire of his heart, he calls the new commandment both 'his' and 'new': it is appropriate to the New Covenant and indispensable for the inauguration of the Kingdom. If this is the Gospel of Christ, if this is the very summit of the Fourth Gospel, how can our understanding of the central Mystery of Faith remain locked into the individual perspective?

How can we tolerate any longer the loss of an 'effective' ('By this all men will know …') and 'fruitful' ('… so that the world will believe') presence or 'sacramentality' in the world?[83] Modern men and women seem less capable of finding God vertically. God must be made present for them by being present among those united in his name (Mt 18:20). This fact, however, shouts out the need to manifest the God of Jesus Christ to them horizontally! The vocation of Christians is to show

God to their brothers and sisters. This call is a fresh opportunity for Christians today to undertake that evangelisation to which recent Popes have called them. How can we continue to close our eyes to the Trinity without which God is not beautiful and Christians are neither credible nor attractive?

The history of the dogma, however, throws up a constant fact, namely, it was theologians who as either great charismatics, or else as the interpreters of a charismatic, often opened up new vistas in our understanding of divine revelation. Is there a charism about today that can fulfil that role for our times? Is there an articulation of that charism or a charismatic that can help us overcome the scandal of the exile of the Trinity from the spiritual and daily life of believers in our times? From the great 'worlds' that create and drive contemporary culture, such as communications, economics, politics, art, education, medicine, social engineering, to name but a few? After all, did not Pope Paul VI describe the separation of faith from contemporary culture as the greatest drama of our times? How can the Trinitarian God of Jesus Christ inspire a new culture as he did so powerfully until the beginning of the modern period and beyond? That is the question. The answer is already hinted at: if someone shows us how to live the Gospel of the words and the deeds of Jesus, just as the great charismatics and their theologians did. It will always be the case that 'only if Christ can be practised is Jesus Lord'.[84]

6. Chiara Lubich (1920–) and the Mystery of the Trinity

In the whole history of Christian spirituality, there has never been a strictly communitarian spirituality. There have of course been instances where charity was put at the basis of the Christian life. It is enough to think of St Basil the Great who founded monasteries for men and women. Stressing the necessity of the other person, he wondered how we can live the Gospel if there is no one to serve and no one to make us practise patience. St Augustine, enamoured as he was by the splendour of love in all its echelons, placed fraternal charity at the basis of his *Rule*. These are exceptions, however, and only prove the rule that there never has been a strictly communitarian spirituality based on the law of the life of the Trinity and incarnating the new commandment!

Or almost never! The last century saw the birth and rapid diffusion of a spirituality that was radically communitarian. During the experience of the mutual hatred of the Second World War, Chiara Lubich and several young companions in Trent discovered that the unity of all humanity according to the pattern of the life of the Trinity is the deepest desire of the heart of Jesus. 'Father, may they be one in us, as you are in me and I am in you' (Jn 17:21). The adventure of living the Gospel of mutual love in a situation of mutual hatred where every day could be their last made them look out for the commandment that was most loved by Jesus: they discovered and lived the New Commandment (Jn 13:34; 15:12) as the way to go. 'Above all, never let your love for each other grow insincere' (IPet 4:8): this and other texts seemed underlined by the Holy Spirit, while the fragility of life in war-torn Trent made them live out these living words as if each day could be their last.

It is enough to quote just two short texts of Chiara Lubich in order to see the form of this new spirituality of Trinitarian communion. 'God who is in me, who has shaped my soul, who dwells in it as Trinity, is also in my neighbour's heart ... And just as I love him in myself, recollecting myself in him when I am alone, so too I love him in my neighbour when he or she is beside me.'[85] The next text underlines how this is the very life of the eternal Three, the Father, the Son and the Holy Spirit:

> The Father generates the Son out of love: he loses himself in the Son, he lives in him; in a certain sense he makes himself 'non-being' out of love, and for this very reason, he is, he is the Father. The Son, as echo of the Father, out of love turns to him, he loses himself in the Father, he lives in him, and in a certain sense he makes himself 'non-being' out of love; and for this very reason, he is, he is the Son. The Holy Spirit, since he is the mutual love between the

> Father and the Son, their bond of unity, in a certain sense
> he also makes himself 'non-being' out of love, and for this
> very reason, he is, he is the Holy Spirit.[86]

What St Augustine aspired to in apostolic church life and wrote
about in the *De Trinitate* has in the Providence of God come about.
The Trinity is the key model for all humankind and all societies!

Writing about the Church of the future, Karl Rahner had this to
say:

> If there is an experience of the Spirit made in common, an
> experience recognised as such,...it is clearly the experience
> of the first Pentecost in the Church, an event – it must be
> presumed – which did not consist surely in the casual
> gathering of a number of individual mystics, but in the
> experience of the Spirit had by the community ... I suspect
> that the element of a fraternal, spiritual fellowship, of a
> communally lived spirituality, can play a greater part and
> be slowly but courageously acquired and developed.[87]

In fact, that is the very route announced at the Council and
underlined at the Extraordinary Synod of 1985 which declared
'communion' to be the encompassing idea of the Council. In his
Apostolic Letter for the new millennium, *Novo Millennio Ineunte*,
Pope John Paul II declared that the greatest task facing the Church
is to make her 'the home and the school of communion'.

Notes

1. George Bernanos, 'Christianity and the Writer's Task', in *Communio*, XXXVIII (2001), 208.

2. St Augustine, *De Trinitate*, VII, 3, 7: translation is from Edmund Hill, *Saint Augustine. The Trinity*, New York 1991, 225.

3. H. de Lubac, *Catholicism. The Social Aspects of Dogma*, London 1950, xiii, quoting Jean Giono, *Les vraies richesses*, 1936, viii.

4. St Augustine, *Homily 26, 4 on St John's Gospel*, PL 35, 1608; see the same argument as employed by Cardinal Newman, *Discourses to Mixed Congregations*, London 1921, 67–72. In the estimation of Henri de Lubac, Newman is 'heir to their way of thought', in *Catholicism*, 150

5. *Dei Verbum*, 1.

6. St Augustine, *De catechizandis rudibus*, IV, 8: PL 40, 316: quoted in DV 1.

7. David Bentley Hart, *The Beauty of the Infinite. The Aesthetics of Christian Truth*, Michigan 2003, 16.

8. Plato, *Symposium, passim*.

9. Simone Weil, *L'ombra e la grazia*, Milano 1985, 156.

10. See St Augustine, *Sermons Guelf*, 3 (Breviary, Holy Week, Monday), 'Why is human weakness slow to believe that men will one day live with God? A much more incredible thing has already happened: God died for men ... Of ourselves we did not have the ability to live, as of himself he did not have the ability to die. Accordingly he carried out a wonderful transaction with us through our mutual sharing: he died from what was ours, we will live from what is his'.

11. See Vera Donnelly, O.P., *Gestalt as the integrating Motif in the Christology of Hans Urs von Balthasar*, doctoral dissertation (DD), St Patrick's College, Maynooth, 2004.

12. St Augustine, *De Trinitate*, VI, 2, 11; St Bonaventure picks up the same idea in the *Itinerarium Mentis in Deum*.

13. Pope John Paul II, *Letter to Artists* (1999), no. 5; see Hans Urs von Balthasar, *The Glory of the Lord: A Theological Aesthetics*, I, *Seeing the Form*, San Francisco 1982, 216.

14. David Bentley Hart, ibid., 4.

15. Henri de Lubac, *La Foi chrétienne*, Paris 1970, 22; see Michael Mullins, *The Gospel of John. A Commentary*, Dublin 2003, 112–120.

16. David Tracy, 'The hidden God: the Divine Other of Liberation', *Cross Currents* 46, 1(1996), 5–6.

17. Dogmatic Constitution on Divine Revelation, *Dei Verbum*, 2.

18. St Irenaeus, *Adversus Haereses*, IV,7,4; IV,20,1; V,1,3; V,5,1; V,6,1;V,28,4; *Demonstratio Apostolica*, 11.

19. Pope John Paul II, *Redemptor hominis*, 8.

20. In the prologue of the work Augustine writes, 'De Trinitate quae Deus summus et verus est libros iuvenis inchoavi, senex edidi'. The work therefore coincides with the central portion of his theological and pastoral adventure.

21. See Enrique Cambon, *Trinità modello sociale*, Rome 1999

22. I. Kant, *Il conflitto delle facolte*, Genoa 1953, 47.

23. Karl Rahner, *Mysterium Salutis* 3, Brescia 1969, 404.

24. Catherine LaCugna, *God for Us. The Trinity and Christian Life*, New York, 1991; see Patricia A. Fox, *God as Communion. John Zizioulas, Elizabeth Johnson, and the Retrieval of the Symbol of the Triune God*, Collegeville, MA 2001.

25. See K. Rahner, *The Trinity*, London 1970.

26. See for example the claim of N. Ciola that 'Trinitarian theology is the grammar of all Theology', in *Teologia trinitaria, storia, metodo, prospettive*, Bologna 1996, 198.

27. See John Paul II, *Novo millennio ineunte*, 43.

28. Marxism, for instance, could be seen as a Messianic and de-divinised version of the communion for which the blessed Trinity was communicated to the world. See Eric Voegelin, *The New Science of Politics*, Chicago and London 1952, 112–132.

29. St Augustine would have been familiar with earlier attempts to write a theology of the Trinity: see *De Trinitate*, I, 2, 7.

30. *De Trinitate*, I, 3, 5.

31. A. Trapè, *Agostino. L'uomo, il pastore, il mistico*, Roma 2001, 358: translation my own.

32. Cardinal Newman makes the comment that 'St Athanasius or St Augustine has a life which a system of theology has not', in *Lectures on Justification*, London 1874, 31, n.1.

33. Hans Urs von Balthasar, *Theo-Logic. III:The Spirit of Truth*, San Francisco 2003, p. 22.

34. St Augustine, *Confessions*, VII, 10.

35. *De Vera Religione*, XXXIX, 72: CCL 32, 234.

36. *Confessions*, III, 4, 'aestu cordis incredibili sapientiam quaerebam'.

37. St Augustine, *Confessions,*VII, 10.

38. Vladimir Solovyov, *Divine Humanity*, New York 1995, 94–95.

39. It is enough to read his *De doctrina Christiana*, I, 35, 39 where he writes, 'This is the summary of all that has been said: that it be understood that the fullness and the purpose of the Law and of all the divine Scriptures is love'. (See ibid., 36, 40). In 16, 15 he writes, 'Christ bonds together his Body, which is composed of many members fulfilling different tasks, by means of the bond of unity and of charity, which is the sign of its health'.

40. Piero Coda, 'Il *De Trinitate* di Agostino e la sua Promessa', in *Nuova Umanità*, XXIV(2002/2–3), 225–226.

41. *De Trinitate*, IV, 9.

42. Ibid, I, 5.

43. St Augustine, *Homily 26, 4 on St John's Gospel*, PL 35, 1608.

44. *De Trinitate*, V, 11, 12; see Joseph Ratzinger, 'Der heilige Geist als Communio' in *Weggemeinschaft des Glaubens*, Augsburg 2002, 34–52, especially at 37 where he writes that 'the communication between Father and Son into full unity is not to be seen as into a general ontic consubstantiality but as communion, not as if from a general metaphysical material (*Wesensstoff*) as it were, but as resulting from the Persons'. Translation my own.

45. Ibid, V, 6.

46. Aristotle, *Categories*, 4 1 b 25; see also his *Metaphysics*, XIV, 1088a, 20–25.

47. *De Trinitate*, V, 6.

48. Piero Coda, ibid.,240.

49. Joseph Ratzinger, ibid., 140–141; Walter Kasper makes a similar claim, 'This entails a revolution in the understanding of being. The ultimate and highest reality is not substance but relation –', *The God of Jesus Christ*, New York 1991, 154–156. In chapter XIII on ontology we shall attempt to suggest an approach towards a Trinitarian ontology.

50. *De Trinitate*, XV, 6, 10,

51. *Confessions*, XIII, 11.

52. *De Trinitate*, VIII, 7, 10; it is quite remarkable how a contemporary author such as Eberhard Jüngel should come to the same position again as Augustine when he writes, 'God is not only I loving and You loved. Rather, God is the irradiating event of love itself ... God in giving himself possesses himself and so is. His self-possession is the event, the history of a giving of self and in this sense the goal of any mere self-possession. As this history he is God. Indeed, this history of love is 'God himself', in *God the Mystery of the World*, Brescia 1982, 427.

53. *De Trinitate*, VIII, 7, 11.

54. Ibid., VIII, 8, 12.

55. Ibid., VIII, 10, 14.

56. Ibid.

57. Ibid., XV, 10; see the study of Maurice Nedoncelle, 'L'intersubjectivité humaine: est-elle pour Saint Augustin in image de la Trinité?' in *idem*, *Explorations personalistes*, Paris 1970, 213–222.

58. *Dei Verbum*, 8.

59. See John Henry Newman's naming of the 'development of dogma' as the tenth 'first principle' of Catholicism in later editions of his *Essay on the Development of Christian Doctrine*.

60. St Augustine, *De Trinitate* XV, 28, 31.

61. See St Thomas, *Summa*, II-II, q.8, a. 6 c; see Bernard Lonergan, 'Theology and Understanding' in *Collection*, London 1967, 121–141.

62. St Thomas, *Summa*, I, qq. 27–43.

63. See Bernard Lonergan, *Verbum. Word and Idea in Aquinas*, London 1968.

64. St Thomas, *Summa*, I, q.29, a.4.

65. Ibid., I, q.37, a.1 c.

66. Walter Kasper, *The God of Jesus Christ*, 156.

67. See the *Processus*, n.79, 376s; Bruno Forte, *Il silenzio di Tommaso*, Napoli 1998.

68. Joseph Ratzinger, *San Bonaventura. La teologia della storia*, Firenze 1991, 147–148.

69. G.K. Chesterton's biography, *St Francis of Assisi*, London 1923 still provides a most exceptional insight into the essential Francis, just as his biography of St Thomas also does for the *Doctor Angelicus*.

70. St Bonaventure, *Legenda*, XIII, 5.

71. Dante Alighieri, *Paradiso*, Canto XI.

72. St Bonaventure, *Itinerarium Mentis in Deum*, Prologue, 3; see also IV, 2–3; VI, 4-7; VII, 1–2.

73. St Teresa of Avila, *The Interior Castle*, vol. VII, 1, 6.

74. St John of the Cross, *The Spiritual Canticle*, A, Stropha 38, 3.

75. Hans Urs von Balthasar, *Word and Redemption*, New York 1965, 65.

76. John Henry Newman, *The Idea of a University*, numerous editions.

77. St Thomas, *Summa*, I, q.39, a.8.

78. Second Vatican Council, Decree on Ecumenism *Unitatis Redintegratio*, 11.

79. See Piero Coda, 'Sulla logica trinitaria della verità cristiana', in *Nuova Umanità*, XXVII 1(2005), 57–75.

80. St Bonaventure, *De reductione artium in Deum*, 20 quoting St Augustine, *De Trinitate*, VI, 10, 11: PL 42, 931.

81. Boethius, *Liber de persona et duabus naturis*, 3: PL 64, 1343.

82. Second Vatican Council, Dogmatic Constitution on the Church *Lumen gentium* 4, quoting Cyprian and Augustine.

83. See *Lumen gentium* 1; 4.

84. David Bentley Hart, ibid., 1.

85. Chiara Lubich, 'Look at all the Flowers' in *An Introduction to the Abba School. Conversations with the Focolare's Interdisciplinary Study Center*, New York 2002, 104.

86. 'Elementi di Spiritualita nella Chiesa del Futiro', in T. Goffi and B. Secondin, *Problemie prospettive di Spiritualità*, Brescia 1983, 440–441.

Epilogue

The cross of our Lord was the key through which the realities that were hidden will be opened.[1]

The God who communicates his life to us in Jesus Christ and in the Holy Spirit chose the way of incarnation. In doing so he elected to die, for to say incarnation is to say cross. He chose not only to be one of us, but also to enter the human condition fully, 'being found in human form' (Phil 2:7) and 'by God's grace experiencing death for all of mankind' (Heb 2:9). This means that Christianity is eminently an historical and existential religion.

Just as in the Word made flesh of our flesh and bone of our bone there is neither separation nor confusion between divinity and humanity, so too the God who joins in the procession of time neither floats above our history nor swallows it up. This 'criterion of Chalcedon'[2] throws light on how the Gospel on its course through time avoids two forms of destruction: first, there is the Scylla of historicism by which the events constituting the history of salvation are increasingly relativised. Second, there is the Charybdis of Platonism which denies substance and significance to these same events. The truth is that time becomes a dimension of divinity through the incarnation, death and resurrection of Christ. The God of Jesus Christ could have been content with a word, but he gave us his very life at the appalling cost of the cross and the abandonment that we 'may have life and have it to the full' (Jn 10:10).

The earliest creeds make the point succinctly, 'We have come to believe in the love which God has for us' (IJn 4:16). Those first Christians had noticed the bridge which God had thrown across the great divide separating God and humankind, for a bridge is needed precisely there where the human pilgrimage can go no further. Now divinity and humanity are one, *with divinity being always more* and so always overtaking us and surprising us. Christ is 'the beginning and the end, Alpha and Omega, all time belongs to him and all the ages', as the vigil liturgy of Easter, itself encapsulating the total mystery of Christ, joyfully proclaims. So taken by this word of life and love were the first Christians that they tried to match such generosity. 'God loved us first' (IJn 4:19), indeed, but they added at once, 'since God has loved us so much, we too should love one another' (I Jn 4:11). St Ignatius of Antioch declared that he was 'an imitator of the passion of my God'.[3] About the same time, the beginning of the second century, the writer of the *Letter to Diognetus* saw the body of Christians in the Empire as the very soul of that great commonwealth.[4] The Church was neither a private corporation nor a spiritual taste, but a visible body with observable social contours and significance. Approximately a century later, Tertullian could write, 'We were born only yesterday and have spread into all the world.' The secret of such diffusion, however, was the life by which they lived, 'Look how these Christians love one another and are willing to die for each other'.[5] In that time and in that way the nascent Church strove and prevailed against the very Empire that persecuted her relentlessly.

This book, however, is not about the early Church. Its focus is a question that is twofold: how did Europe, where the first great evangelisation occurred with the resultant first striking inculturation of the Gospel, come to reject the paschal mystery of Christ in the era of the Enlightenment? And how did that phenomenon actually *open up a surprisingly fresh reading of hitherto undetected dimensions of divine revelation?*[6] The rejection did not occur outside of Europe, as Pope John Paul II reminded the bishops of Europe in 1982. '... we can affirm that these trials, these temptations and this result of the European drama not only question Christianity and the Church from outside as a difficulty or an external obstacle, but in a certain sense, they occur within Christianity and within the Church.'[7] How did this dark night of God, this 'collective' and 'epochal dark night', emerge? It leads in fact to a schizophrenia in Europe, a schizophrenia that separates Church from society, revelation from history, and faith from reason. The study you have just read deals, in part one, with this separation, describing and, as far as practicable, speaking to that separation. The second part of the work begins a 'dialogue of insight' from out of the very core of the Christian faith *as studied in the context of the loss of God.* In the words of the renowned Orthodox theologian, Sergei Bulgakov, could it be the case that 'the total problematic of our times, with its premonitions and omens, is nothing other than the shadow thrown by the One who is coming?'[8]

The first chapter provides a brief account of how Europe lost that home in which Europeans had lived for almost two millennia *and now exports that loss to other continents.* In the second chapter, three thinkers respond to this schizophrenia of our times. In very different contexts and within very different ecclesial settings, John Henry Newman, Eric Voegelin and Bernard Lonergan articulate the dimensions of the separation between the components of reality. The result is an understanding of the origin of 'weak reason' and its functioning. If the access to spiritual reality is declared impassible or delusory, then great indeed will be the resulting night.

This contention is confirmed in the next chapter where the drama of revelation's relation to the human search is highlighted. The fracturing of that relationship stands out as the greatest drama of our time. Yes, it is true, as Vatican I stresses, that the question of God falls within the range of human reason. However, that reason has been so fractured and so confined to its scientific and technological deployments that it has forgotten its more original and daring accomplishments in religion, philosophy and theology. 'What then has been the radical drama of the West? That the subject, a providential and irreversible conquest of humanity, absolutises itself, places itself outside God, asking questions about him "from outside". From being mystery, God becomes a problem.'[9] Accordingly, we now face the fact of a reason too little converted (Henri de Lubac).

This scenario needs one thing above all else: it needs to hear again the good news of Jesus Christ, 'your hope of glory' (Col 1:27). It needs to perceive the inbreaking beauty of the Father's glory in his Son crucified (2Cor 4:6) for us (Rom 8:32; Gal 2:20). As the beloved Son of the Father, he brings with him the life of the Trinity. Jesus announces the one God, but he opens him out to us and for us *as a Trinity of Persons.* 'On that day you will understand that I am in my Father and you in me and I in you' (Jn 14:20). Chapters four and five attempt to propose the biblically grounded history of 'God with us,' a God who, according to Pope Benedict's first encyclical, in 'his death on the Cross is the culmination of that turning of God against himself in which he gives himself in order to raise man up and save him'.[10] The objective of Part II of this book is to propose 'the word of faith' (Rom 10:8) again, *but in the light of the loss of God in our culture, as well as in the light of the appalling impact of this loss.*

Very concrete and radical questions arise. Have we understood the kind of God revealed in the abandonment on the Cross (Mk 15:34; Mt 27:46)? 'Is the God of Christians Christian?', inquires Bruno Forte.[11] At the summit of salvation history, the Son of the Father dies in our godforsaken distance from the one he called 'Abba' (Mk 14:36). He is accursed because hanging on the cross (Gal 3:13; Dt 21:23) and still fulfils superabundantly the drama of God's struggle, begun in the Old Covenant, for the heart of humankind. Here is the Word that has been growing down the ages fully unfolded, totally 'exegeted' (Jn 1:18). Have we looked upon him whom we have pierced, particularly with the sword of his awful God-abandonment (Jn 19:37; Zc 12:10)? The Son wishes us to have his Father, and in *giving* us that Father the Son has the experience of *losing* him. Is not this the Face of God for today (chapter six)? He is the God who cancels himself out of love for us: He is because he is a nothing-out-of-love-for-us who wound him with our unlove (Is 53:5).

It was necessary, as the Scriptures like to repeat (Lk 24:26), for the Son to do it that way. Here is the mind of Christ. St Paul tells us in *First Corinthians*, however, that 'we have the mind (*nous*) of Christ' (2:16).

Now, since it is Jesus who both knows the Father and wishes to reveal him to us, we must speak of 'the Theology of Jesus' *and our participation in that very Theology*. We have not dared to think of *where the redeeming Son and the sanctifying Spirit want to place us*! In chapter Seven, however, we dare to look at, and to spell out, the amazing relationships that define our life in Christ, relationship becoming as important as substance, indeed even more so! 'Father, I want those you have given me to be with me where I am, so that they may always see the glory you have given me' (Jn 17:24). And since Vatican II's constitution on divine revelation emphasises this re-location, chapter eight articulates the Trinitarian milieu where we now live and move and have our being.

'We have the mind of Christ', then. Notice that St Paul says 'we'. He highlights the significance of that plural when he writes, 'All of you are one person in Christ Jesus' (Gal 3:28). A new subject exists in history as the fruit of the Son's forsakenness, glorification and prayer. This is the Church properly understood, as the great Council stressed. The practical implications are immediate. 'We have to discover, first of all in life, then in thought – because thought always follows life – a kind of thinking, a culture, that would be as *perichoretic*, as reciprocally interpersonal as the life of the Trinity.'[12] The truth is that the incarnate Son gives us access in the Holy Spirit to the Father (Eph 2:18). In the love of the divine Persons for each Other, one understands that love is a personal exodus. Accordingly, each divine Person lives in the Others, thereby setting up the eternal being-in-one-another-through-love that is the life of our homeland, the Trinity. This means that each divine Person is a nothingness of love. He both *is* and *is not*, but even when he *is not* he *is*, because he is a nothingness of love, the nothingness that is total being-for-the-Others. Now this great truth finds its historical economy in the cry of abandonment of the Father-forsaken Son on the wood of the Cross.

Only if we understand this do we understand that 'God is love'. Otherwise the summit of New Testament revelation becomes a pious platitude. The kenotic and forsaken Son not only redeems, he also manifests the truth of reality *and so also the contours of an authentic culture*. I am if I am not, out of love! I am not if I am not loving. As the Italian theologian, Piero Coda, shows, the Word and Nothingness coincide in the *kenosis*, this nothingness that is total love, a Love that is Trinitarian, forsaken and glorified.[13]

Perhaps it is now possible to appreciate the centrality of Jesus' teaching on the life of love in the gospels. The culture of the Trinity had become flesh on earth at the cost and in the measure of the forsakenness on the wood of the Cross. Jesus, in fact, had translated that culture of love into our world, showing by his doing and his teaching (A 1:1) a very *concrete art of loving*. The key to the new culture that the Father of our Lord Jesus Christ offers to men and women in the third millennium is that very art of loving. This art will be able to mend the fracture of the relationship between Christian faith and the culture of the West.

Notes

1. St Augustine, *In Psalmum XLC*, 1 in CCL, 38, 518.
2. Bernard Sesbouë, *Jésus-Christ dans la tradition de l'Eglise* (coll. 'Jésus et Jésus-Christ', 17), Paris 1982, 165–174.
3. Ignatius of Antioch, *Epistle to the Romans*, 6.
4. *The Epistle to Diognetus*, 5–6.
5. Tertullian, *Apologeticum*, 37,4 and 39,7 in CSEL 69.
6. Pope John Paul II, *Memory and Identity*, London 2005, 109–110.
7. *Idem*, Address to the Fifth Conference of European Bishops in 1982, as quoted by Giuseppe Zanghí, 'A Reflection on Postmodernity' in *Being One*, 7(1998), 80–81.
8. Sergei Bulgakov, *La luce senza tramonto*, Rome 2002, 4. Translation my own.
9. Giuseppe Zanghí, 'A Reflection on Postmodernity', ibid., 83; see his recent *Notte della cultura europea. Agonia della terra del tramonto?*, Rome 2007.
10. Pope Benedict XVI, Encyclical *Deus caritas est*, 12.
11. Bruno Forte, *Trinità come storia*, Milano 1988, 13.
12. G. Zanghí, 'A Reflection on Postmodernity', ibid., 84.
13. Piero Coda, *Il Logos e il nulla. Trinità, religioni, mistica*, Rome 2003.

Index